The Future of Social Theory

NICHOLAS GANE

continuum
LONDON • NEW YORK

CONTINUUM

The Tower Building	15 East 26th Street
11 York Road	New York
London SE1 7NX	NY 10010

British Library Cataloguing-in-Publication Data
A catalogue record for this book is available from the British Library.
  ISBN: 0–8264–7065–3 (HB)   0–8264–7066–1 (PB)

Library of Congress Cataloging-in-Publication Data

Typeset by YHT Ltd, London
Printed and bound in Great Britain by CPI Bath, Bath

For Antonia

Contents

Acknowledgements

The idea for this project was aired over lunch with Tristan Palmer (my then editor at Continuum) in a small Italian restaurant in London in the summer of 2002. I would like to thank Tristan for greeting my initial ideas with such enthusiasm, and for supporting the project through to its final stages. Many others encouraged and influenced me along the way. In particular, I would like to thank Thomas Kemple and my uncle, Mike Gane, for the many stimulating conversations and e-mail exchanges that inspired me to complete this work. Special thanks also go to Antonia Luther-Jones (to whom this book is dedicated), who lived through every twist and turn of this project (and my obsession with it!), and who helped keep it on track with many practical ideas and suggestions. Above all, however, I would like to thank each contributor for responding to my questions with such energy and passion, and for making this book what it is.

Notes on Contributors

Zygmunt Bauman is Emeritus Professor of Sociology at the University of Leeds and the University of Warsaw. His recent books include *Postmodernity and Its Discontents* (Polity, 1997), *Work, Consumerism and the New Poor* (Open University Press, 1998), *Globalization: The Human Consequences* (Polity, 1998), *In Search of Politics* (Polity, 1999), *Liquid Modernity* (Polity, 2000), *The Individualized Society* (Polity, 2001), *Community* (Polity, 2001), *Society Under Siege* (Polity, 2002) and *Liquid Love* (Polity, 2003).

Ulrich Beck is Professor of Sociology at the University of Munich, British Journal of Sociology Visiting Centennial Professor of the London School of Economics and Political Science, and Director of the Research Centre for Reflexive Modernization (*Deutsche Forschungsgemeinschaft*) in Munich. His publications include *Risk Society* (Sage, 1992), *Reflexive Modernization*, with Anthony Giddens and Scott Lash (Polity, 1994), *Ecological Politics in an Age of Risk* (Polity, 1995), *Ecological Enlightenment* (Prometheus, 1995), *The Normal Chaos of Love*, with E. Beck-Gernsheim (Polity, 1995), *The Reinvention of Politics* (Polity, 1996), *Democracy Without Enemies* (Polity, 1998), *World Risk Society* (Polity, 1999), *What is Globalization?* (Polity, 2000), *The Brave New World of Work* (Polity, 2000) and *Individualization* (Polity, 2002).

Judith Butler is Maxine Elliot Professor in the Departments of Rhetoric and Comparative Literature at the University of California, Berkeley. She received her Ph.D. in Philosophy from Yale University in 1984. She is the author of *Antigone's Claim: Kinship Between Life and Death* (Columbia University Press, 2000), *Hegemony, Contingency, Universality*, with Ernesto Laclau and Slavoj Žižek (Verso, 2000), *Subjects of Desire: Hegelian Reflections in Twentieth-Century France* (Columbia University Press, 1987), *Gender Trouble: Feminism and the Subversion of Identity* (Routledge, 1990), *Bodies That Matter: On the Discursive Limits of 'Sex'* (Routledge, 1993), *The Psychic Life of Power: Theories of Subjection* (Stanford University Press, 1997), *Excitable Speech* (Routledge, 1997), as well as numerous articles and contributions on philosophy, feminist and queer theory. Her recent project is a critique of ethical violence and an effort to formulate a theory of responsibility for a subject who cannot always know herself. This manuscript works with Kafka, Freud, Foucault, Adorno, and Levinas. She is also working on a set of essays engaged with grievable and ungrievable lives, war, politics and the suspension of civil liberties.

Scott Lash is Professor of Sociology and Director of the Centre for Cultural Studies at Goldsmiths' College, University of London. He is the author of *The Militant Worker* (Heinemann, 1984), *Sociology of Postmodernism* (Routledge, 1990), *Another Modernity, A Different Rationality* (Blackwell, 1999) and *Critique of Information* (Sage, 2002). He is the co-author of *The End of Organized Capitalism*, with John Urry (Polity, 1987), *Economies of Signs and Space*, with John Urry (Polity, 1994), and *Reflexive Modernization*, with Ulrich Beck and Anthony Giddens (Polity, 1994). He is also the co-editor of *Max Weber, Rationality and Modernity*, with Sam Whimster (Allen & Unwin, 1987), *Modernity and Identity*, with Jonathan Friedman (Blackwell, 1992), *Global Modernities*, with Mike Featherstone (Sage, 1995), *Detraditionalization*, with Paul Heelas and Paul Morris (Blackwell, 1996), *Risk, Environment and Modernity*, with Brian Wynne and Bronislaw Szerszynski (Sage, 1996), *Time and Value*, with Andrew Quick and Richard Roberts (Blackwell, 1998), and *Spaces of Culture: City, Nation, World*, with Mike Featherstone (Sage, 1999).

Bruno Latour has been Professor at the Centre de Sociologie de l'Innovation at the Ecole Nationale Supérieure des Mines in Paris since 1982. He has also held visiting Professorships at the University of California, San Diego, at the London School of Economics and in the History of Science Department of Harvard University. His books include *Laboratory Life: The Construction of Scientific Facts* (Princeton University Press, 1981), *Science in Action* (Open University Press, 1987), *The Pasteurization of France* (Harvard University Press, 1993), and *Pandora's Hope: Essays in the Reality of Science Studies* (Harvard University Press, 1999). He has also published a field study on an automatic subway system *Aramis, or the Love of Technology* (Harvard University Press, 1996), and an essay on symmetric anthropology *We Have Never Been Modern* (Harvard University Press, 1993, and now translated into 15 languages). Recent publications in French include *Paris ville invisible* (La Découverte, 1999) – a photographic essay on the technical and social aspects of the city of Paris, and *Politiques de la nature* (La Découverte, 1999, and soon to be published in English by Harvard University Press).

Nikolas Rose is Professor of Sociology and Convenor of the Department of Sociology at the London School of Economics where he also directs the BIOS research centre for the study of Bioscience, Biomedicine, Biotechnology and Society. His most recent books are *Governing the Soul: The Shaping of the Private Self* (2nd edition, Free Assocation Books, 1999) and *Powers of Freedom: Reframing Political Thought* (Cambridge University Press, 1999). He is Managing Editor of the journal *Economy and Society* and, together with Paul Rabinow, he is currently editing the Fourth Volume of Michel Foucault's *Essential Works*. His current research concerns biological and genetic psychiatry and behavioural neuroscience, and its social, ethical, cultural and legal implications.

Saskia Sassen is the Ralph Lewis Professor of Sociology at the University of Chicago, and Centennial Visiting Professor at the London School of Economics. She is currently completing her forthcoming book *Denationalization: Territory, Authority and Rights in a Global Digital Age* (Princeton University Press, 2004) based on her five-year project on governance and accountability in a global economy. She has also just completed for UNESCO a five-year project on sustainable human settlement for which she set up a network of researchers and activists in over 50 countries. Her most recent books are *Guests and Aliens* (New Press, 1999) and the edited *Global Networks, Linked Cities* (Routledge, 2002). *The Global City* is out in a new fully updated edition (Princeton University Press, 2001). Her books have been translated into 14 languages. She is a Member of the US National Academy of Sciences Panel on Cities, and Chair of the newly formed Information Technology, International Cooperation and Global Security Committee of the Social Science Research Council (USA).

John Urry is Professor of Sociology at Lancaster University, UK. Recent books include *Contested Natures*, with Phil Macnaghten (Sage, 1998), *Sociology Beyond Societies* (Routledge, 2000), *Bodies of Nature*, co-edited with Phil Macnaghten (Sage, 2001), *The Tourist Gaze* (2nd edition, Sage, 2002), *Global Complexity* (Polity, 2003), 'Presence Absence' (special issue of *Society and Space*, 2003, co-edited with Michel Callon and John Law), and 'Cultures of Automobility' (special issue of *Theory, Culture and Society*, 2003, co-edited with Mike Featherstone and Nigel Thrift).

Françoise Vergès is Reader in the Centre for Cultural Studies, Goldsmiths' College, University of London. Her publications include *Abolir l'esclavage: une utopie coloniale. Les ambiguïtés d'une politique humanitaire* (Albin, 2001), 'The Island of Wandering Souls: Processes of Creolization, Politics of Emancipation and the Problematic of Absence on Réunion Island', in Rod Edmond and Vanessa Smith (eds), *Islands in History and Representation* (Routledge, 2003), 'Post-Scriptum', in David Theo Goldberg and Ato Quayson (eds), *Relocating*

Postcolonialism (Blackwell, 2002), and 'Vertigo and Emancipation. Creole Cosmopolitanism and Cultural Politics', *Theory, Culture and Society*, Vol. 18, Nos 2–3, April–June 2001, pp. 169–84. Her research interests centre on postcoloniality, the economy of plunder, politics of predation and force, slavery and humanitarian politics, Indian Ocean cultural and political formations. Currently she is consultant for the exhibition 'Dé-placements' at Musée d'Art Moderne de la Ville de Paris and for the Maison des civilisations et de l'unité réunionnaise (MCUR), a cultural project on intercultural processes in the Indian Ocean region, based on Réunion Island.

CHAPTER I

Introduction: Rethinking Social Theory

The world today is passing through a number of dramatic transformations, not least those arising from the increased technological mediation of interpersonal relations, the blurring of boundaries between human subjects and impersonal objects, and the proliferation of new global social and cultural forms. These developments demand a new sociological imagination and perhaps, in turn, a new conceptual vocabulary, one better equipped to negotiate the daunting complexity of the contemporary world than the classical one that is still commonplace today. For no longer is it possible to treat social relations as arising simply from human relations (as did Marx and Weber), to confine social interaction to the face-to-face interactions of human 'agents', or to talk of society in the same breath as the social (as was the trend for the majority of the twentieth century). Objects and technologies now exercise an increasing power over our lives, to the extent that we can no longer place humans as all-powerful agents at the centre of all analysis, or even presuppose what it means to be human (it is now far easier to define the characteristics of an object). This question of the (in)human is more important than ever, and is tied, in turn, to the heightened intervention of advanced media technologies (or technological objects) into the social world, a development which itself poses sociology a whole new set of problems. For example: an increasing number of working and personal relationships are now mediated by digital technologies that remove many of the physical barriers of time and space. But are such 'tele-relationships' truly social relationships, and, if so, what is to be meant now by the term 'social'? Moreover, how might we begin to track, let alone understand, these new, accelerated relationships, and what methodologies might we use to do so? This is an especially difficult question given that such relationships play out at an unprecedented speed across time and space, and are conducted through networks and exchanges so fluid and complex that they are characterized more by a blizzard of connections than by fixed, clearly delineated social structures. Such questions raise important issues of spatiality and scale (see Chapter 7), and, in turn, urge us to reconsider structural connections between the 'local', 'national' and the 'global'. Increasing numbers of social relationships (more than often mediated by new information communication technologies) now cut across traditional nation-state boundaries. Could it be that 'society' (which tended to be theorized as being contained within the territorial limits of the nation-state) is all but dead, or is it possible that (capitalist) society is recasting itself in new global, post-national directions? Or might it be that the social itself is no longer confined (if it ever was) within the limits of society or the nation-state, and is increasingly fluid and diverse in form? Such questions are crucial to the immediate future of social theory, and the aim of this book is to push them a little further, if not to provide any final answers.

EXISTING LIMITS

While such issues and questions are more urgent than ever, for the most part, however, they have yet to penetrate the core of mainstream sociology. In many respects, social theory is still built on foundations that date from the mid- to late nineteenth century, in spite of isolated attempts to re- or *un*think the discipline from within (see, for example, Wallerstein, 1991). More often than not it is still presumed without question, for example, that 'humans' exist at the centre of the universe, and that these beings are discrete entities immune to technological intervention and so endowed with the capacity to exercise 'agency' (and thus some kind of control) over the world. Beyond this, these agents, because of their nature as humans (regardless of what this 'nature' might actually be), are treated as intrinsically *social* beings (one famous formulation (from Weber, 1978) being that social relations are meaningful relations between *humans*). This basic connection between the human and the social remains relatively unexplored (at least from within the discipline of sociology), but is the bedrock upon which classical social theory is built (at least in the interpretive tradition). A prominent development of this attempted separation of 'the human' (and thus 'the social') from objects or technologies, and with this the defence of the human subject, is the work of Manuel Castells, which treats new media technologies as 'the expression of ourselves' (2001: 6) and looks not at the transformative powers of these technologies but at the ways in which they extend existing forms of 'human action'. This position, in fact, replicates an argument made by Max Weber over 80 years ago, one that reduces all interest in technologies, objects or machines to the purposes or meanings bestowed on them by human actors:

> To be devoid of meaning is not identical with being lifeless or non-human: every artifact, such as for example a machine, can be understood only in terms of the meaning which its production and use have had or were

intended to have; a meaning which may derive from a relation to exceedingly various purposes. Without reference to this meaning such an object remains wholly unintelligible. That which is intelligible or understandable about it is thus its relation to human action in the role either of means or of end; a relation of which the actor or actors can be said to have been aware and to which their action has been oriented. (Weber, 1978: 7)

In this perspective (which runs from the nineteenth century through to today), sociology is only to be concerned with objects and technologies in relation to their intended uses or meanings, so that, ultimately, they are to be understood in terms of the known intentions of human activity.

But such a position is today increasingly difficult to maintain. What if, for example, objects and technologies today exceed their intended capacities and meanings? What if these technologies now exercise power over our lives rather than vice versa (as Marshall McLuhan (1964) and, more recently, Jean Baudrillard (1993) have suggested)? What if we are no longer aware (if we ever were) of the ways in which technologies mediate our actions? To what extent can relations between humans that are mediated through new communications technologies and virtual environments be designated *social* in the traditional sense? And if we can no longer presuppose or agree on what it means to be 'human', what might this mean for social theory built on understanding and interpreting human relations? Does the loss of a discrete and clearly definable human subject spell the end for the discipline of sociology, or alternatively mark an exciting new beginning?

NEW BEGINNINGS

These types of questions have been asked outside of the discipline by thinkers as diverse as Jean-François Lyotard, who, in *The Inhuman* (1991), addressed the impact of technologized (or accelerated) time on the so-called 'human condition', Donna Haraway (1991), who questions the boundaries between humans and machines in her analysis of the cyborg, and N. Katherine Hayles (1999), who has examined the emergence of the 'post-human' in cybernetic theory. More recently, important debates have taken place over the bearing of genetic engineering on 'the human', fired, in particular, by Francis Fukuyama's *The Great Disruption* (2000) and *Our Posthuman Future* (2003). The impact of these broadly philosophical writings are starting to be felt within the field of sociology (for example, in the growing sociological literature on genetics), and new attempts at rethinking the social are emerging as a consequence. Meanwhile, elsewhere in the discipline, similar things are happening: the basic categories of sociology are being called into question and, with this, new social theories being forged. Debates, for example, which have raged over the changing status of human identity, the emergence of new hybridized cultural forms or even the transfiguration of the nation-state are today feeding into analysis of the social, and new theories and methods are emerging, if rather slowly, in turn.

These are exciting times for social theory, and for the social sciences more generally. This situation is a far cry from the late 1980s when, with the demise of Marxist thought, social theory looked to be in decline. For while the collapse of the Marxist orthodoxy loosened the traditional binding of the social with a theory of production or *class*, few alternative conceptions of the social (either new or re-invented from the writings of Durkheim, Weber or Simmel) immediately came to the fore. This, in part, was due to the emergence of new postmodern approaches that privileged aesthetics, language and singularity over the analysis of social institutions and social structures, and in their most extreme and polemical form declared the social to be dead (Baudrillard, 1983, see below). At this point, social theory appeared to have little future. But new prospects opened, in turn, with the construction of postmodern theories of sociality (for example, Maffesoli, 1995), new approaches to reflexive moder-nization, risk society (Beck, Giddens and Lash, 1994) and globalization (for example, Roland Robertson (1992), Malcolm Waters (2000)), and exciting developments in political, cultural, media, feminist and literary theory, as well as in the discipline of history (see Joyce, 2002). Today, these approaches and theories are *beginning* to impact upon the form and content of mainstream sociology, which until now has tended to comfort itself with a rather traditional theoretical and conceptual vocabulary. There is still much work to be done, but nevertheless things are changing: sociology is once again broadening its ima-gination, and new spaces are opening up for dynamic thinking and for theo-retical and conceptual invention.

THE DEATH OF THE SOCIAL?

The primary rationale of the present work is to explore some of the directions that new theory might take, and, with this, to call into question the changing basis of the social today. A key proposition of the present book is that 'the social' is *changing* in form rather than disappearing. This position goes firmly against the grain of the more extreme visions of the 1980s that pronounced the social (along with modern ideas of history and class) to be dead. The most famous declaration of this sort came from Jean Baudrillard, who, in his work *In the Shadow of the Silent Majorities* (1983), presented three alternative scenarios: that the social never existed in reality ('there has never been anything but *simulation* of the social and the social relation' (1983: 71; original emphasis)), that the social now exists everywhere and invests everything (with the implication that it exists everywhere and nowhere), or that the social really did exist, but does so no longer. For the most part, Baudrillard pushes the logic of this latter position, and treats the social as an effect of second-order simulacra – the order of mass production and class relations (Baudrillard, 1993) – that disappears with the emergence of digitalized forms of simulation and the mass circulation of signs (or codes). He declares: 'The social only exists in a perspective space, it dies in the space of simulation . . .' (1983: 83). Put simply, Baudrillard treats the social as an effect of 'reality', which is not understood as a universal truth, but rather as the temporary outcome of mass commodity production. With the digitalization of the mechanical forces of production (and hence the advent of new virtual or hyperreal forms), reality is seen to disappear, along with traditional class oppositions based upon the private ownership of physical property or the means of production. And with the disappearance of reality, class is said to go too, and with it the whole sphere of social relations. For with the advent of new forms of simulation and simulacra, the social ('a people, a class, a proletariat'), along with related oppositions (in particular, class struggle), is neutralized and effectively vanishes: it implodes in on itself and is absorbed into the masses (which, unlike classes, are undifferentiated and non-stratified), which, in turn, become increasingly silent and apolitical (Baudrillard, 1983: 19). Hence, with the transition from class-based to mass consumer society, politics and the social are seen to be all but dead.

MARX AND BEYOND

It is worth pausing for a moment to consider the logic of Baudrillard's argument, not least because it is one of the most striking positions on the social (and its apparent demise) since the early 1980s. What is interesting about Baudrillard's position is that (like so many theories of the social) it is tied to a one-dimensional reading of Marx, and in no way considers alternative (non-Marxist) lines along which a theory of the social might be developed. Marx's own use of the term social is, in fact, complex, and shifts from text to text. One reading of the term social (that Baudrillard in no way adopts) comes at the conclusion to 'On the Jewish Question', where Marx talks not of political emancipation (like Bruno Bauer) but of 'social emancipation'. The difference, in short, is that whereas political emancipation involves the granting of political rights to individuals (a process which reduces 'man on the one hand to the member of civil society, the *egoistic, independent* individual, and on the other to the *citizen*, the moral person' (Marx, 1992: 234; original emphasis)), social emancipation instead attacks the very ideology of rights and citizenship (which fetishize the individual) and demands that we restore ourselves to communal species-beings. Marx's emphasis, then, is placed not on the political right to be Jewish, but on the passage beyond both religion and rights (which are, at the same time, a source of freedom and subjection) to a society that is emancipated from the bourgeois and self-interested politics of capitalist society. In other words, social emancipation is essentially the same thing as human emancipation, and lies a step beyond politics: the social is the utopian form of the post-political.

In these terms, it would be very easy to take a 'post-social' position, for the decline of revolutionary politics would seem to spell the end of the social as Marx defines it here (meaning that there is no such thing as the post-political). But Baudrillard does not formulate his argument in quite this way. Instead, his emphasis is placed firmly on production and class. This argument draws its understanding of the social from the pages of a quite different text, namely Marx's 'German Ideology', in which, particularly in the section 'Premises of the Materialist Method', it is argued that the social is less tied to emancipation than to production (that 'first historical act'). In this work, Marx traces the history of production through different historical configurations before tying it firmly to a conception of the social: 'By social we understand the co-operation of several individuals, no matter under what conditions, in what manner, and to what end. It follows from this that a certain mode of production, or industrial stage, is always combined with a certain mode of co-operation, or social stage, and this mode of co-operation is itself a "productive force"' (1978: 157). Curiously, while Baudrillard subjects Marx's arguments regarding the necessity of production (along with the concepts of need and use-value) to harsh critique in his early work (see Baudrillard, 1975; 1981), in *In the Shadow of the Silent Majorities* (1983) he develops exactly the same understanding of the social as the later Marx: it is tied to production, and thus to class (the first and second orders of simulacra). But, as always with Baudrillard, there is a twist: with the implosion of commodity production into the production of signs, and with the accompanying shift from reality to hyperreality, the social is doomed. The basic concept of the social, then, is much the same for both Baudrillard and the later Marx, but for Baudrillard the social neither disappears with the overcoming of historical modes of production through revolutionary struggle (as in 'The German Ideology') nor emerges in the passage to utopia ('On the Jewish Question'), but rather dies with the shift beyond commodity production and class politics to a coded world of simulation and signs.

Baudrillard's position here, though, is a little odd to say the least, not least because in this argument he presents his orders of simulacra as linear stages in capitalist development: with the passage to third-order simulacra, the social as class simply disappears along with the era of mass production and political engagement. But mass production clearly has not ceased. Rather, the production of signs sits alongside the production of physical commodities in the capitalist economy, meaning that the world is made up of a complex configuration of different forms of simulacra rather than simply one dominant order. This might mean that rather than the social disappearing, it might simply have mutated in form. It might be tied more now to consumption, for example, than physical commodity production (something suggested, in fact, by Weber in his famous 'Class, Status, Party' (1978: 926–40)).

THE HYPER-SOCIAL?

Unwittingly, however, Baudrillard reveals the weaknesses of his early position, and of theories that conflate class and the social, in his later book *Seduction* (1990). In this work, he attacks the concept of the social from a different angle, saying that 'The age of law has passed, and with it that of the socius and the social contract' (1990: 155). This statement is intended to draw attention to the precariousness of law and the concept of value as Western culture passes through the second order of simulacra (the era of mass production) to a third order characterized by the mass circulation of signs and new forms of digital modelling and simulation. This instability becomes increasingly evident in *The Transparency of Evil*, in which Baudrillard talks of a fourth stage of chaos and certainty, where 'Properly speaking there is now no law of value, merely a sort of *epidemic of value*, a sort of metastasis of value, a haphazard proliferation and dispersal of value' (1993: 5; original emphasis). The important point here, however, is the underlying connection between modern contractual law, or more specifically the 'Rights of Man', and the birth of the social. What Baudrillard suggests here (but never follows through in detail) is that the social is not simply the effect of mass production and class relations, but is tied more fundamentally to the historical pursuit of political rights based on a claim to universality (an issue addressed in Chapter 3). What is strong in Baudrillard's account is the attempt to show that the claim for universality (especially the universality of the social) is, in fact, highly particular (and tied to a specific phase of Western industrial development). What is weaker is his explanation of the ways in which institutional and ideological systems of contractual law and positive right, particularly those that developed out of the French Revolution, were intimately connected to the social from its outset. Such a connection is, in fact, crucial to the understanding of the social in its classical form. Indeed, changes in the legal structures of modern societies provide the backdrop to what we know as classical social theory: Rousseau spoke famously of the emergence of the social contract, Comte formulated the law of the three states (theological, metaphysical and *positive*), Durkheim analysed the rise of new forms of sanction and the shift from repressive to restitutive law, Weber opposed legal-rational domination to earlier traditional and charismatic forms, Hegel spoke of the birth of subjectivity accompanying the emergence of positive rights, and Marx, at least in his early work, exposed the difference between political emancipation (based on the limited freedoms of political rights) and human emancipation (which transcended the very ideal of rights and duties). In view of this, Baudrillard's earlier declaration of the death of the social based on the disappearance of class is clearly one-sided, for if anything the social (as a concept) emerged in the attempt to understand changes in the structural basis of law that accompanied (or perhaps underpinned) the transition to the modern world. This connection requires detailed analysis, but there would seem to be some complicity between positive law and rights, the birth of modern subjectivity, the development of modern legal institutions and (contractual or capitalist) social relations. And this connection, if it holds (and the work of Gillian Rose (1984; 1992) suggests it does), is more important than ever, for rather than witnessing the end of law, as Baudrillard suggests, discourses on international law and global human rights are proliferating and today dominate the political arena (even if there is no international law as such), which, following the above logic, signals, in turn, that the social is now more alive than ever. Indeed, if this reading is correct, it is possible to argue that globalization marks not the death of the social, but rather the birth of a new era of rights and citizenships, or what might be termed the era of the *hyper-social*.

THE INTERVIEWS

There is clearly life, then, beyond Marx (and also Baudrillard). One way forward may be to turn back to alternative conceptions of the social or sociality that remain buried in the work of other thinkers such as Durkheim, Weber and Simmel. Maffesoli (1995) has attempted to do this in his work on postmodern tribes, while Lyotard (no doubt drawing on the work of Lévi-Strauss) developed Durkheim's idea of a social bond into a linguistic bond through the course of his *Postmodern Condition* (1984: 14–17). Meanwhile, others have developed an explicitly political approach to the idea of the social bond through an application of Michel Foucault's (1991) writings on governmentality. Key figures here include Jacques Donzelot (1979; 1984), Nikolas Rose (see Chapter 9 of the present work) and Mitchell Dean, who defines the social as: 'The plural and heterogeneous forms of interventions that cross and connect various formally separate public and private spheres in response to and sometimes in opposition to the effects of a liberal governmental economy and a depoliticised sphere of the family' (1999: 212). In this view, the social bond is produced and maintained by an underlying body of power relations, relations that underpin liberal strategies of governments and which are concealed (and very often forgotten) in contemporary discourses about 'freedom'.

But if one strategy is to rethink old texts in creative ways in a bid to revitalize the present (what might be called a genealogical strategy), another is to push current ideas and theories as far as possible to open up new ways of thinking (what might be called an agonistic strategy). It is towards this latter aim that the present book works. It does so through a series of dialogues with key thinkers in the field (even if their primary academic affiliation is not to the discipline of sociology), thinkers who have formulated challenging new ways of theorizing the social or social relations, and who, in the process, have called into question many of the basic assumptions of mainstream theory and practice. Of course, not every such thinker could be (or would want to be) part of this book, but those who are are renowned for the striking originality of their work – each has developed new, critical and inventive ways of thinking, and each offers a distinct theoretical perspective to the question of the social (which is related, in turn, to a range of different substantive interests). The methodology of this work is simple. The interviews were conducted over the course of one year (from June 2002 to June 2003). They took the form of face-to-face meetings where possible (Butler, Lash, Rose, Latour, Beck, Urry) and written questions and responses where not (Sassen, Vergès, Bauman), with all interviewees having the option of reviewing their answers prior to them going into print.

Each interview is designed to explore a different dimension of, and theoretical approach to, the social. In Chapter 2, Zygmunt Bauman explains his recent shift from postmodern sociology or a sociology of postmodernism towards analysis of what he calls *liquid modernity*. He explains: 'the "postmodern" was but a stopgap choice, a "career report" of a search far from completion. It signalled that the social world has ceased to be like the one mapped using the "modernity" grid ... but was singularly uncommittal as to the features the world has acquired instead.' Bauman's stance is that we are now in the position to risk a '*positive* theory' of this new situation. His theory is that we have entered a new era of *liquid modernity*, one marked by the increased transience, uncertainty and insecurity (*Unsicherheit*) of all social forms. Underpinning this shift, he argues, is a process of individualization that has unlocked individual choices from collective projects and actions, so that today individuals are left to confront their life-choices in increasing isolation. Life in liquid modernity may, as a consequence, appear freer than ever, but this 'freedom' comes at a price, for individuals now have no choice but to take responsibility for their own self-determination, but without the traditional support of collective agency. At the same time, new forms of global class are said to be emerging on the basis of an increased polarization between the global elites (who are free to move across the globe and thus disengaged spatially and politically from those who stand opposed to them) and the local masses (who are not only tied to their localities but are occupied, for the most part, with individual rather than collective freedoms, without seeing the connection between the two). One answer suggested by Bauman is a reworking of the relation of public and private space so that, first, public space (the *ecclesia*) is protected from the invasion of private interests, and second, public-private space (the *agora*) is revitalized to enable the collective basis of private or personal troubles to be brought to the fore.

Chapter 3 explores the boundaries between literary and social theory. Here, Judith Butler proposes that literary works may be used to conceptualize the domain of the social, not because they simply mimic or reflect social reality, but because they help expose the ways in which social norms are instated at the level of 'voice and diction' (or alternatively through what is not said or what is absent from the text). Butler is careful, however, not to reduce social theory simply to discursive or linguistic analysis, for language and the social are not one and the same thing. She explains: 'the social can neither be reduced to discourse (understood as a historical configuration of language; a shifting configuration subject to rupture and transformation) nor to the linguistic, but language emerges precisely at the juncture when we try to make the distinction between language and the social'. Moreover: 'There is no way to peel off the linguistic dimension from any social theory. But that is not the same thing as saying that all social theory is reducible to linguistic theory, it just means that social theory *cannot do without* the linguistic.' Further to this, Butler sees any definition of the social as proceeding through an act of demarcation or circumscription, or, put simply, through the selection of basic criteria that lend the concept, in turn, its value and legitimacy. This practice is effectively based upon a principle of exclusion, for, according to the criteria selected, a line is drawn in theory and practice between what is to be counted as 'social' and what is to be deemed 'a-social, anti-social, pre-social or even post-social'. Butler calls into question the principles of exclusion that frame current understandings of the social, and in so doing emphasizes the historical limits and power relations that condition and constrain the workings of this concept. This critical analysis is positive rather than negative in tone, for it seeks to open up the concept of social to contestation and to stimulate thereby the possibility of change: 'I think that reinvigorating the notion of the social can give us back a notion of the transformability of social structure. So, it is with a certain hopefulness that I am reanimating the term.'

In Chapter 4, Bruno Latour attacks the idea of the social from a very different angle, arguing that the social, in its classical sense (as *society*), is merely a screen that sociologists project their data onto, and in itself explains nothing. In his words, the concept of society 'does nothing but reassures, gives moral comfort, and allows the sociologist to have an overview. It does moral things but has no empirical grasp.' Latour, in response, develops a theory in which the social is not tied to a static conception of society (which is said not to exist), but arises instead from the mobile connections between things, or what might be called *associations*. This approach, inspired by the work of Gabriel Tarde, is part of a 'sociology of mobilities', and is one that has been excluded from, or repressed by, the sociological tradition since its inception. Such an approach, Latour insists, is empirical in orientation, but with a twist: it attempts to follow what actors say and do rather than to unmask the truths that lie behind their actions. Further to this, it places the analysis of objects at the centre of its concerns, and does so by treating them not simply as the cause or effect of social relations, but rather as hybrids of nature and culture that have their own dynamic forms of agency.

This idea of object-agency surfaces again in Chapter 5, in which Scott Lash, like Zygmunt Bauman, attempts to move beyond some of the time-worn ideas of postmodern theory. He does so not by taking a stance against postmodernism *per se*, but rather by shifting the focus of his analysis to what he calls 'technological forms of life'. What emerges in this shift is a new form of sociological vitalism. He explains: 'For me ... postmodernity is identified with postmodern architecture and also certain kinds of pastiche. And those kinds of pastiche and those kinds of architecture are mish-mashes of dead forms. They don't connect to the intensity of desire, to lines of flight, to life and the way we live today ... I have been using the term "vitalism" and not "postmodern". I am not anti-postmodern at all, but concepts like "communication", "information", "life" and "media" now do the same sort of work that postmodernism did for me in the late 1980s.' This vitalism, inspired by figures as diverse as Henri Bergson, Georg Simmel and Gilles Deleuze, crosses over into a media theory that posits no separation between media and society, and which sees instead a world where classical social relations have become mediated or *communicational* relations. This disappearance of the social bond into the communicational bond, however, is not something Lash mourns, for he rightly observes that technological development is not simply something that can be undone. Given this, Lash makes a positive declaration: 'We are living in a technological culture and this means affirming it and using it.' This means, by extension, that social theory (which Lash still accords an important role) is to technologize itself, and, if it is to keep up with the pace of the mediated world, become *performative* – it is to play out through new forms of critical intervention that are 'more event-like, more like art events, installations and performances'.

Many of the themes of the previous two chapters are picked up again in Chapter 6, where John Urry, in similar vein to Latour, seeks to shift 'sociology from the study of society to the study of mobility'. Unlike Latour, however, Urry applies this argument to the study of globalization by looking at the ways in which relationships are networked across the globe. His position is that neither nation-states nor societies have simply disappeared, but that their tying together (in classical sociological discourse), along with their power to limit the mobility of social forms, has become significantly weaker. Urry's response is to shift away from analysis of the nation-state or, more broadly, societal forma-tions to study instead the ways in which entities now flow across time and space through global scapes. But whereas in previous formulations such entities or flows have tended to be studied in separation from the structures through which they travel, Urry asserts the need to theorize flows and structures together, which can be done through analysis of *networks*: 'dynamic open sys-tems that partly are reproduced through the very processes through which the flows take place'. And this, in turn, requires new methods of study, ones that can address the emergent properties of systems in new, dynamic ways. Urry calls these 'mobile methods', and these address not only different connections between 'human powers' and 'material objects', but track different entities – 'the people, the objects or the informational or cultural flows' – across time and space to see how they flow, how they shape the network, and how they themselves are transformed in the process.

Chapter 7 stays with this question of globalization, but centres more explicitly on the connection between space and power. Like Urry, Saskia Sassen sees a shift away from the 'inter-state system' as the dominant organi-zational form of social relations, and, at the same time, the proliferation of new cross-border exchanges and flows. She explains: 'With the partial unbundling or at least weakening of the national as a spatial unit come conditions for the ascendance of other spatial units and scales ... The dynamics and processes that get territorialized or are sited at these diverse scales can in principle be regional, national and global.' On top of this, there are new global circuits of capitalist activity that both contribute to and constitute these new scales, and that are enhanced by them in return. Sassen theorizes this new situation through a socio-geographical approach, one that pays close attention to city structures and networks and in the process bypasses simple oppositions of 'the national' to 'the global'. In this perspective, the global is not treated as that which lies outside of the national but is rather seen to filter through ' "national" institutional orders and imaginaries'. And to study this interplay, along with the emergence of new transnational social forms, new conceptual architectures are called for, in particular those that can 'accommodate multiple diverse components operating at different scales ... without losing analytic closure'.

Ulrich Beck also addresses the question of globalization in Chapter 8, and does so by taking issue with what he calls 'methodological nationalism', or rather the 'situation where the social sciences – not only sociology but also political science, law, history, economics and so on – are to some extent still prisoners of the nation-state'. In response, he proposes that there are two directions in which we can proceed. The first is to recognize that spaces of lived experience are no longer nationally exclusive, not least because increasing numbers of people are living in two or more national spaces. Beck argues that the world today is distinguished by increasingly fluid life-forms and by a proliferation of new *transnational realities*, and that new sociological methods are needed to study these changes. This leads us, in turn, in a second direction, which is towards new forms of empirical work. Beck proposes that we 'build a new frame of reference which redefines the basic concepts of the social sciences from transnational and cosmopolitan perspectives', and adds that '[t]his is to be done by empirical research in different areas in order to find out how reality beyond sociological categories is transforming itself'. But this can happen only if we shift beyond methodological nationalism towards 'methodological cosmopolitanism', which redefines key concepts (such as power) from a cosmopolitan perspective. And, for Beck, this means, above all, overcoming the limitations of national sociology and, with this, *'thinking society anew'*.

In Chapter 9, Nikolas Rose ties analysis of the social to questions of power and government in an approach inspired by the work of Michel Foucault. Rose's position is that '[t]he social is not the same as "society", it is not the same as "social life", and it is not the same as "social relations"'. Rather, the social is said to have emerged in the nineteenth century out of 'liberal' governmental strategies that gave rise, in turn, to new welfare regimes and a range of associated individual obligations. Rose observes that from this point onwards the term is 'used as the qualifier for all sorts of things, including social insurance, social rights, social workers and indeed of a whole discipline of the social that is sociology'. His question is why the social came into existence in this way, and how it developed subsequently into both a political imperative ('if government is to be legitimate or effective, it must be social') and an intellectual imperative ('if this or that feature of human life is to be understood, we must pay attention to its social aspects'). These developments are analysed with the aid of a genealogical method, or rather through a range of historical methods that look not for a general truth to history, but at small (often repressed or excluded) fragments of the past that expose 'the profusion and diversity of entangled events' leading to the present. It is through such historical work that, for Rose, a critical understanding of current developments (such as the recent rise of the 'etho-politics' of community) may be gained, and, with this, new possibilities for the future perhaps opened (through, for example, the invention of a radical post-social politics).

In the final chapter, Françoise Vergès uses genealogy along with a range of other interdisciplinary tools to remind us of the intimate relation that has existed, or perhaps still even exists, between Western modernity and the quest for empire. In particular, she maps out a series of historical and *political* connections between republicanism and colonization. These connections in many respects underpin modern notions of citizenship, rights, freedom, 'nation' and even the social, yet their social, political or philosophical dimensions have yet to be fully explored. For Vergès, however, the question of colonization remains pivotal, not least because 'republicanism is again a central question of the political debate' and 'because aspects of French colonial republicanism, such as the "civilizing mission" and justified interference in sovereign countries, have returned to haunt us'. Beyond this, attention is drawn to the continued existence of 'postcolonial colonies'; societies freed of their colonial status but not freed of their colonial structure, or which remain tied to a colonial model of the political insofar as freedom is conceived through an idealistic or romantic view of the nation-state. These colonies exist alongside or within new 'grey zones' of globalization, zones which have all too easily fallen away from Western consciousness and which today are scarred by increased 'poverty, corruption and violence'. Vergès employs a range of concepts, including creolization, hybridity, *métissage* and bio-power, to understand this new situation, and, while taking care not to be caught in the rush to theorize, accords social theory an important role, part of which is to 'perform critical analysis of notions such as the nation, immaterial work, transnational capital and resistance'.

These interviews present a range of different theoretical approaches to the study of the contemporary world, and with this map out possible directions in which social theory might be developed. They are designed to orientate critical thought to the study of major transformations that are taking place today, including the globalization or transnationalization of certain social and political relations, the heightened mediation of social life through new communications technologies, the increased power or 'agency' of technologies or objects, and the emergence of increasingly fluid and transient forms of sociality. This list of transformations is certainly not exhaustive, and there are other important developments not covered here. But these interviews in no way seek to bring theoretical resolution or closure. Rather, their aim is to prompt further questioning and debate, and such questioning might proceed along a number of different lines. For example: what new types of power are emerging in the course of contemporary social and political transformation? How might theory encounter those 'grey zones' of globalization that so rarely enter the socio-logical gaze? What is the future of the human subject, and is it possible to conceive of a post-human conception of the social? How might we think of gender against this backdrop of socio-technical change? And, given the speed of change in the contemporary world, what is the future for theory, which has always been a patient and slow affair? Should it technologize itself in order to keep pace?

Such questions, among others, are broached during the course of these interviews, and demand detailed and sustained work. It is hoped that this book will open new directions in which such work can take place. Exciting things can happen during the course of an interview, not least because underpinning critical dialogue is a practice of challenge and counter-challenge, out of which new ideas, perspectives or, at the very least, openings can emerge (it is prac-tically impossible to leave a dialogue at the same point one enters it, for something always changes). With this in mind, it is not my purpose to say what one should take from this work, for such a prescription would run counter to the agonistic and aporetic basis of the interview format. All that can be hoped is that readers of this book will be prompted to ask their own questions about the worlds in which they live, and that new futures for social theory will emerge as a consequence.

REFERENCES

Baudrillard, J. (1975) *The Mirror of Production*. St Louis: Telos.

Baudrillard, J. (1981) *For a Critique of the Political Economy of the Sign*. St Louis: Telos.

Baudrillard, J. (1983) *In the Shadow of the Silent Majorities*. New York: Semio-text(e).

Baudrillard, J. (1990) *Seduction*. Basingstoke: Macmillan.

Baudrillard, J. (1993) *The Transparency of Evil*. London: Verso.

Beck, U., Giddens, A. and Lash, S. (1994) *Reflexive Modernization*. Cambridge: Polity.

Castells, M. (2001) *The Internet Galaxy*. Oxford: Oxford University Press.

Dean, M. (1999) *Governmentality*. London: Sage.

Donzelot, J. (1979) *The Policing of Families*. London: Hutchinson.

Donzelot, J. (1984) *L'invention du social*. Paris: Fayard.

Foucault, M. (1991) 'Governmentality', in G. Burchell, C. Gordon and P. Miller (eds) *The Foucault Effect*. London: Harvester Wheatsheaf.

Fukuyama, F. (2000) *The Great Disruption*. London: Profile.

Fukuyama, F. (2003) *Our Posthuman Future*. London: Profile.

Haraway, D. (1991) *Simians, Cyborgs and Women*. London: Free Association Books.

Hayles, N.K. (1999) *How We Became Posthuman*. Chicago, IL: University of Chicago Press.

Joyce, P. (ed.) (2002) *The Social in Question*. London: Routledge.

Lyotard, J.-F. (1984) *The Postmodern Condition*. Manchester: Manchester University Press.

Lyotard, J.-F. (1991) *The Inhuman: Reflections on Time*. Cambridge: Polity.

Maffesoli, M. (1995) *The Time of the Tribes*. London: Sage.

Marx, K. (1978) 'The German Ideology', in R. C. Tucker (ed.) *The Marx-Engels Reader* (2nd ed). New York: Norton.

Marx, K. (1992) 'On the Jewish Question', in L. Colletti (ed.) *Karl Marx: Early Writings*. Harmondsworth: Penguin.

McLuhan, M. (1964) *Understanding Media*. London: Routledge.

Robertson, R. (1992) *Globalization*. London: Sage.

Rose, G. (1984) *Dialectic of Nihilism*. Oxford: Blackwell.

Rose, G. (1992) *The Broken Middle*. Oxford: Blackwell.

Wallerstein, I. (1991) *Unthinking Social Science*. Cambridge: Polity.

Waters, M. (2000) *Globalization*. London: Routledge.

Weber, M. (1970) *From Max Weber: Essays in Sociology*. London: Routledge and Kegan Paul.

Weber, M. (1978) *Economy and Society*. Berkeley, CA: University of California Press.

CHAPTER 2

Zygmunt Bauman: Liquid Sociality

NG You are known by many (rightly or wrongly) as a sociologist of post-modernity or even as a postmodern sociologist. Recently, however, you have announced the emergence of a new, liquid state of modernity, and with this you seem to have distanced yourself from 'the postmodern'. But how is 'liquid' modernity different from industrial modernity, postmodernity, and from what other thinkers have called 'reflexive modernity'?

ZB All theory is selective; there can't be a theory of everything, just as there can't be a map of everything, as Jorge Luis Borges showed beyond reasonable doubt. As a matter of fact, I suppose that theorizing is triggered by the need of selecting (that is, a decision about 'topical relevancies', as Alfred Schutz would say – lightening some spots and shading all others). The *compleat mappa mundi* may be a bookworm's attractive idea, but would leave what has been mapped as messy and impenetrable as it was before mapping, and would leave the traveller as sunk in the flood of signals and lost as before. Theories differ not by their appetite for selection, but by what they select. Selection as such they cannot (and shall not, if they wish to be of use) avoid; the point is to make the right selection, or rather a better selection than the one the theory intends to improve on, complement or replace. That is, to focus the searchlights and the spotlights in a way that would assist orientation and help to find the way; on paths and crossroads, but also on bogs and landmines...

You are right; I have some time ago distanced myself from the 'postmodern' grid of the world-map. A number of reasons contributed.

To start with, the 'postmodern' was but a stopgap choice, a 'career report' of a search far from completion. It signalled that the social world has ceased to be like the one mapped using the 'modernity' grid (notably, the paths and the traps changed places), but was singularly uncommittal as to the features the world has acquired instead. The 'postmodern' has done its preliminary, site-clearing job: it aroused vigilance and sent the exploration in the right direction. It could not do much more, and so after that it outlived its usefulness; or, rather, it worked itself out of a job ... And we can now say more about the present-day world than it is *unlike* the old familiar one. We have, so to speak, matured to afford (to risk?) a *positive* theory of its novelty.

'The postmodern' was also flawed from the beginning: all disclaimers not-withstanding, it did suggest that modernity was over. Protestations did not help much, even ones as strong as Lyotard's ('one cannot be modern without being first postmodern') – let alone my insistence that 'postmodernity is modernity minus its illusion'. Nothing would help; if words mean anything, then a 'postX' will always mean something that has left X behind...

In time, more flaws became clearer to me – I'll mention but two of them.

One was, so to speak, objective: 'postmodern' barred the much needed break or rupture, taking a distance to certain theorizing habits, cognitive frames and tacit assumptions sedimented in the wake of a century-long deployment of the 'modernity grid'. 'Postmodern' thinking could not but adhere to the agenda set by the 'modern', limiting itself mostly to the rearrangement of pluses and minuses. To let the theorizing, the effort to grasp the novelty of the present-day social condition follow its own and that condition's logic by constructing its own agenda, the umbilical cord had to be cut. Symbolically, this meant the need to abandon the terminology that sapped the courage, resolution, and the freedom of thought necessary to do this.

The second was subjective. I prefer to select my bedfellows and affinities myself. Ascription to the 'postmodernist' camp grew more unsavoury and unpalatable by the day as the 'postmodern' writings went further and further astray and 'postmodernism' came to mean, more than anything else, singing praise of the new brave world of ultimate liberation rather than subjecting it to a critical scrutiny. The pain grew more acute yet, since using a term already wrapped in a thick and dense layer of imputed meanings I found it difficult to get my own message through; many a reader, with some justification, read into my sentences quite unintended meanings.

I had (and still have) reservations towards alternative names suggested for our contemporaneity. 'Late modernity'? How would we know that it is 'late'? The word 'late', if legitimately used, assumes closure, the last stage (indeed – what else would one expect to come after 'late'? Very late? Post-late?) – and so it suggests much more than we (as sociologists, who unlike the soothsayers and clairvoyants have no tools to predict the future and must limit ourselves to taking inventories of trends) are entitled responsibly to propose. 'Reflexive'? I smelled a rat here. I suspected that in coining this term we are projecting our own (professional thinkers') cognitive uncertainty upon the social world at large, or reforging quite real professional puzzlement into imaginary popular prudence – whereas that world out there is marked by the fading and wilting of the art of reflection (ours is a culture of forgetting and short-termism – of the two arch-enemies of reflection). I would perhaps embrace George Balandier's *surmodernité* or Paul Virilio/John Armitage's *hypermodernity*, were not these terms, like the term 'postmodern', too shell-like, too uncommittal to guide and target the theoretical effort.

NG You use the metaphor of 'liquid' to suggest that the solid, heavy social structures of the past are becoming lighter, diffuse and more mobile. But, at the risk of reading this metaphor too literally, all fluids are not free flowing. Some are heavier than solids, some need shaping, and others need restraining. And different fluids (blood or semen for example) signify quite different things. What, then, does the 'liquid' of liquid modernity refer to? What does it mean *to flow*? Exactly *what* flows: people, information, signs, 'hard' commodities (for these are not the same thing, the same 'liquid')? Are there different rates of flow for different types of 'liquid'? And between *where* do these liquids flow? Are there, for example, regular exchanges between certain key nodes (such as cities) that make up a network of advanced capitalist relations?

ZB I have tried to explain as clearly as I could why I have chosen the 'liquid' or 'fluid' as the metaphor for the present-day state of modernity – see particularly the foreword to my *Liquid Modernity* (Bauman, 2000). I made a point there not to confuse 'liquidity' or 'fluidity' with 'lightness' – an error firmly entrenched in our linguistic usages ('we associate "lightness" or "weightlessness" with mobility and inconstancy' – I wrote; but that association rests on an unwarranted extrapolation of travelling experience . . .). What sets liquids apart from solids is the looseness and frailty of their bonds, *not* their specific gravity. One attribute that liquids possess and solids do not, an attribute that makes liquids an apt metaphor for our times, is the intrinsic inability of fluids to hold their shape for long on their own. The 'flow', the defining characteristic of all liquids, means a continuous and irreversible change of mutual position of parts that (due to the faintness of intermolecular bonds) can be triggered by even the weakest of stresses. Fluids, according to *Encyclopaedia Britannica*, undergo for that reason 'a continuous change in shape when subjected to stress'. Used as a metaphor for the present phase of modernity, 'liquid' makes salient the brittleness, breakability, *ad hoc* modality of inter-human bonds. Another trait contributes to the metaphorical usefulness of liquids: their, so to speak, 'time sensitivity' – again contrary to the solids, which could be described as contraptions to cancel the impact of time.

Many things 'flow' in a liquid-modern setting – but in most cases this is a trivial, even banal observation. After all, to say that commodities and information 'flow' is as pleonastic as the statements 'winds blow' or 'rivers flow'. What is a truly novel feature of this social world, and makes it sensible to call the current kind of modernity 'liquid' in opposition to the other, earlier known forms of modern world, is the continuous and irreparable fluidity of things which modernity in its initial shape was bent on solidifying and fixing: of human locations in the social world and inter-human bonds – and particularly the latter, since their liquidity conditions (though does not determine on its own) the fluidity of the first. It is the 'relationships' that are progressively elbowed out and replaced by the activity of 'relating'. If one still unpacks the meaning of the word 'relationship' in the pristine, and still the dictionary, fashion, one can only use it, as Derrida suggested, *sous rature*; or one ought at least to remember that it is, to use Ulrich Beck's terminology, a *zombie term*.

All modernity means incessant, obsessive modernization (there is no *state* of modernity; only a *process*; modernity would cease being modernity the moment that process ground to a halt); and *all* modernization consists in 'disembedding', 'disencumbering', 'melting the solids', etc.; in other words, in dismantling the received structures or at least weakening their grip. From the start, modernity deprived the web of human relationships of its past holding force; 'disembedded' and set loose, humans were expected to seek new beds and dig themselves in them using their own skills and resources, even if they chose to stay in the bed in which they germinated ('it is not enough to be a bourgeois', warned Jean-Paul Sartre; 'one needs to live one's life as a bourgeois'). So what is new here?

New is that the 'disembedding' goes on unabated, while the prospects of 're-embedding' are nowhere in sight and unlikely to appear. In the incipient, 'solid' variety of modernity, disembedding was a necessary stage on the road to re-embedding; it had merely an instrumental value in transforming what used to be 'the given' into a task (much like the intermediary 'disrobing' or 'dismantling' stage in the three-partite Arnold Van Gennep/Victor Turner scheme of the passage rites). Solids were not melted in order to stay molten, but in order to be recast in moulds up to the standard of better designed, rationally arranged society. If there ever was a 'project of modernity', it was the search for the state of perfection, a state that puts paid to all further change, having first made change uncalled-for and undesirable. All further change would be for the worse . . .

This is no more the case, though. Bonds are easily entered but even easier to abandon. Much is done (and more yet is wished to be done) to prevent them from developing any holding power; long-term commitments with no option of termination on demand are decidedly out of fashion and not what a 'rational chooser' would choose . . . Relationships, like love in Anthony Giddens' portrayal, are 'confluent' – they last (or at least are expected to last) as long as *both* sides find them satisfactory. According to Judith Baker, author of bestselling 'relationship' handbooks, most relationships are designed to last no more than five years – enough time to pass from infatuation through the attachment phase and land down in the 'why am I here?' phase. With partnerships and other bonds in flux, the *Lebenswelt* is fluid. Or, to put it in a different idiom – the world, once the stolid, rule-following umpire, has become one of the players in a game that changes the rules as it goes – in an apparently whimsical and hard-to-predict fashion.

NG   What might the social look like in liquid modernity? Does it still exist? And does the onset of liquid modernity necessarily mean changes in the way we study social forms? Do we need to develop new methods and concepts to do so?

ZB   To teach me social psychology half a century ago, my university teachers used laboratory experiments with rats learning their way through the maze in search of a piece of lard. My fellow students like our teachers found the rats-in-the-maze allegory quite resonant with the gist of their life experience. Indeed, the social world felt to us like the cut-in-rock labyrinth must have appeared to Theseus. And in a solid world with its hard-and-fast, firmly fixed division of labour, career tracks, class distinctions, power hierarchies, marriages bound to last 'till death do us part', etc., social skills – the sole social skills ever to be required – seemed to consist in memorizing the immutable shape of the world and adjusting one's own conduct to that shape. It seemed sensible to measure the rats' (and the humans' by proxy) intelligence by the rats' or humans' ability to do just that: to acquire, by learning, routines that will be perpetually of service. 'Adaptation', 'adjustment', 'habituation' cropped up invariably as key terms whenever 'the social' was discussed. 'The social' was about conformity; the rest was anomie, anomaly, pathology or deviance: the a-social, the *anti-social*.

What, however, if the maze were made of partitions on castors, if the walls changed their position as fast, perhaps faster yet than the rats could scurry in search of food, and if the tasty rewards were moved as well, and quickly, and if the targets of the search tended to lose their attraction well before the rats could reach them, while other, similarly short-lived allurements diverted their attention and drew away their desire? No such setting occurred to the behaviourists running the laboratory, and in the world of half a century ago it would have been indeed bizarre if it had: it would have been jarringly at odds with the experience of those whom the laboratory findings were to enlighten.

This is, nevertheless, the liquid-modern setting of the 'social'. In such setting one would expect, as Americans would say, 'a quite different ball game' . . . And it is a different game.

In the changed setting, learning (which used to be in the previous setting the principal modality of being-in-the-world and the key to all life success) has lost much of the 'survival value' which it claimed and boasted at a time when it was assumed, with good reason, that success depended on the acquisition and entrenchment of *habitual* responses to *repetitive* situations. That assumption, though, made sense only if supported by another assumption: that situations would indeed repeat and each time call for the same responses as before. Routine behaviour was a bonus – in a routinized world. Now, however, the bottom has fallen out of that compact, solidly built container in which the challenges and responses could be fitted to each other once and for all, and stay this way for as long as it takes to see life-tasks to their completion.

Routine, the habits it requires, and the learning that results in both, do not pay any longer. In a fluid setting, flexibility is the name of rationality. Skills do not retain usefulness for long, for what was yesterday a masterstroke may prove today inane or downright suicidal. Just as long-term commitments threaten to mortgage the future, habits too tightly embraced burden the present; learning may in the long run disempower as it empowers in the short. A promising life-strategy is one that combines learning with forgetting, though how to mix them in the right proportions is anybody's guess. 'You are as good as your last project', warn the career experts. 'Your skills and know-how are as good as their last application', we may add.

The interplay of learning and de-learning, memory and forgetting converges on *experiment*: the major – optimal – modality of acting in a liquid-modern setting. Immersed in a liquid-modern context, though, 'experiment', unlike the leopard, changes its spots. For the solid-modern mind, to 'experiment' meant to try various means until the means best fitting to the given end were found, and to test (or refute as the case may be) a hypothesis – an anticipation of regularity. To experiment in liquid-modern times means trying to deploy the resources at hand in a way hoped to bring the most satisfactory returns, and no regularity is expected to be discovered whatever the results, and hardly ever a hypothesis is there to be tested – trials follow each other at random. Experimenting can be structured no more tightly than the setting in which it is conducted – and the setting of the liquid-modern is more akin to a gambling casino than to a scientific laboratory.

'The social', whatever that awkward word may mean, is under such circumstances reminiscent of the kind of activity of which Odysseus' wife, Penelope, was a past master, and which made her famous: at night she ripped apart the cloth she had woven during the day. Liquid-modern sociality (the term I prefer, since it emphasizes the processuality of relationships; it calls to mind patterning rather than patterns, structuring rather than structures, something constantly in-the-state-of-becoming, unfinished and revocable) manifests itself as much in the assembling of relations as in keeping them eminently 'dismantlable'.

Do we need new methods and concepts to deal with this new reality?

Obviously. But presenting the issue in this way means putting the cart before the horse. Concepts are needed to grasp the objects of cognition, and methods are called for to render them graspable. And so we work out the concepts and the methods as we struggle, laboriously, tortuously and through an unending series of trials and errors, to come to grips with infuriatingly evasive, protean realities. In the course of my work I found it useful, for instance, to distinguish between cognitive, moral and aesthetical socialities, and then to explore their interplay as one of the causes of the mobility and volatility of bonds. Or to deploy, metaphorically, the concept of a 'swarm' to account for the 'unmanaged' uniformity of our times – units of the swarm are known to go through similar motions without commanding officers, marching orders and daily briefings.

As to the method – as you may know, I came to appreciate the way of proceeding which I call 'sociological hermeneutics' (don't confuse, please, with hermeneutical sociology!). It consists, in a nutshell, in reading the observed behavioural tendencies against the conditions under which actors find themselves obliged to go about their life-tasks. The tendencies in question can be seen as the sediments of the search for adequacy – but though the actors do their best to act reasonably, their actions are all too often off the targets that could secure that adequacy, targets that stay essentially out of the actors' reach and so render 'really existing' adequacy permanently wanting.

NG In your book *Globalization: The Human Consequences* (Bauman, 1998) you present a case for the emergence of a new social hierarchy, one that reflects an increasingly rigid class polarization. Is this theory of class also a theory of the social?

ZB A liquid-modern setting is a habitat shared by all denizens of the increasingly globalized planet, but with sharply varying effects: globalization is as divisive in its outcomes as it is unifying. Indeed, we may say that the 'unification' of the planet consists, thus far, mostly in the global reach of the dependencies that ground the new social divisions or new social stratification. Access to mobility is now, in my view, the main stratifying factor on the inner-societal as well as inter-societal scale – but there is a qualitative break in the middle of the hierarchy that prompts us to speak of polarization rather than stratification. That break – rupture, hiatus – separates the extraterritorial realm of 'cyberspace' from the realm of 'places'. The appearance of that break changes radically the stakes and the strategies of power struggles and the nature of domination.

In its 'solid' phase, modernity lived, fought and triumphed under the sign of managerial rule. Management meant detailed design for action, meticulous supervision and continuous disciplinary/corrective intervention. It cast the managed into the 'agentic state' (the modality of acting-on-behest, of being an agent of someone else's will), and placed the responsibility for their performance squarely on the managers' shoulders: the assembly line of a Fordist factory was the managerial dream come true. But the same pattern applied to all cases of domination. That pattern has become now all but redundant: it has been gradually eliminated from the competition on account of its high and unstoppably rising costs.

That pattern (let me call it 'panoptical', in reference to the Foucaldian version of Jeremy Bentham's 'universal solution to all problems of control') made the dependence between the managers and the managed mutual (the managed depended on the managers for their livelihood, the managers depended on the managed for their profits); both sides were 'tied to the place', and both sides knew well that that was the case and was likely to remain the case for a long time to come. That knowledge prompted them to seek improved *modus covivendi*; it induced the managed to fight for favourable changes in the managerial code and learn to deploy their 'nuisance power' in bargaining for such changes. This made the managed an 'unknown variable' in the managers' equations, and thereby a source of uncertainty from which there was no escape due to the mutuality of dependence.

With capital emigrating to the newly emerged 'cyberspace' and the new global frontier-land of fleeting engagements, floating coalitions and few if any binding rules (as described in the last chapter of *Society Under Siege* (Bauman, 2002)), the missing escape-route, and so the capacity of neutralizing the uncertainty generated by the old-type management-related tensions, has been found. Under new conditions of a radical polarization of mobility chances, domination need no longer be grounded in constant and ubiquitous managerial intervention. It is now *disengagement*, or more exactly the unshared capacity of unilateral disengagement and the constantly realistic threat of disengagement, that secures domination. And it does it not just at a much lesser cost than did the old-style management, but also with an added benefit of recasting liabilities into assets, and expenditures into profits.

Of course, disengagement and its threat remain effective as instruments of domination only in as far as the capacity of disengaging remains a privilege – as it is confined to only one, the dominating side of the confrontation. This one-sidedness renders those in control of the movement of capital – the managers or shareholders – a source of perpetual uncertainty in the situation of the dominated, who unlike in the past cannot respond in a similar manner. The new strategy of domination, to remain effective, requires therefore two policies entangled in a blatant, though eagerly hushed, contradiction with each other. On the one hand, promotion of an unbridled freedom of movement for the dominant elite (and for all it stands for – capital, commodities, information). On the other, imposition of ever tighter restrictions on movements of the rest (as manifested most spectacularly, though not exclusively, in the ever more severe anti-migration policies, coupled with the hiving-off of the job of human-waste disposal to global men-smuggling mafia).

Pierre Bourdieu conflated the two mutually complementary policies of domination in the concept of *precarization* – the deliberate expansion of the element of uncertainty in the existential modality of the dominated. To try to control the future, Bourdieu pointed out, one needs to have a grip on the present; *precarization* sees to it that such a grip is weakened or non-existing.

If you wish, you may call the resulting polarization of existential modalities a class system. And any class theory cannot but be a theory of the social – just as class division cannot but be a social division...

NG Do you see there to be a contradiction to your position here? For your theory of liquid modernity posits the new-found fluidity of all social forms, while at the same time you argue that this condition is scarred by an increasingly rigid class polarization. How do these two halves of your argument add up?

ZB Do you see a contradiction here? I cannot, and not just because the 'fluidity of social forms' *does not clash* with the 'rigidity of polarization'. In our new global unsystemic system, they *condition* each other and *reinforce* each other. They would be inconceivable – unthinkable – otherwise than in each other's company and co-operation. 'Rigidity' of the setting is a projection of the helplessness of actors. It is because of the ambient, all-penetrating mood of *precarité* – uncertainty/insecurity (*Unsicherheit*), lack of safety – that the mechanisms that churn out daily polarization seem to be infinitely remote and well off limits, and the gap between what needs to be done and the capacity for doing is widening.

NG Your argument seems to be that the new polarization is based upon a capacity for *movement*, or rather that the 'contemporary global elites' are those 'absentee landlords' who can travel light and at will, while the masses have little choice but to remain tied to their locality. This is all very well, but does this not mean, in essence, that nothing much has changed? For are the boundaries between the extraterritorial elites and the masses still not as *solid* as ever, the only real difference being that you have replaced capital with mobility as the yardstick for 'measuring' class? In practice, are not those with capital (albeit 'light', 'extraterritorial' capital) the ones that also have the ability to move? And if this is the case, have you not simply reproduced, albeit inadvertently, a classical Marxist position: material differences are *the* criteria for defining class?

ZB 'Nothing much has changed?' On the contrary, a lot has changed, and domination-through-disengagement is the difference that has made the difference . . .

This way of muscle-flexing used to be the speciality of highway robbers and robber-barons, appearing from nowhere and in nowhere dissolving – evasive, unpinpointable, uncatchable . . . It was also the common stratagem of the power games played in frontier-lands, as vividly depicted in Hollywood westerns. But now the unregulated, under-institutionalized, all-control-rejecting-and-eliding global space has turned into a frontier-land, where cattle-barons and gunslingers co-operate in exorcizing and keeping away the spectre of control. It is not just that the 'boundaries between extraterritorial elites and the (*glebae adscripti!*) masses are as solid as ever'; the point (a new point!) is precisely that the elites are *extraterritorial*, whereas the rest are, as before, *localized*, as are all the means and agencies of collective action, self-defence and self-government that humanity discovered/invented/deployed and learned to use in the modern era.

The 'solid-modern' setting made the mutual engagement and confrontation of the 'elite' and the 'masses' (capital and labour, as it happened) direct, close, inevitable, inescapable and permanent. Both sides were locality-dependent; they fought for control over the same place while being acutely aware that in that place they were both bound to remain for a very long time to come, that they would share that place tomorrow and the day after, and meet again day in day out. As one would expect in such circumstances, conflict was profound and battles ferocious, but also the desperate search for a liveable *modus covivendi* was earnest and intense. The history of the nineteenth century and a good part of the twentieth was the story of both – culminating in one or another form of a settlement, protracted armistice, 'social compact', welfare state . . . As if following Simmel's formula, conflict was a form of sociation – a preliminary stage and breeding ground of togetherness.

This has changed, and must have changed, when the sides of the conflict disengaged – one side moving into a different space and emancipating from its local bonds and commitments, while the other side stays tied to the place, or is forced to stay tied. By comparison with the new option of breaking bonds and annulling commitments, a permanent engagement based on a negotiated settlement becomes a needless luxury. Hit-and-run tactics may achieve at a lesser cost (and without mortgaging future catch-the-opportunity chances) the same purpose that the building and manning of permanent garrisons, daily policing and the carrying of responsibility for the law, order, welfare and social peace, pursued with much greater expense and laborious effort.

May I remind you that according to the foremost authority – Marx himself – there is nothing 'Marxist' in the observation that 'material differences' separate classes. It was only the proof of the inevitability of the proletarian revolution as the ultimate outcome of class struggle that Marx believed to be his original contribution to what has been the common sense of the time – the *doxa* of the boffins and the newspapermen alike. But Marx's proof rested on the assumption that the exploited and their exploiters are bound to stay in each other's embrace indefinitely, united for better or worse in the managed reproduction of capital. It is that assumption that no longer rings true.

As to the impact of what you call 'material differences' in diversifying human conditions: do you have any doubt that it has retained its full significance now, more than two hundred years after it had turned into the canon of political economy and historiography? I believe that relegating 'material differences' to the rank of lesser, even if unpleasant, traits of our world is a snub and an offence to the 40 per cent of mankind who live on two dollars a day or less on a planet shared with Enron or World.com bosses, their accountants and lawyers . . .

NG Following on from this, in your recent books you repeatedly remind us that large numbers of the world's population continue to live in desperate poverty, and beyond this that the gap between the rich and poor is continuing to grow. In *Globalization: The Human Consequences* (Bauman, 1998: 70), for example, you say that 'the total wealth of the top 358 "global billionaires" equals the combined incomes of 2.3 billion poorest people (45 per cent of the world's population)'. In *In Search of Politics* (1999: 175–6): 'Among 4.5 billions of the residents of the "developing" countries, three in every five are deprived access to basic infrastructures: a third has no access to drinkable water, a quarter has no accommodation worthy of the name, one-fifth has no use of sanitary and medical services ... In 70–80 of the 100 or so "developing" countries the average income per head of population is today lower than ten or even thirty years ago. 120 million people live on less than one dollar a day.' And once again, in *The Individualized Society*: 'in the USA, by far the richest country in the world and the homeland of the world's wealthiest people, 16.5 per cent of the population live in poverty; one-fifth of adult men and women can neither read nor write, while 13 per cent have a life expectancy shorter than sixty years' (Bauman, 2001: 115). Do you have an idea of how 'international development' should take place (if indeed it is desirable)?

ZB I am not quite sure what do you mean by 'international development', but if you mean what I suppose you do – the taming, 'civilizing' of the new global frontier-land, the seeking and finding of a global equivalent of the tools of democratic control and justice-oriented politics that have been developed throughout the modern era at the nation-state level, but not beyond – then the answer is yes, it is desirable, and it is, in addition, imperative. But I leave to history (operated by our shared human inventiveness) the way and form in which this task, certainly through a long series of trials and errors, will be eventually accomplished . . .

For better or worse, we have now entered the times of *convergence between the interest in self-preservation and the obedience to ethical command*. Today, self-preservation and morality dictate the same policy and strategy. Your loss is no more my gain. Cohabitation on a full planet is *not* a zero-sum game. In these turbulent times we are all in the same boat now. *We will sail safely together – or together will we sink*.

And so self-preservation and ethics have finally met – but only because social realities, through history, have reached a moment that philosophers, through the ingenuity of reason, were vainly trying to reach.

Only a few wise men predicted that this would happen and that it would happen in the way it did. Immanuel Kant was one of the most outstanding among those few. In 1784 – more than two centuries ago, when few if any signs, and certainly no symptoms visible to the residents of the tranquil town of Königsberg where he lived and thought, augured the imminent filling up of the human planet – Kant sent to the publishers a little book titled *Idee zu einer allgemeinen Geshichte in weltbürgerlicher Absicht* [*Idea for a Universal History With a Cosmopolitan Intent* (Kant, 1983)]. In this book, Kant observed that the planet we inhabit is a sphere – and that in the consequence of that admittedly banal fact we all can only move on the surface of that sphere. Since we have nowhere else to go, we are bound to live forever in each other's neighbourhood and company. And if you move on a spherical surface, you will sooner rather than later find that the distance shrinks as you try to stretch it. All effort to lengthen a distance between you and the others and to keep it long cannot but be ultimately self-defeating. And so *die volkommene bürgerliche Vereinigung in der Menschengattung* ['the perfect unification of the human species through common citizenship'], Kant concluded, is the destiny Nature has chosen for us – the ultimate horizon of our *allgemeine Geschichte* that, prompted and guided by reason and the instinct of self-preservation, we are bound to pursue, and in the fullness of time reach. This is what Kant found out – but it took the world more than two hundred years of experimenting, blundering, trials and errors, to find out how right the Königsberg philosopher was.

Kant's foresight has been, ultimately, vindicated – when it became obvious that the *era of space* (the time when space was the most coveted of prizes, the prime stake in the power struggle and the cure-it-all medicine for apparent and putative social troubles) has come to its close.

Throughout that era, territory was the most avidly desired of resources, the plum prize in any power struggle, while its acquisition or loss was the mark of distinction between the victors and the defeated. But above all, territory was throughout that era the prime guarantor of security. 'Security' was a territorial matter: the era of space was the time of 'deep hinterland', *Lebensraum*, 'sanitary belts' – and the Englishmen's homes that were their castles. Power itself was territorial, and so was the privacy and freedom from power's interference. Land was a shelter, and a hideout: a place to which one could escape and inside which one could lock oneself up, 'go underground' and feel safe. The powers-that-be which one wished to escape and hide from stopped at the borders.

This is all over now, and has been over for some considerable time – but that it is indeed definitely over has become dazzlingly evident only after 11 September 2001. The events of 11 September made obvious that no one, however resourceful, distant and aloof, can cut oneself off from the rest of the world.

It has also become clear that the annihilation of the protective capacity of space is a double-edged sword: no one can hide from blows, and blows can be plotted and delivered from however enormous a distance. Places no longer protect, however strongly they are armed and fortified. Strength and weakness, security and danger have now become essentially *extraterritorial* (diffuse) *issues that evade territorial* (and focused) *solutions*. However fortified and armed, *any place and any population can be truly secure only inside a secure world*; a world in which no one has reason or desire to shoot one's own way to survival, to the escape from one's own humiliation or to the destruction or the humiliation of others. We need to repeat the immortal truth of Aristotle: outside a *polis*, only a beast or an angel can live; but in our time we need also add that no human *polis* can survive for long unless there is a will to remake the world into a shared *polis*.

Nothing done today in any, however remote and secluded, part of the world can be guaranteed to remain indifferent and with no influence on the fate of all the rest of the planet. And nothing can be done in any, however powerful and fortified, segment of the globe without counting the consequences for, and the response of, all the other sectors. For all practical intents and purposes, we are all dependent on each other, and so we bear responsibility for each other's fate whether we know it or not and whether we like it or not. The problem – the life and death problem – is whether we 'take responsibility for that responsibility' and make the planet our shared home and the human species, as Kant suggested we should, our joint community.

All communities are imagined: the 'global community' is no exception. But imagination turns into an effective integrating force when aided by socially produced and socially sustained institutions of collective self-identification and self-government. As far as the imagined *global* community is concerned, such an institutional network (woven of global agencies of democratic control, globally binding legal systems and globally upheld ethical principles) is today largely absent. And little has been done to make it reality.

In his recent sober assessment of the current tendency, David Held (2002) observed 'strong temptations to simply put up the shutters and defend the position of some nations and countries only'. He did not find the post-11 September prospects particularly encouraging. They contain a chance to 'strengthen our multilateral institutions and international legal agreements', but there is also a possibility of responses that 'could take us away from these fragile gains toward a world of further antagonisms and divisions – a distinctively uncivil society'. Held's overall summary is anything but optimistic: 'At the time of writing,' he says, 'the signs are not good'. Our consolation, though (the *only* consolation available, but also – let me add – the *only one* humankind needs when falling on dark times) is the fact the 'history is still with us and can be made'.

Yes, indeed – history is anything but finished, the choices still can and, inevitably, will be made. And, as Hannah Arendt told us:

> The world is not humane just because it is made by human beings, and it does not become humane just because the human voice sounds in it, but only when it has become the object of discourse ... We humanize what is going on in the world and in ourselves only by speaking of it, and in the course of speaking of it we learn to be human. The Greeks called this humanness which is achieved in the discourse of friendship *philanthropia*, 'love of man', since it manifests itself in a readiness to share the world with other men. (1968: 24–5)

The above words of Hannah Arendt could be – should be – read as prolegomena to all future efforts aimed at arresting the reverse drift and bringing history closer to the ideal of 'human community'. Following Gottlieb Ephraim Lessing, one of her intellectual heroes, Arendt avers that 'openness to others' is 'the precondition of "humanity" in every sense of the word ... [T]ruly human dialogue differs from mere talk or even discussion in that it is entirely permeated by pleasure in the other person and what he says' (1968: 15).

Willingly, if with sadness, I admit that the odds against common humanity seem overwhelming. Looking around the world we share one is tempted to dream of a better place from which to start on the road to the planet-wide humanity. In one of those incisive and uncompromising Irish jokes, a passer-by asked by a driver 'how to get from here to Dublin', answers: 'If I wished to go to Dublin, I wouldn't start from here.' Indeed, one can imagine a world better fit to journey towards Kant's 'universal unity of mankind'. But there is no such alternative world, and so no other site from which to start the journey. And yet not starting it, and starting with no more delay, is – in this case beyond doubt – *not an option.*

The unity of human species that Kant postulated may be indeed, as he suggested, resonant with Nature's intention – but it certainly does not seem 'historically determined'. The continuing uncontrollability of the already global network of mutual dependence and 'mutually assured vulnerability' most certainly does not increase the chance of such unity. This only means, however, that at no other time has the keen search for common humanity, and the practice that follows such an assumption, been as urgent and imperative as it is now.

NG So far we have concentrated on the negative side of liquid modernity (as you yourself tend to in your recent books) – as characterized, for example, by the increased transience, uncertainty and insecurity of all social forms. But is there not also a positive side to the 'liquefaction' and individualization of society? For example, take the question of identity. You say that individualization transforms identity 'from a given into a task' (one accompanied by a *de jure* autonomy but not necessarily a *de facto* one) (Bauman, 2001: 144). This is because individualization attacks the traditional supports and agencies that previously aided the individual in constructing and fixing his or her identity, and as a result leaves us to pursue the task of identity formation in increasing isolation. At this point, identity becomes privatized, and transformed into a matter of 'obligatory' self-determination, meaning that identity formation becomes divorced from all collective or *social* responsibility, and in the process becomes an individual *burden*, with 'pattern-weaving and the responsibility for failure' falling 'primarily on the individual's shoulders' (Bauman, 2000: 7–8). This might indeed be the case, but need this situation necessarily be seen as a burden? What, for example, of the political gains that have accompanied 'liquid modernization'? And what, to use Castells' (1997) term, of 'the power of identity'? These seem, to me at least, to be important questions, for liquid modernity might also contain exciting opportunities for breaking from the institutional constraints of the first modernity. It might, for example, contain the possibility for transcending rigid class identities and fictional ties with nature, and, as a result, open new political questions about what it means to be black, a woman, gay, or simply to *be*. In this light, identity formation need not be seen as a burden but perhaps as a positive site for the expression of a new cultural politics. It is at precisely this point, however, that the question of identity becomes, for you, a problem. Why is this? In speaking of the negative

attributes of liquid modernization, are you also placing a positive value on
things that have been lost, including class, the family or other institutions that
you see as being successful in protecting collective freedoms or in taking
responsibility for individual failures? In this respect, is there a slight nostalgia
for the stability and rigidness of the past that underlies your critique of liquid
modernity?

ZB   The bane of one type of human togetherness is not a cure for the banes of
another. This is the sad truth that could be easily gained from even a cursory
look at societies of the past, none of them known to be free of its own well-
justified discontents, and the ill-conceived or abortive (but atrocious whenever
their implementation was attempted) programmes of replacing them with a
made-to-order society without blemish. Projectionism is fraught with risks,
nostalgia is naïve – though being what we are, the chance that we will stop
indulging in one or another is, to say the least, slim.

Being free of chains is wonderful, but so is the possibility of knowing how to
proceed and act with a degree of certainty. Having one's hands and feet tied is
awful, but so is living in a state of a prospect-less uncertainty and never being
sure whether the step about to be taken, or just taken, does not lead into a trap
or into a blind alley. Freedom and security are two values indispensable for
decent human life – but all too often they resist reconciliation. We have kept
seeking an optimal balance between the two throughout human history, but all
attempts to find such a balance, let alone to keep it in place once found, have
thus far failed. It seems that freedom and security are horizons rather than
realities, always 'not yet' (for keen reformers) or 'have been' (for conservatives),
but always wanting in their 'really existing' versions. There is always too little of
one or the other, and the more we get of one, the more poignantly we feel the
dearth of the other. One recalls the famous parable of a bed-sheet too short:
when you cover your nose, your feet get frozen – when you cover your feet,
your nose gets cold . . .

I have already mentioned that modernity was from its birth an era of 'disembedding'. In the garden called 'modern society', human plants were set free
from the plot in which they germinated and from which they sprouted. But for
the better part of modern history they did not shed their floral nature: unless
replanted in a different flowerbed, they were bound to wilt and fade. During
the 'solid' phase of modernity, the 'disembedding' was to be promptly followed
by a 're-embedding'. Once classes replaced the estates, human plants were no
longer bound to remain in the same bed for the duration of their life – but each
bed to which they could be transferred was as clearly delineated as the
ascriptive estates used to be. Individuals' social places could be no longer
'ascribed', but the alternative positions on offer now had their rules of

admission (even the position of origin had acquired its rules of acceptance), and the rules of conduct remained class-ascribed, combining into strict, legible and learnable membership conditions. As Jean-Paul Sartre put it – 'it is not enough to be born as a bourgeois. One needs to live all his life as a bourgeois.' And there was little doubt as to what the 'living of a bourgeois life' should be like; little room was left for experimentation.

Like in its first stage, modernity in its later 'liquid' phase remains the era of disembedding. No longer, though, is the disembedding promptly followed by a 're-embedding'. It is not just that alternative beds on offer have become more profuse and that therefore the act of replanting can be repeated more often. The change has reached further and deeper: at no stretch of their life-itinerary can individuals be correctly described as 'embedded' (even if only temporarily and 'until further notice') because flowerbeds have ceased to be as clearly defined as before; their boundaries are now unclear if not washed out altogether. Instead of seeking their proper, prefabricated locations, individuals must conjure up the locations as they go – and the only roads in sight are the lines of footprints they have left behind. Society no longer looks like a garden; it seems to have returned to a state of wilderness, or rather a 'secondary wilderness', a frontier-land, where locations need to be first carved and fenced off to be fit for settlement.

Alberto Melucci, in *The Playing Self*, is most emphatic in his description of the seminal change in the conditions of life and the life-strategies they require:

> We can no longer conceive of our needs as compelling and instinctual urges, or as transparent manifestations of a benevolent nature that guides us. But nor can we continue to labour under the illusion that nature can be substituted by a society to which we assign the task of instructing us or which we accuse of repression. Needs are a signal of something that we lack, and it is up to us to recognize these needs and to give them cultural expression. (1996: 28)

We can skip the 'needs' word; the important thing is the (however called) sense of lack: of un-finishedness, of un-accomplishment, of something continually, harrowingly missing and missed, of a road ahead stubbornly refusing to shorten, let alone promising to reach its (vexingly invisible) destination. That eerie feeling – that the world around and the world inside are both (to deploy the never bettered expression of Ernst Bloch) *noch nicht geworden*. It is the sense of lack so understood (or rather so experienced) that makes us all compulsive and obsessive identity-seekers, but also prevents us from ever finishing the search. We are, so to speak, bound to remain the 'also-runs' in the lifelong chase after identity: identity's failed discoverers or industrious yet hapless constructors.

Freedom to choose identity, like all freedoms, has its positive and negative aspects. What is celebrated in most postmodernist literature is the positive aspect: freedom to choose at will the difference of one's liking and to 'make it stick' come what may. Such *positive* freedom is today a privilege of the global elite and off limits for a great majority of the planet's residents. A substantial part of that majority, though, have not as yet come anywhere near obtaining and securing their *negative* freedom: freedom to refute and reject the differences enforced by others, and to resist being 'socially recognized', against their will, for what they resent to be, and would actively refuse to be were it in their power.

Freedom to choose and keep an identity is, like all freedoms, a social relation; freedom of some *presumes* un-freedom of some others, and more often than not is enjoyed as a *privilege* – no privilege being conceivable unless coupled with someone else's deprivation. Like most new departures in history, the liquid-modern version of the 'identity problem' and of self-formation is not a blessing uniformly enjoyed by all. It only augurs a new mechanism of redistribution of blessings and banes and a new method of counting gains and losses.

Anthony Elliot attempted to grasp the dual nature of the present-day transformations and the duality of reactions they prompt by suggesting the co-presence of two sharply distinct 'object-relational configurations' (Elliot, 1996: 4). The first, 'modern', 'suggests a mode of fantasy in which security and enjoyment are derived by attempting to control, order and regulate the self, others, and sociopolitical world'. The second, 'postmodern', 'suggests a mode of fantasy in which reflective space is more central to identity and politics, the creation of open spaces to embrace plurality, ambiguity, ambivalence, contingency and uncertainty'. Elliot's main point, though, is that in contemporary society *both* 'reveries', modern and postmodern, are deployed – with, inevitably, a considerable amount of tensions and contradictions.

The two 'reveries' (manifested in two diametrically opposed life-strategies, or two mutually contradictory political predilections/impulses, or both) are indeed present in a liquid-modern context, but they are not, let me comment, *class-ascribed*. Neither are the two actual, feared or desired social conditions (of freedom and un-freedom) with which they correlate. The two 'reveries' and the two social contexts in which they tend to arise are rather the ideal-typical extremal points of a continuum along which the perceived condition, as well as the strategies deemed appropriate to such conditions, are plotted – and along which they vacillate.

Regarding the identity-related issues, both freedom and un-freedom are realistic prospects for *each and any* resident of a liquid-modern society. None of the currently privileged and enjoyable situations is guaranteed to last, while most of the currently handicapped and resented positions can be in principle renegotiated using the rules of the liquid-modern game. There is, accordingly, a mixture of hope and fear in every heart, spread over the whole spectrum of the emergent planetary stratification. And so is the perpetual ambivalence about the strategy most appropriate in a stubbornly ambiguous world. Inter-mittently actors and victims, torn between joyful bouts of self-confidence and sinister premonitions of vulnerability and doom, the denizens of the planet may be excused for their volatile moods, schizophrenic demeanour, inclination to panic and lust for witch-hunting.

NG   A key idea of the liquid modernity thesis is that society is undergoing a process of individualization, by which you mean (as I read it) that agency is becoming disengaged from the social system, and individual choices and lives are becoming isolated from collective projects and actions. When this happens, what is left of 'society'? And how is the process connected to the rise of 'community' or 'communitarian' ideas?

ZB   As the received structures are one by one thrown into a melting pot, as no new reliably solid structures seem likely to be moulded in the foreseeable future, and as the fast filling-up planet turns into an all-embracing and all-inclusive frontier-land – *all* denizens of our crowded planet tend to be simul-taneously the subjects and the objects of interminable re-identification pressures and recognition claims. Groups obliged to struggle for the right to self-identification and to demand and obtain recognition for their choices are not necessarily confined to the lower rungs of the planetary hierarchy. The struggle is no longer vertical (nor as a rule up-hill), and is not confined to groups and categories clamouring or fighting for admission to some higher, more comfortable locations in a multi-storey building. It is rather a struggle for a legitimate, reserved and secure (not necessarily 'superior') place on a horizontal and essentially flat terrain.

On a crowded planet, such a struggle can be hardly successful without encroaching upon, and in the end limiting, some other groups' property rights and bids. Identity, as it were, defines one's own difference from others, but such a self-definition inevitably entails the definition of differences that dis-tinguish and separate others from the self-defining agent. In most cases, therefore, the purpose of 'recognition wars' tends to be twofold: gaining recognition for one's own chosen identity, and disqualifying or overpowering the others' refusal to accept the identities one had composed for them and would wish them to be known for. 'Identity' is, to sum it all up, a multiply contested, intrinsically agonistic concept. The process of self-identification cannot but generate conflicts, and on many fronts simultaneously.

Like in all verbal or armed conflicts, success depends ultimately on the volume and quality of resources the warring sides can muster, and the skill with which available resources are deployed and operated. Effective imposition of a self-definition calls for legions of make-up experts, public-personae designers, dressers, public-conduct trainers and spin-doctors. Alongside the factories of security gadgets and security agencies, PR is nowadays the most profitable and expansive of industries.

Entering the recognition game, collectivities cannot bypass the media. Only some groups and associations are, however, prosperous enough to buy their entry. The others, too numerous and varied to be listed, need to resort to other resources – their nuisance-making power being arguably the most prominent among them. Once upon a time, the ability of industrial or service workers to bring a significant fraction of daily functions to a standstill used to be the decisive factor in gaining recognition for the rights and dignity of labour. Today's terrorists resort to much more violent, gory and shocking demonstrations of their nuisance-making capacity, but they follow a similar pattern. Indeed, the same pattern is likely to be followed whatever measures are undertaken to suppress it and force it out of use. Terror, after all, is the poorman's version of PR.

'When contemplating change,' Melucci pointed out, 'we are always torn between desire and fear, anticipation and uncertainty' (Melucci, 1996: 45). The point is, however, that in the liquid-modern world, *not* contemplating change is no longer an option. And on a full planet you can no longer ask for whom the bells toll, since no attempted change, by whomever it has been contemplated and tried, is likely to bypass you and leave you unaffected, just as no change you contemplate yourself would leave unaffected the rest of the planet's residents. The compound of desire and fear is the *milieu* in which we conduct our daily life-pursuits, just as the mixture of nitrogen and oxygen is the air we breathe.

Hence a spectre hovers over the planet: a spectre of xenophobia. Old and new, never extinguished or freshly unfrozen and warmed-up tribal suspicions and animosities have mixed and blended with the brand-new fear for safety distilled from old and new uncertainties and insecurities of liquid-modern existence.

People worn-out and dead-tired by the forever inconclusive tests of adequacy, and frightened to the raw by the mysterious, inexplicable precariousness of their fortunes and by global mists hiding their prospects from view, desperately seek the culprits of their trials and tribulations. They find them, unsurprisingly, under the nearest lamppost – in the only spot obligingly illuminated by the forces of law and order. 'It is the criminals who make you feel insecure, and it is the outsiders who cause crime'; and so 'it is the rounding up, incarcerating and deporting of outsiders that will restore the lost or stolen security'. Donald G. McNeil Jr (2002) titled his summary of the most recent shifts in the European political spectrum 'Politicians pander to fear of crime'. Indeed, throughout the world ruled by democratically elected governments, the 'I'll be tough on crime' slogan has turned out to be the trump card, but the winning hand is almost invariably a combination of a 'more prisons, more policemen, longer sentences' promise with a 'no immigration, no asylum rights, no naturalization' oath. As McNeil (2002) put it: 'Politicians across Europe use the "outsiders cause crime" stereotype to link ethnic hatred, which is unfashionable, to the more palatable fear for one's own safety.'

NG You also say that the primary threat to democratic society is no longer authoritarian in nature (as it was in industrial society), but comes instead from the individualization of all public and collective forms. In other words, the danger no longer lies in the homogenization of private (the *oikos*) and public/ private space (the *agora*) by totalitarian public powers (the predominance of the *ecclesia*), but in the reverse: the reduction of public issues to private concerns, and, beyond this, the increased inability to link the two. In response to this situation, you suggest that the object of critical theory should change: it should no longer be centred on exposing and countering the threat of totalitarianism (as it was for Adorno, Horkheimer and also Arendt), but should address the problem of individualization, and with this the reduction of social critique to *self*-critique, as its main priority. This appears to mean tackling democracy on two fronts, so that both individuals (or rather citizens) *and* society retain their autonomy: rendering the former 'free to form their own opinions and to cooperate in order to make words flesh', and the latter 'free to set its laws and knowing that there is no other warrant of the goodness of the law than the earnest and diligent exercise of that freedom' (Bauman, 2001: 202). The role of critical theory here seems to be to redefine the relation of public and private space: the *ecclesia* must be protected from the invasion of private interests, while at the same time the *agora* is to be revitalized so that the collective (*social*) basis of private/personal troubles can be brought to the fore. A number of questions might be addressed to this position (if, indeed, I have understood it correctly). First, exactly *how* is such a critical theory to play a role in reconfiguring public-private space, or, more precisely, how do you suggest moving from theory to practice? For example, you say, following Castoriadis I believe, that society is to 'put itself into question'. But how might social theory, or sociology more generally, set about translating this into a public concern? And second, your response to the threat of individualization seems to have shifted from an emphasis on asceticism or *self-limitation* in *In Search of Politics* (Bauman, 1999: 4) to a demand for a stronger and more autonomous ecclesia in *Liquid Modernity* (Bauman, 2000: 51). Why is this?

ZB   You have represented my views faithfully and you have flawlessly spotted all the axial points. I am, indeed, grateful. And you have unerringly articulated the most seminal of questions that follow: 'how is critical theory to play a role in reconfiguring the private-public sphere?' Since I have insisted all along that sociology, whether by design or by default, cannot help but be critical about society, its object (through sapping its foundational confidence in the 'naturalness' or, what amounts in practice to much the same, in the 'rationality' of its ways and means), I take it that your question can be stretched to overlap with the functions of sociology as a whole.

I believe that no one better than Pierre Bourdieu answered that question – and I fully endorse his answer, albeit with a few added clarifications. With a whole-hearted approval, Bourdieu quoted Emmanuel Terray, who in his turn draws inspiration from the ancient wisdom of Hippocrates: 'A passive recording of the symptoms as described in the confessions of the sick can be done by anybody. If that were enough to intervene effectively, there would be no need of the medics' (Terray, 1990: 92–3). But the commonly available diagnostic ability does not suffice. Hence the need of medics when it comes to the cure of bodily ailments, and of sociologists when it is the *social* body that falls victim of a disease. And so genuine medicine starts 'with the cognition of the invisible illnesses, that is facts of which the sick person does not speak, of which he is not aware or which he has forgotten to mention'. Among such invisible and unspoken-of facts are social realities that constitute the domain of sociological study . . .

'Genuine medicine starts here.' But where do we go from here? A moment of reflection would show that 'to make people aware of the mechanism that makes their life miserable, perhaps even unliveable, does not mean to neutralize them; bring into light the contradictions does not mean to resolve them'. A long and tortuous road stretches between the recognition of the roots of trouble and their eradication, and making the first step in no way assures that further steps will be taken, let alone that the road will be followed to the end. And yet there is no denying the crucial importance of beginning – of laying bare the complex network of causal links between pains suffered individually and conditions collectively produced. In sociology, and even more in a sociology which strives to be up to its task inside our *Risikogesellschaft* ['Risk Society'], the beginning is yet more decisive than elsewhere; it is this first step that designates and paves the road to rectification which otherwise would not exist, let alone be noticed. And this is so for two reasons.

To start with, the *risks* that have taken over the role of the major threats to human existence from the traditional *dangers* of the past, differ from their predecessors in one paramount respect. Old-style troubles were straightforward and all too obvious to the sufferers. There was no doubt that they were real, nor was there any question that something had to be done to stave them off, defuse, rectify, mitigate, or at least alleviate. There was no mystery either about what was to be done, even though the means to do it were often difficult to come by (in the case of hunger, for instance, it was self-evident to the point of banality that food, and food alone, was the remedy). Not so in the case of risks. Most of them are neither seen nor felt. Though we are all exposed to their consequences and to one degree or another suffer in their result, we can neither smell, hear, see nor touch the slowly but unstoppably worsening climatic patterns, rising levels of radiation and pollution, fast shrinking supplies of non-renewable raw materials and sources of energy; and, indeed (it is here that sociology comes fully and truly into its own), the politically and ethically uncontrolled processes of globalization that sap the roots of our existence, dismantle safety networks together with the social bonds that sustained them, and infuse individual life with unprecedented volumes of anxiety-generating uncertainty. And when we hear of 'sustainable growth', as Jeremy Seabrook (2002) recently commented, we are made to believe that it means 'what the market, not the earth, can bear'.

We would hardly know of all this happening were we not told that this is the case and alerted to the possible consequences of the processes under way. Singly, severally or even all together we would not come to that knowledge were we to confine ourselves to the individually available experiences. As Ulrich Beck, who more than anyone else alerted us to the intricate mechanisms of *Risikogesellschaft*, put it, 'we the citizens have lost sovereignty over our senses and thus the residual sovereignty over our judgment . . . [N]one are so blind to the danger as those who continue to trust their eyes' (Beck, 1995: 66–7). The direct link between perception and effective (remedial or reforming) action has been broken – and cannot be tied up again without assistance. The new, repaired link can be only a *mediated* one. To confront their existential condition and come to grips with its challenges, humans need to step beyond the individually accessible experiential data; call it critique – it most certainly is a critique of the 'obvious' and the 'self-evident'. And the sought-after adequacy between condition and action will not be established without *interpretation*. This circumstance assigns a totally new role to the interpreters armed with an access to data not available inside, and only obliquely accessible from individual experience.

Unlike orthodox dangers, the risks saturating the human condition in the world of global dependencies may be not only overlooked, but also 'interpreted away' even when noticed. They may be denied, unduly played down, assigned to putative causes. Accordingly, actions that need to be undertaken to thwart or limit the risks may be diverted away from the true sources of danger, and the diffuse anxiety generated by ambient fear and endemic uncertainty may be channelled against the wrong targets. The urge to act, instead of being systematically deployed in confronting the risks point-blank, may be used up in sporadic and random outbursts that leave the founts of uncertainty by and large unscathed and intact. Scattered, unfocused uncertainty, in which *Risikoleben* (life of risk) is soaked even at its most tranquil and enjoyable moments, lends itself, notoriously, to many, often incompatible, interpretations.

The locating of the social factories of the anxiety-ridden products is a contentious matter. Answers to the vexing question 'what is to be done?' are, as a rule, hotly contested. Interpretation is an ongoing, perpetually inconclusive process, full of trials and errors and of frustrated, though seldom if ever ultimately defeated, hopes. Sociology is an integral part of the interpretative process, a potentially powerful voice in the never-ending dialogue; a real-life version of the hermeneutic spiral, in which not just the understanding, but the quality of the human condition is at stake. Much in the success or failure of the interpretation-targeted public dialogue hangs on sociology acquitting itself, as it should, of the task of stretching the cognitive horizons of interpretative effort.

And so we come to the second reason for which 'the first step' acquires a uniquely decisive role in coping effectively with the trials and tribulations of *Risikoleben*, and for which sociology, as long as it makes the widening of its interpretative frame the focus of its vocation, acquires an added significance. This second reason lies in the process of individualization – one of the most prominent and seminal aspects of the great social transformation that leads to the present-day 'liquid-modern' condition.

Casting members as 'individuals' is the trademark of modern society. That casting, however, is not a one-off act; it is an activity re-enacted daily. Now, as before – in the 'fluid' as much as in the 'solid' stage of modernity – individuality is a universal human fate, not a matter of individual choice.

The individual's self-containment and self-sufficiency, which is sometimes taken to be the substance of 'individualization', may be an illusion. That men and women have no one to blame for their frustrations and troubles does not need to mean now, anymore than it did in the past, that they can protect themselves against frustration using their own domestic appliances, or pull themselves out of trouble, Baron Munchausen style, by their bootstraps. Risks and contradictions go on being socially produced; it is our duty and necessity to cope with those that are being individualized. The self-assertive capacity of individualized men and women, however, falls short, as a rule, of what a genuine self-constitution would require. And yet this sad truth has been made difficult to grasp. Troubles may be similar, but they no longer seem to form a 'totality greater than the sum of its parts'; they neither acquire a new quality nor become easier to handle by being faced in company. The sole 'advantage' that being in the company of other sufferers may bring is to reassure each individual that fighting troubles alone is what all others do daily – so as to refresh and boost once more the flagging resolve to go on doing just that.

The overall effects of 'individualization by decree of fate' are what Dany-Robert Dufour (2001) described recently as 'new forms of alienation and inequality'. All 'grand figures placed in the centre of symbolic configurations' – like *physis*, God, King, people, nation, race or proletariat, have one by one disappeared from the horizon of life-projects, intestate and without successors. In the absence of the Other to which one could relate the logic of one's own life-pursuits, the individual is doomed to seek, zealously yet in vain, 'a self-referential definition'. 'The new individuals are abandoned rather than liberated.'

Abandoned to the Sisyphean labours of self-reference, individuals are drawn away from the idea that the collectively designed, shaped up and run mechanisms of their individually suffered troubles could be changed and made more human-friendly. They are prevented thereby from embarking on the sole expedition that may lead to the promotion of their 'individuality by decree' to the rank of individuality *de facto*, and to the genuine self-assertion that defines it. In the absence of credible translations between the languages of private worries and public issues, and with dedicated and trustworthy translators conspicuous mostly by their non-availability, the *agora* loses its past charms and attraction. The individual, as Alexis de Tocqueville prophetically declared, is an enemy of the citizen. Citizens reincarnated as individual consumers leave the *agora* in droves. But the vacated space does not stay empty for long. It is populated once more, this time, though, by individuals wishing to be reassured in the irreversibility of their fate. The new *agora* has become a stage where private individuals confess and rehearse in public their private struggles with privately suffered and privately confronted individual adversities. From this *agora*, both the actors and the spectators emerge reinforced in their belief that this is exactly how the world is constructed and how its residents need to live their lives.[1]

In other words, the *agora*, in Castoriadis' spot-on definition 'public/private space', ceases to be the site of translation between private and public, that substance of all politics, and particularly of democratic politics. If the new 'individualized' predicament and the consequent disempowerment of citizens *qua* citizens is to be confronted point-blank, the art of the translation needs to be relearned and the *agora* made once more available for practising it. It is in this awesomely difficult yet imperative task that sociology is to take, as Pierre Bourdieu keeps reminding us, the crucial role. This is a life-and-death matter for the sociological vocation – not another manifestation of scientist conceit and unwarranted pretension. This is also the condition of reuniting the *vita contemplativa* and *vita activa* and so salvaging them both of the impotence and irrelevance unavoidable in separation. This is, finally, the task in pursuit of which the intellectual vocation is formed, or rather, stands a chance of resurrection at a time when the dismantling of bridges connecting the *Lebenswelt* of individuals and the real world shaped up by forces unknown to them and escaping their control is fast turning into the major cause of the new *misère du monde*.

Indeed, we need to repeat after Pierre Bourdieu: 'those who have the opportunity to devote their lives to the study of the social world, cannot rest neutral and indifferent regarding the struggles in which the future of humanity is at stake' (quoted in Lanzmann and Redeker, 1998: 14).

NG   It seems to me that in your 'search for politics' your sociology takes a legislative rather than interpretive form. For example, you say that an empowered public/private sphere is tied to a more inclusive ideal of citizenship, which in turn rests upon work to alleviate mass poverty. This, you suggest, could be achieved through the introduction of a basic income (Bauman, 1999: 182–3), and through the pursuit, more generally, of a new republicanism (1999: 168). This is all very well, but why should sociology be a legislative science? You say that value-freedom (*Wertfreiheit*) is 'as human silences are concerned – not just a pipe-dream, but also an utterly inhuman delusion ...' (Bauman and Beilharz, 2001: 335). Does this mean that sociology is to be political in nature, and with this abandon any attempt to be either scientific or objective? If this is the case, then why not simply write a political manifesto that tells us *how* individuals are to be transformed into citizens, how the *agora* is to be rebuilt, or what rules should be implemented to protect the public sphere? Why write sociology? What is its continuing appeal?

ZB   I guess you can easily predict my answer to this question from what I said a moment ago, commenting on Bourdieu's ideas of *vita activa* being, in the case of the sociologist, a natural consequence of *vita contemplativa*. But let me restate this point with stronger emphasis – and falling yet deeper in debt to Bourdieu...

Reviewing the latest collection of Bourdieu's trenchant essays and public statements, Thomas Ferenczi noted that in recent years Bourdieu 'renounced in a number of his interventions the attitude of a scientist in order to assume the posture of a militant' (Ferenczi, 2001: 8). One may question, however, Ferenczi's interpretation of the shift. Did the ever more active presence of Bourdieu on the public stage and his increasing tendency to focus on the most topical issues of the day (issues that happened as well to occupy the attention of the politically alert and attuned part of the public) signal renunciation of the scholarly, academic role? Is the abandonment of scholarly, academic values a price one is bound to pay for political commitment? Scientist *or* a militant – either/or?

Himself, Bourdieu would deny the dilemma, as we can judge from the following admission: 'I found myself led by the logic of my work to transgress the limits assigned to me in the name of the idea of objectivity – that appeared to me more like an idea of censorship'. Far from being either an act of treachery or a feat of reincarnation, the new militancy has been brought about and moved to the fore by the professional logic which sociologists need to obey for the sake of their professional integrity. The logic of sociology leads inescapably to transgression – to the *transcendence* of genuine or putative 'objectivity' of research and its interpretation. Sociology cannot but trespass, continuously and resolutely, on the boundaries drawn between academic study *sine ira et studio* and the always-already-engaged-and-committed, subjective experience of its human objects/partners-in-conversation.

Bourdieu's sudden and widely publicized entry into political debate might be seen as a U-turn for someone preaching for years the purity and impartiality of objective science, but looking back on the way the subject matter of sociology was construed by Bourdieu from the very start of his academic life, one could conclude that rather than a change of course, this entry was pre-determined, perhaps even over-determined, by the whole development of his social theory. As Philippe Frisch points out, political confrontation was inevitable for a thinker who as far back as 1972 asserted that 'power of the words and power over words always suppose others kinds of power' (Frisch, 2000: 11). Already in 1984, Bourdieu defined political struggle as a 'struggle to maintain or change a vision of the social world, through the conservation or modification of the categories of the world-perception and working on the constitution of common sense that appears as the truth of the social world' (Bourdieu, 1984: 3). From there, just a small step led to his conclusion about the contestation between 'three camps vying for the same stake: imposition of legitimate vision of the social world' (Bourdieu, 1996: 13), and that the pragmatic precept which follows is to focus on 'the access to the means of legitimate manipulation of the world visions' (Bourdieu, 1996: 16).

To sum it all up: the *vita contemplativa* of a sociologist, however earnestly and resolutely s/he observes the rules of impartiality, leads irrevocably to a *vita activa*. More precisely, both kinds of life are begotten and spend their time in each other's immediate and intimate company. It is *the purely professional requirements of objectivity and reliability that make the sociologist a 'man of action'.* Inserted, by choice or by the nature of things, in the competitive struggle over the substance and shape of world visions, sociology cannot but carve itself upon the reality which it investigates; it transforms the human world as it goes on examining its credentials. This is, one may say, the fate of a sociologist, someone who takes it upon her/himself to practise the social-scientific profession. Like anyone else, though, the sociologist, knowingly or not, confronts the possibility of reforging fate into a vocation. Unlike fate, vocation is a matter of choice and responsibility. One thing is to go on practising a profession which willingly or not interferes in the areas where political and 'mediatic' powers would prefer to rule undisturbed. Quite another is to challenge the adversary to a duel and openly declare the start of the contest.

By occupying her/himself with things that by their very nature are not neutral, the sociologist is already responsible for the shape of the world s/he investigates. Entering political battle signals nothing more, yet nothing less either, than assuming responsibility for that responsibility; taking such a step is an ethical demand and a moral act. It is also a 'citizen duty'. Assuming responsibility – the transformation of a sociologist into an intellectual – is an act of 'transgression', but such transgression arises organically out of loyalty to the vocation.

NG   Finally, you once said that you believed sociology could change the world (Bauman and Tester, 2001: 18). Do you still believe this is the case? And if so how should sociology go about doing so, and in pursuit of what ends?

ZB   Sociology is one voice among a cacophony of other voices, and its audibility is not assured. Most of the time, sociology is a voice crying in the wilderness. What sets it apart, however, from many other voices that share this fate is that it speaks of the ways in which the wilderness turns wild and the ways in which it sheds the wildest of its qualities, so that, hopefully, no human voices need cry in the wilderness...

NOTES

1. In *L'individu incertain*, Alain Ehrenberg (1995) picks up a Wednesday evening in October 1983 as the watershed date (at least for France). On that evening, Viviane and Michel, an ordinary and on the whole unremarkable couple easily dissolved in a city crowd, appeared in front of French TV cameras, and millions of TV viewers, so that Viviane could say of Michel: my husband suffers from *ejaculatio praecox*, and complain that when with him, she never experienced pleasure. A watershed, indeed. Not just the boundary between the private and the public has been erased, but the spaces in public view have been captured for the display of sentiments

and deeds heretofore reserved solely for the most intimate confessions. Since that Wednesday evening, of course, Viviane's pioneering act has been endlessly reiterated in millions of TV chat shows and newspaper 'exclusive stories', the contemporary replicas of the *agora*. Far from shocking, it has become the daily intake of hundreds of millions of individuals 'like her' and the only publicly staged events in 'public interest'.

REFERENCES

Arendt, H. (1968) *Men in Dark Times*. Orlando, FL: Harcourt Brace.

Bauman, Z. (1998) *Globalization: The Human Consequences*. Cambridge: Polity.

Bauman, Z. (1999) *In Search of Politics*. Cambridge: Polity.

Bauman, Z. (2000) *Liquid Modernity*. Cambridge: Polity.

Bauman, Z. (2001) *The Individualized Society*. Cambridge: Polity.

Bauman, Z. (2002) *Society Under Siege*. Cambridge: Polity.

Bauman, Z. and Beilharz, P. (2001) *The Bauman Reader*. Oxford: Blackwell.

Bauman, Z. and Tester, K. (2001) *Conversations with Zygmunt Bauman*. Cambridge: Polity.

Beck, U. (1995) *Ecological Enlightenment*. Atlantic Highlands, NJ: Humanities Press.

Bourdieu, P. (1984) 'Espace social et genèse des classes', *Actes de la recherche des sciences sociales*, June, pp. 3–14.

Bourdieu, P. (1996) 'Champ politique, champ des sciences sociales, champ journalistique', *Cahiers de recherche*, Vol. 15, pp. 1–48.

Castells, M. (1997) *The Power of Identity*. Oxford: Blackwell.

Dufour, D.-R. (2001) 'Les désarrois de l'individu-sujet', *Le Monde diplomatique*, February, pp.16–17.

Ehrenberg, A. (1995) *L'individu incertain*. Paris: Calman-Lévy.

Elliot, A. (1996) *Subject to Ourselves: Social Theory, Psychoanalysis and Postmodernity*. Cambridge: Polity.

Ferenczi, T. (2001) 'Les intellectuels dans la bataille', *Le Monde*, 19 January, p. 8.

Frisch, P. (2000) 'Introduction', in P. Bourdieu, *Propos sur le champ politique*. Lyon: Presses Universitaires de Lyon.

Held, D. (2002) 'Violence, Law and Justice in a Global Age', *Constellations*, March, pp. 74–88.

Kant, I. (1983) *Idea for a Universal History With a Cosmopolitan Intent*. Indianapolis, IN: Hackett.

Lanzmann, C. and Redeker, R. (1998) 'Les méfaits d'un rationalisme simplificateur', *Le Monde*, 18 September, p. 14.

McNeil Jr, D. G. (2002) 'Politicians pander to fear of crime', *New York Times*, 5–6 May.

Melucci, A. (1996) *The Playing Self: Person and Meaning in the Planetary Society*. Cambridge: Cambridge University Press.

Seabrook, J. (2002) 'Sustainable growth is a hoax; we cannot have it all', *Guardian*, 5 August, p. 16.

Terray, E. (1990) *La politique dans la caverne*. Paris: Éditions de Seuil.

CHAPTER 3

Judith Butler: Reanimating the Social[1]

NG   In 2000 you co-edited (with John Guillory and Kendall Thomas) a book called *What's Left of Theory?* In the introduction to this book you talk of the connection of literary theory to politics, and of the recent redirection of the field of literary studies towards 'political themes and active political invest-ments in justice, freedom and equality' (Butler, Guillory and Thomas, 2000: xi). With this redirection it seems that literary theory and social theory are coming ever closer. This is presented as a positive process, insofar as 'insightful forms of reading' are being brought to bear on social and political texts, while at the same time literary scholars are overcoming their 'ignorance of the law, of political theory, of the shape and structure of social movements' (Butler, Guillory and Thomas, 2000: xii). But where do you work within this land-scape? Would you call yourself a social theorist? And where would you draw the line between social and literary theory? Is not all theory a form of fiction?

JB   I was trained in philosophy but I was also trained in what we call 'con-tinental philosophy' here in the United States. That meant that from early on I was reading nineteenth-century German social theory and political philosophy, and later phenomenology and structuralism and then, much later, post-structuralism. So, prior to my move into post-structuralism and even literary analysis, I was studying social theory. I was also, even as an undergraduate, working in economic anthropology and then dividing my time between phi-losophy and literature, so it was not as if literary studies came late, but literary studies did turn out to be, for me, a better place to work, mainly because it allowed me a certain kind of interdisciplinary range as well as a rhetorical approach to texts. It was possible to use a theory like Foucault's on power to talk about a theme like gender in the context of a memoir or a literary text of some kind, whether it be *Herculine Barbin* (Foucault, 1980) or Willa Cather's novels, and one could move in that way without too much of a problem. It is important to note, though, that there are people in literary studies that decry the entrance of social theory into literary analysis. Richard Rorty has written on this. He thinks that work like John Guillory's on social capital uses social science categories and forgets the inspirational role of literature. Others worry about the lack of linguistic and literary specificity that has emerged within some forms of literary studies deeply influenced by social theory. They tend to argue that when social theory enters literary analysis, it becomes heavy handed. Yet it seems to me that there are ways of reading literature, fiction, drama and poetry that ask about its form, and the way that history becomes lodged in form, and so attend to what is specifically literary about any particular piece of work. What distinguishes that kind of reading from formalism is the way that it questions what is being socially articulated at the level of form. Lukács (1974) understood this in *The Theory of the Novel*; Adorno recast this interconnection differently in his approach to music, while Benjamin understood this differently in his approach to Baudelaire and Kafka, for example. I would say that the Frankfurt School prior to the communicative turn was constantly looking at aesthetic form as a place where social meanings were being articulated in very specific ways. Social and historical meanings were regarded as immanent to literary form, and it might be said that the move beyond ideology critique by Habermas and Apel, for instance, was an effort to move beyond the interest in relations of immanence such as these. But my view is that critique deserves a serious rehabilitation, and that the aesthetic domain needs to be re-engaged precisely at the level of historical meaning and artistic form.

I think that there is also a second part to this answer that has to do with how literature helps us to conceptualize the domain of the social. It would be a mistake if we took the world as it is depicted in a novel, say Henry James' *Washington Square*, and decided that that *was* the social world, and that a mimetic relationship existed between the world portrayed in the novel and the world as it truly existed. I don't think we can consult literary works as mimetic reflections of social reality. On the other hand, if you look at the diction, even in the opening paragraph of this particular novel, you will see something about the operation of bourgeois norms in spoken social encounters that is very hard to capture through another kind of social analysis. We might say that literature enhances the descriptive domain of social theory, but here it does something more: it tells us something about how norms work to produce what can be speakable, and what cannot. The narrator speaks or bespeaks a certain kind of failing aristocratic position, replicating a certain kind of high diction and social judgement but also belying the impossibility of that diction and judgement to sustain itself. So you actually get something of the very voice of class privilege as it falters, or in its faltering, and you read as well the strategies of its shoring up. I think that the literary rendition of class gives you that in a more textual form than you would be able to find in any kind of more general description. At the same time, I would say that this is theoretical – it is implicitly and radically theoretical for it shows us the operation of norms at the moment of their iterability and fragility. In the case of James' novella, we can read that norm as it is instated, and instates itself at the level of voice and diction. My work tends to cut across social theory, philosophy, and literary studies, so it would be difficult for me to call myself a 'social theorist'. I have a problem with identity generally – indeed, that may well be my *identity* – but I would not be offended by being called a social theorist, although I'm not sure I have ever offered a theory of the social *per se*.

NG   In the introduction to *What's Left of Theory?* it is also said that 'the texts produced in social theory and social science rely on metaphor, metonymy, ellipsis, and allegory, and these dimensions of meaning production go unnoticed by those who do not engage a literary analysis' (Butler, Guillory and Thomas, 2000: xii). This, in general, is true. But what might be gained by adopting a literary perspective? And, beyond this, is there a danger that the application of literary methods and practices to the study of social issues might reduce all events or actions to linguistic or narrative forms? Or, rather than this being the case, is the very strength of literary theory that it can be used to unmask the underlying politics of language and performativity (see Butler, 1997)?

JB   I think it would be a mistake if all social theory were reduced to discursive or linguistic analysis, and I'm not in favour of that. Very often my positions are construed this way, and I can understand why. But there are two different issues here. The first is the status of language or discourse, which are themselves distinct from one another, and the second is the status of the literary. With respect to the first question, the social can neither be reduced to discourse (understood as a historical configuration of language; a shifting configuration subject to rupture and transformation) nor to the linguistic, but language emerges precisely at the juncture when we try to make the distinction between language and the social. I would certainly say that any description of the social would have to take place through a language that contributes to the demarcation of the social itself. There is no way to peel off the linguistic dimension from any social theory. But that is not the same as saying that all social theory is reducible to linguistic theory, it just means that social theory *cannot do without* the linguistic. But there are other issues at stake. There is the question of what kind of social practice language is, and what place it occupies within a more general account of the social. Bourdieu certainly tried to give a sustained answer to this question, but it is probably not possible to understand his contribution without reconsidering Lévi-Strauss.

Lévi-Strauss (1969, orig. 1949) sought to identify the primary social bond with a linguistic bond in *The Elementary Structures of Kinship*. He isolated the structuralist economy of the sign and sought to trace the ways that signs, in the form of women, were meant to travel between linguistic-social clans, understood as relatively autonomous economies. It seemed that if he could find the linguistic bond or the linguistic means by which a communication takes place between clans, he could find the bond that sealed or constituted an entire community on the basis of its capacity for communication. Women were exported as wives, and, in return, symbolic bonds were struck between clans, and these bonds became the model for thinking about kinship, communication, and translation. The theoretical implication for the theory of sexual difference was, of course, enormous, since it turns out that women, as travelling signs, were at the basis of all communication and of all language. Thus, feminists could say in the late 1970s that there can be no language without sexual difference.

Of course, the Lévi-Straussian model has been criticized from many directions, and the only people who still adhere to it as a viable model of the social seem to be orthodox Lacanians or others within the French structuralist school. Pierre Clastres made the important criticism of Lévi-Strauss that the social could not be reduced to the linguistic bond and neither could it, by the way, be reduced to the bonds of kinship. Rather, both language and kinship have to be understood in terms of other kinds of circulations of power. Foucault clearly offered the same critique, but in another way. I think the structuralist conceit that one might discover and articulate a single and recurring structure of linguistic communication and thus to the bond of sociality itself is a mistake. Such an approach abstracts from history, from power, and indeed from the practices of gender in favour of a kind of linguistification of sexual difference, understood as the bedrock of kinship, as a constitutive social difference. I am opposed to this, not only because it divorces language from considerations of power, but also because it assimilates gender (which takes many forms) to sexual difference (whose theorization is constrained by heterosexuality), and because it makes sexual difference into the precondition of a viable condition (thus, dismissing forms of kinship not ordered on the heterosexual bond).

Nevertheless, I do think that very often when we ask how theories of the social are demarcated and circumscribed, or what belongs to the social and what does not, we have to be able to see that any given account of the social is committed to a practice of demarcation or circumscription. This means that every such theory, by virtue of its very definition, decides what is not social, what is a-social, anti-social, pre-social or even post-social. So, any account of the social is making decisions and invoking a criterion of selectivity by which the social will or will not be constituted and in that sense is part of the practice of constituting the social as such. How, then, do we think about what is not part of the social as an excluded domain which is structurally constitutive of the social? Is there a kind of exclusion, or a refusal of sites of contact, blending, hybridity, or proximity, by which the social itself is constituted?

NG   How might we proceed to answer such questions?

JB   In my early work I considered some of what Kristeva did in thinking about what is properly social and what is understood as the domain of communicability. There were obviously forms of psychosis which she thought were pre-social and even threats to the enduring fabric of the social itself. There were also certain forms of sexuality which she understood as pre-social, and it seemed to me that she cast most, if not all, of lesbian sexuality as part of the pre-social. This strikes me as a tactical move: the sphere of the social is identified with the sphere of the linguistically communicable which in turn is inaugurated by an Oedipal scene that secures heterosexuality as a precondition of communicability and of a viable speaking subject. But there are other ways of understanding who qualifies to become part of the social.

One of the things that is happening presently within the United States (December 2002) is that a certain nationalist grip on the *socius* is taking place. The United States says in its public voice that certain kinds of people are not properly part of the social. Or the question is asked, publicly and without shame, whether Islam has had its modernity, whether it has 'achieved modernity'? When you go on to ask people what they mean by modernity usually they invoke Weber or some notion of a complex social organization that is capable of internal division and integration of some kind. Or they invoke the social conditions for constitutional democracy. Oddly, it is precisely the ones who ask this question who also, by virtue of the answer they imagine ('no, it has not'), make the argument to suspend the rights and obligations of constitutional democracy (including the protection of civil liberties, rights of privacy, rights of due process, habeas corpus). Those who pose this question assume a monolithic Islam – they are not thinking of downtown Cairo, for instance – and they are effectively saying that Islam belongs to the pre-social or cannot be understood as part of the social, properly understood. Something similar happens with anti-immigrant politics within Europe. There you get a very specific version of European modernity laying claim to the social as its privileged instrument, and being used in effect to cast the non-European or questionably European as the pre-social or anti-social. So, I think we need to be very careful when we see how the social is invoked since every invocation works by virtue of a principle of exclusion or selectivity that is not always thematized within the theory. One might say that at a logical level the invocation of 'the social' tends to work through the production of the a-social, the anti-social or the pre-social, and sometimes we run into theories about socialization which seek to instruct us as to how the social is achieved, or let us know the developmental problems, individual and cultural, that attend to those who fail to achieve them. At this point, we see that the invocation of the social is implicated in power relations. This may be one reason why the turn to *the political* seems to have in some instances supplanted the interest in the social: there is a working of power in the circumscription of the social itself.

NG   You mentioned the term 'post-social' above. What does this term mean?

JB   I guess that if you subscribe to a kind of progressive or developmental narrative in which you see the social as being constituted through overcoming or excluding the pre-social you could postulate a post-social as a Utopian beyond, and you could come to imagine that any radical transformation would entail transcending the social itself. It is not my position but I think one could go there. There is a fair amount of scepticism of the social as a category precisely because it seems to lack a certain critical dimension. You would even have to ask Habermas, interestingly enough, whether communicative action is an account of the social or whether it is an account of structures which can be understood to be anterior to the social. He speaks, for instance, of 'pre-conventional' structures of linguistic exchange. And he seems to associate the conventional with the parochial. One might see the utopian dimension of his theory in the practice of anticipating a form of communication where validity claims are not dependent on social conventions for their legitimation.

NG   In this context, the title of *What's Left of Theory?* is interesting. This title asks what is left of literary theory following its redirection towards new political themes, but also what is Left about theory in the political sense. Exactly the same question might be asked of social theory. For example: what is left of social theory after the collapse of what classical sociological theorists saw as 'the social', and what is Left about such theory (if it remains at all) following the demise of Marxism? Do you see any similarities here between the political orientations of literary and social theory?

JB   I look at this from a very particular point of view since it is difficult to know how best to identify the place of social theory in the US university. I am always struck by the enormous difference between sociology in Germany, sociology as I know it in the United Kingdom and even France and Holland, and sociology as it is practised in the United States. It is very hard to find social theory in sociology these days in the United States. There are some people who do it, and some institutions that support it (mainly Canadian), but it is almost as if sociology has become a place in the United States where scepticism towards theory is voiced. Instead of 'the social' you will hear about social practice, and you won't necessarily even get an account of what a social practice is. It seems to be a term that is used as if it maintains a transparent referent to that to which it refers.

That is hard because I was actually trained in a European philosophy department in the United States, Yale University in the early 1980s, before it lost almost all of its important faculty in that area. Back then it seemed to me that social theory was not just a descriptive enterprise but also a critical and even a normative one. When you took a course in social theory with a European emphasis you would take a course that read Durkheim and Weber but also read Sheldon Wolin and some Nietzsche, Marx, and the Frankfurt School. Certainly Arendt would be understood as a social theorist regardless of the fact that she herself had such a negative view of the social, equating it as she did with the uniformity and homogeneity of 'the masses'. And the work of Talcott Parsons would be included as part of what we would learn. These were venues in which you would ask what human action was, what the conventions were that conditioned human agency, what the norms were by which you distinguished legitimate from illegitimate action, and ask about the public/private distinction, and how it mapped onto an understanding of the social. One would also consider the social as a domain in which you might look at the functioning of populations in ways that were not always explicitly political, that is, pertaining to modes of governance or even managed by modes of governmentality. I do not know of a course now where I could send my students to study these topics in this way. So when you ask me 'what is left of social theory?', I would say that in the United States what is left is mainly a European inheritance that is sustained with difficulty, at least in the universities I know, and which is struggling to defend itself from an overwhelming positivism on the one hand, and a kind of pragmatic descriptive project on the other. People here are likely to say: 'I don't know how to talk about the social, but if you give me this social context and this problem to look at, I can generate a response'. But if you are looking at a problem – say reproductive technology in the social context of the urban United States – the question you do not ask in American sociology for the most part is how is it that the topic, the issue and the problems raised by it effect a reconstitution of the social itself. American society is often treated as if it is an unproblematic context, or something which is 'affected' by an issue such as reproductive technology; but few ask how such issues can and do prompt a definition of what counts as the American *socius*. It doesn't work that way around. Instead, one presumes the context and works within it and that gives one a geographical anchor and even a disciplinary field, understood as a territory. What is more difficult to ask, however, is how the context – namely the social itself – is reconstituted, reframed or reworked by virtue of the problem that has entered into its frame. It is this critical moment that I am missing from contemporary sociology in the United States. I am probably saying very general and rash things, but I think they have a general truth to them.

NG   The second half of my previous question asked of the play on the word 'Left' here. It seems to me that following the demise of Marxism it has become difficult for sociologists to talk about the social because this concept had been tied for the most part to a political conception of class relations. In this sense, the political question of what is Left of literary theory also applies to what is Left of social theory, for as social theory, like sociology more generally, has moved away from the work of Marx it seems that theoretical interest in 'the social' has all but disappeared as well.

JB   Bourdieu, of course, rejuvenates the concept in many important ways, but the lack of dynamism in his account can be read as a part of the post-Marxist malaise. I would imagine that in the British context one could follow what happened to the work of E. P. Thompson, the critiques made of it, and see what has survived and what has not. But I think there is another category we are missing here, and that is the cultural. It seems to me that very often what we hear about now in the post-Marxist terrain are quarrels between the economic, on one hand, and the cultural, on the other. Those who stand for the political very often invoke the economic on their side, and worry that the cultural has deflected from the economic and the political. While on the other hand, there are cultural studies practitioners who say – with some justification – that cultural studies is a place for political critique, and that culture, and popular culture, has to be a bona fide terrain for political analysis. In this debate – in this almost binary standoff between the political and the cultural – the social does fall away as a category. I had the feeling that I was smuggling in the word when I used it my recent book, *Antigone's Claim* (Butler, 2002a). And I do use it polemically – I have just published a piece on kinship in which I also use it as a polemical instrument. People do stop me and ask what I mean by it, but I tend to defer my answer. The reason I use it is to put it into play again, and I hope to make clear why I think that is important.

Perhaps one approach would be to return to the question of the play on the word 'Left', since there is a Left that is left. There were certain perspectives that socialist feminism provided on the organization of the family that were clearly from the Left, and which clearly talked about the social organization of kinship in a way that could not be understood as only cultural, that is to say, not in the Lévi-Straussian sense, but also not simply at the levels of representation or language. In the past few decades, there have been important efforts, mainly within anthropology, to try to think about how kinship was organized (Mitchell, Strathern, Yanagisako, Weston, Schneider, Borneman), how the maternal function was organized, how reproduction was organized, and there were critical questions that came out of that kind of social theory: 'by what rules of organization did kinship come into being in its form, say, as the nuclear family?', 'what other forms of organization might there be?' and 'how can we imagine new forms of organization?' It seemed to me that there was not only a Left project of disputing a natural law of the family, but also a Left project of imagining various ways in which that social organization could still occur. I think it was only under the rubric of social theory that you could answer that question in that way. If you were a Lacanian or you were a Lévi-Straussian you asked about the variable rules of kinship because any variation you saw was bound to be a modification of a perennial structure, so you ended up returning to something like a symbolic law as a relatively stable and permanent structure. Social organizations and their contingency and their malleability were seen as instances of a more permanent law. And there were, and remain, insoluble problems for structuralism in accounting for the transition or link between the symbolic and social realms. If, on the other hand, one wanted to say that *there could be no permanent law*, that all there can be are historical modes of organizing this particular human function, then one had to return to social criticism, and seek recourse to the social to pose that question in that way.

I have returned to the social more recently in order to pose this question to not only those who believe in natural family forms but to those who believe that the family form is finally regulated by a structuralist law that has a kind of transcultural permanence. When I invoke 'the social' polemically, I do so in order to signal and to reanimate, in a new venue, a certain kind of question that I think has become difficult to voice in debates on kinship.

NG In your final contribution ('Dynamic Conclusions') to the book *Contingency, Hegemony, Universality* you say that a truly radical theory is one that enquires into the presuppositions of its own enterprise. Further to this, you say that 'to question a form of activity or a conceptual terrain is not to banish or censor it; it is, for the duration, to suspend its ordinary play in order to ask of its constitution'. In other words, 'a concept can be put under erasure *and* played at the same time' (Butler, Laclau and Žižek, 2000: 264; original emphasis). You call this practice 'affirmative deconstruction'. But what are the methods of such a practice? How, for example, might one place a concept such as 'the social' under erasure yet at the same time continue to play with this concept? Is it by suspending a concept from its ordinary usage that we find new forms of play and with this discover (and perhaps even change) the conditions of its possibility? And is this your aim in agreeing to use the term 'the social' while at the same time not taking it as 'a given' (Butler, Laclau and Žižek, 2000: 269–70)?

JB 'Yes' is the short answer! My sense is that when one speaks the term 'social' now, one is taking up a position with respect to a certain set of historical developments. One of those developments is the exclusion of the word social precisely because it is associated either, in the American context, with descriptive sociology and so robbed of its critical capacity, or some European contexts where a Marxian historiography has come under such strong critique for its progressivism that it is not intellectually plausible. It is perhaps a mis-nomer, though, that we talk here of the demise of Marxism because I actually think there are certain Marxist problematics that are still circulating rather strongly, so I am not fully convinced of this demise. Obviously there is the demise of state communism in most places in the globe, but there are other contemporary critical projects that rely on Marxist theory. I wonder whether the preoccupation with the 'demise' is still a way of working with a continuous notion of history. Under the sign of Marxism many questions are still circu-lating that are still quite urgent.

NG Such as?

JB For instance, one of the points Žižek has made about contemporary dis-course of multiculturalism, and here cites Wendy Brown to this effect, is that very often the list of identities included under multiculturalism does not include class, or that class remains the unspoken presupposition of multi-cultural subjectivities. Stuart Hall, Paul Gilroy, and Angela McRobbie have all clearly made this point in a different way. If this is true, then it would become important to try to rethink class in terms of multiculturalism, and not simply set them up as antagonistic projects as if class belongs to the past and multi-culturalism belongs to the present and future. That would be a mistake. There are obviously huge class issues in trying to think through the way in which cultural identities are lived. So, I think there are lots of debates that are hap-pening in the so-called aftermath of Marxism that are keeping Marxist issues alive, including the relationship between the economic and cultural sphere, which has not been answered. But just because the older ways of answering the question of that relationship do not work does not mean the question cannot be pursued in new ways or that it is no longer a question.

I have some students who are working on questions of colonialism in spe-cifically economic tracts who are also reading literary works in the light of the history of United States colonialism. You read a literary work differently when colonialism is the problematic in mind – you don't just look for the references to the economy in the literary text but you also consider, as I suggested earlier with James, what is unspeakable between characters or in a narrative voice and what is effaced from speakability. You look at terms that over-determined, how narrative temporality is staged, what implicit notions of history and expansion inform narrative structure. Edward Said (1995) surely offered an important and provocative thesis in *Orientalism* when he suggested that the novel form was bound up with imperialism. But here it is important to note that imperialism is not always explicit in the novel form. Literary forms give the lie to positivism. Very often it is in the effacements, in what cannot be said or what cannot be admitted into the realm of appearance, that the economic, as a structuring principle of social life, is signified within a literary text. If one were a simple positivist or offered a naïve realist reading of a literary text in the hope of getting a picture of the world through the representation of the text, then one would miss something of the economic and social resonance in the text itself.

As for the method of affirmative deconstruction, the 'social' can be taken as an example of how this works. I accept, for instance, as a presupposition that the social has become contested. Very often people do not know how to use the term and so do not use it, and it is within this discursive context, a discursive context of reticence, that I use it. By using it, say, in my work on kinship, I am effectively trying to show that the category of the social is not dead. I am not doing foundational work, i.e. here is my idea of the social and here are the implications of this theory for thinking about kinship. I am using it instead in order to signal that a certain kind of question has not been posed and might still be posed. That is strategic, and it takes its bearing within a specific historical juncture of discourse. The usage is, I hope, also consequential in the sense that it matters that we are living in a world in which people are not asking the questions: 'what are the ways in which kinship has been organized?', 'what are the ways in which it might be organized?' and 'what are the consequences of this or that organization?' We tend to hear instead: 'what is a real family, what is not a real family?', 'what counts as family?' and 'what are the rules by which legitimate family can be constituted and known?' These are good questions, necessary questions, but they do not go far enough. With these questions, we are not asking about social transformability or changeability. I think that reinvigorating the notion of the social can give us back a notion of the trans-formability of social structure. So, it is with a certain form of hopefulness that I am reanimating the term. It does not mean that I have an ontological account of the social, that I can step back from the particular context in which I am working to say 'here is my definition of the social'. The point is that the 'the social' in its generality emerges precisely by virtue of the particular social practice under consideration; it is implied, invoked, and performatively insta-ted in any given particular analysis.

NG   Do you do this by placing the social under erasure?

JB   If by 'placing the social under erasure' you are saying that one does not have a full and grounded philosophical account of what the social is in all situations; one that has enough generality to be applied broadly to any given analysis, then OK. But just because you don't have that account does not mean that you cannot use the term, because the term has a certain usefulness pre-cisely because it carries a historical resonance and because it opens up a certain notion of transformation and change. It asks you to perceive social structure as contingently organized and capable of transformation. One uses it because one wants to produce this effect and to reanimate this effect, but one puts it under erasure because one cannot step back and give a full philosophical account of what one means by the term. But I don't think we need do that anyway: terms do not need to be foundational in order to be used.

NG   You also say that the category of the social is tied to 'a conception of language as a practice, a conception of language in relation to power, and hence, a theory of discourse' (Butler, Laclau and Žižek, 2000: 270). What do you mean by this?

JB   There is part of Pierre Bourdieu's theory that I like and there is part that I have trouble with. The part that I find interesting is his conception of the *habitus*. What he was trying to describe by this are certain patterned, regular or even ritualized operations of the body, gestures, practices, habits or patterns of behaviour that are reproduced in a daily and inchoate way. 'Reproducing a social reality' means not only signifying a certain notion of what it is to be a corporeal human being in a social world, but operating within a system of signs that makes one recognizable to others. It seems to me that we have to understand speech acts, that is to say, acts that come from the body that are performed, as social performances that are part of the domain of the *habitus*. This means that the ways in which we speak, in which we represent ourselves, in which we address others are not only performances of voice and of the body but they also operate socially in terms of a shared system of signs, or at least a system of signs that can in some sense receive what one says or can be rattled by what one says. It would be a mistake to have any conception of language that does not take into account the sphere of the speech act and understand the speech act as part of the domain of the *habitus*, and by that I mean a kind of social performance of the body which is not always fully deliberate but which is one way of reconstituting social reality. I am not saying that all of language is reducible to the speech act. I am simply saying that it would be a mistake not to understand that speech is acted, and that the performed or acted dimension of speech is part of language but also part of the social reproduction of reality, and might almost be understood to be a chiasmic site that relates the social to the linguistic in an important way. I hope, though, that what I am saying can be understood such that these categories do not become fully collapsible into one another.

The fact that language is imbued with power, that it acts by speaking, and that it produces and sustains effects through silence, means that it is implicated in power. But the forms that power takes are historical, and once we see this we can no longer refer simply to language but to discourses, in their plurality and historicity.

NG Further to this, you ask of the status of logic 'in describing social and political processes and in the description of subject-formation' (Butler, Laclau and Žižek, 2000: 6). At the outset of *Contingency, Hegemony, Universality*, for example, you pose a number of questions, one of which is: 'What is the relation between logic and social practice?' Do you yourself have an answer to this question?

JB I have some thoughts. And here is the other thing: when I say 'social practice' to someone like Ernesto Laclau, for whom I have enormous respect, I am nevertheless doing it in a scandalous way. One of the things that Ernesto does, and does well, is to try to give a logical explanation of social relations. For him, the questions have become increasingly transcendental: what are the conditions under which the social might emerge and what are the structures that would permit the social to emerge? In this kind of quasi-Kantian trans-cendental approach, the assumption is always that there are structures or there is a logic that precedes the constitution of the social. In this scheme, the 'social' is always thematic and based on content, and something beyond the social is what conditions its possibility, and accounts for its emergence and its ani-mating structure. But if one can actually give an account that isolates these formal principles, it commits one to the view that there are formal principles that precede the emergence of the social, and that these principles are not social. Which means what? That they are not historically specific? That they are not changeable structures? That they are not open to transformation? I have always thought that there was a problem with this kind of formalism and have always preferred Hegel to Kant precisely for the critique of formalism that Hegel provides (just because Hegel may be an idealist does not mean that he is a formalist).

Although there is much in Kant that I appreciate, especially his way of inaugurating the tradition of critique, one of the aims of the first chapter of *Contingency, Hegemony, Universality* (Butler, Laclau and Žižek, 2000) was to show what Hegel's critique of formalism was, and how formalism has to be understood as a kind of abstracted version of a specifically social rationality. I continue to believe that we have to be suspicious of formalisms of all kinds, even when they seem to promise a kind of universality that gets us out of various social antagonisms. The positing of those kinds of formalisms keeps certain kinds of philosophers employed, but that may not be reason enough to continue to believe in their plausibility. I think seeking recourse to formal principles as if they are pre-social or transcendental or, following Apel, quasi-transcendental, is a mistake because this posits a timeless set of principles prior to the social itself. My worry is that if those are reifications of very specific social rationalities, then these specific rationalities get elevated to the status of timeless eternal truths.

I must also admit here that being a part of US political culture at this time I can see no more nefarious thing because this is precisely the social logic by which this culture works: it elaborates a set of formal principles that encodes its own social rationality and imposes this as the universal. And through this route I think we get back to a very problematic epistemological imperialism. I know that Laclau and others might say that my approach leads to cultural relativism or to a purely descriptive sociologism, but I don't think that is true. One always has to be asking how this specific organization of social reality became constituted; not what are the formal conditions of its constitution, but how it came about and how it was able to establish itself *as if it were* timeless, how it was able *to establish itself as a formalism*. It is the tacit logic of cultural imperialism, and the problem with human rights work that is not context-sensitive. This is the historical situation in which I am living and it is the one I feel obligated to develop some critical perspectives on.

NG   One of your aims, then, is to pursue a critical interrogation of the concept of universality (see Butler, Laclau and Žižek, 2000: 264). Why is this such an important task? Why is it that you see the universal 'as simultaneously impossible and necessary' (Butler, Laclau and Žižek, 2000: 10)? For what reasons do you talk of 'competing universalities' rather than of competing local knowledges (Foucault) or *différends* (Lyotard)? And how is your attempt to 'restage the universal' connected to the practice of deconstruction?

JB   I am worried that you hold me accountable for deconstruction, or assume that that is the mantle under which I am supposed to appear, and this is somewhat confusing to me. I am certainly indebted to deconstruction, but it is not the only theoretical project with which I work.

Thirteen years ago I could only see what was pernicious in the concept of universality – I could only see it as a kind of imperialist ruse, a formal effort to espouse a set of values that were then unilaterally imposed upon all cultures at all times. I was particularly worried about people who wanted to claim that there was something universally true about women. I disputed that, or at least tried to dispute it. There have been some important efforts within Third World feminism – Chandra Mohanty and also the work of Gayatri Spivak – that have also raised questions about how universality works in women's rights movements. And, indeed, I also think there has been a resurgence of a mainly American notion of universality within feminism, in the work of Susan Okin, for instance, or even Martha Nussbaum. This kind of work maintains the right to espouse what universal rights should be and to dispute and call wrong anyone from a cultural perspective who disagrees with this formulation. This resurgence of a liberal feminism that wants to lay claim to universal human rights regardless of the various cultural articulations of issues of justice and entitlement is often done in the name of reason, and against irrationality, in the name of civilization, and against barbarism. But it is only an elevated form of barbarism.

There seems to me now to be a difference between a notion of universality that makes the claim of being transcultural and one that would be more speculative or utopian, and based on the difficult struggle of cultural translation on these issues. If I put the notion of universality under erasure, to use your phrase, and say that I don't know in what universality might finally consist, then I open up the question of universality as a site of struggle or contest. And it is, and always has been, precisely that. Look what happened at the United Nations meetings on the status of women in Beijing, for instance. Women from various countries came and argued about what should and should not be included in the term 'universal'. You hear again and again people saying 'I'm not included in your idea of the universal' or 'I don't want my issue included in that notion of the universal' or 'you've conceived of the universal in such a way that my particular rights claims could never be defended or supported within its terms'. Then, what ends up happening is that the positing of the universal inaugurates a set of debates and produces a set of challenges that demands its rearticulation again and again. This is an ongoing process that can have no end, in which the universal is posited, challenged and rearticulated. This struggle itself is of value because it is the site of a democratic contestation, a contestation that has to be open-ended in order to maintain its claim as a democratic process. Its value does not consist in the certainty that we will arrive finally at a true and comprehensive notion of universality. We will never arrive there (if we did, it would be a Kafkaesque nightmare, I fear). We will always have struggle and something of the democratic process will remain alive as a result. As an impossible concept, it will be a site for a certain kind of cultural struggle in which questions of cultural translation will be paramount. One has to learn what the idioms of political demands are that take place outside of dominant conceptions of universality. One cannot hold on to a dominant conception of universality if it is exclusionary, if it actively contradicts the all-inclusive meaning of universality itself. And yet, it is precisely because universal claims are always running up against their own contradictions, foundering on what they exclude, that they have to be ceded and renewed on a different basis. Instead of regarding this process as one that will eventually be fulfilled, one has to take it seriously as a project that can never be fulfilled, and therefore as a place where certain kinds of cultural challenges are perpetually negotiated.

NG I guess I am still stuck in the position you were in 13 years ago! Could you explain why you have become so interested in 'restaging' the universal? What is so important about such a project? And what is the purpose of talking about competing universalities rather than local knowledges?

JB If you just talk about local knowledges then you leave universality intact, and I would like to see universality come undone. Laclau said to me that he thought the notion of a 'competing universality' was a contradiction in terms. What I would want to say in return is that performative contradiction is one way by which politics happens. It is precisely when one group speaks in the name of the universal and another speaks in an opposite way, or some dissenting voices within the group lay claim to the universal, that an antagonism is put into play and it is shown that the universal cannot do its job. Now why care about the universal at all, you might ask? It seems to me that there is enormous power invested in the concept and if you have any hope for human rights work you have to negotiate with it.

Last year, I wrote something on the status of the prisoners held in Guantanamo Bay by the United States. Astonishing was the way the US decided to suspend the Geneva Convention and also other international human rights decisions that had been made in international courts that were clearly intended to protect prisoners from inhumane treatment and to guarantee them legal representation. It was very clear that the reading of the Geneva Convention that the US sought to defend was one in which there were only some populations – those who belonged to states who were signatories to the Convention and who were at war in the conventional sense – who fell under the rubric of universality. So, universal rights were selectively applied to subjects who belonged to certain nation-states who engaged in conventional forms of war, which means that universality was understood as something that could be selectively applied, which means that universality was not universality at all. There you see the contradiction that the notion of universality produced in that context and you also see where the political work to be done is. It seems to me that one has to be able to come back and work that contradiction, expose the way in which state support operates as a more or less explicit condition of 'universal' rights, and move towards claiming another universality in its place. This would mean making a bid for hegemonic control over the term, and accepting that universality is a term over which bids for hegemony are happening: which one shall it be, how will they rearticulate one another and how will they produce problems for applicability? And that is certainly a place for political struggle, especially if you want to see certain rights extended or certain populations humanized who have not previously been understood to be covered by international human rights law. In this case, that would be stateless peoples, above all.

NG   It is interesting that you say that if you just talk about local knowledges then you leave claims to universality intact. Is this really the case? Or can local knowledges be used to destabilize or undermine such claims?

JB   If a local knowledge makes a bid for recognition it is making a bid to be recognized within terms that are not purely local, by those who do not inhabit that locality. And so it is, already, engaged in an act of translation, or demanding a translation from elsewhere. And there is an even more radical point to be made, one Spivak makes, which is that there are ways of universalizing experience from the point of view of various subaltern communities. There are many different practices of universalization other than those currently encoded by Western-based human rights law. In this sense, universalization is a kind of cultural practice, one that ends up demanding cultural translation. There are different ways to make this argument, but I like the idea of competing universalities not because it vacates the notion of the local but because the local makes an implicitly universalist claim or exemplifies a mode of universalizing which is very different from imperialist modes of universalizing.

NG   What about the work of someone like Foucault, where you get the presentation of subjugated knowledges – say in *I, Pierre Rivière* ... (Foucault, 1982a) or *Herculine Barbin* (Foucault, 1980) – which don't make an implicit claim to the universal, or even to be formulated as an argument about universality, but still work against this concept at some level?

JB   Right, let us think about *Herculine Barbin* whose life is pathologized and criminalized both because of her hermaphroditism and her sexuality. She pursues a knowledge that is hardly public, hardly admitted within the codes of universality that operate within the social world she inhabits. But if one is finally going to make a claim on behalf of that life, that this was a life that ought to have been given the conditions to live, that this was a body that ought to be liveable within the social world, and that the social world ought to become one that can house and support Herculine Barbin and others like her, then we are already on the way towards an alternative universalization.

NG   But isn't this a different thing from 'restaging the universal'?

JB   It is, especially if someone like Herculine wants to make a rights claim. I know there are all kinds of critiques of rights claims but I think there are certain conditions under which rights claims are crucial – certain kinds of prison reforms or the decriminalization of sexuality, to name but two. But if you want to make a rights claim then you are going to speak in the name of what? Personhood, or the human? Even as you have been excluded from that very conception of what a person or a human is? The Guantanamo Bay prisoners are excluded from the universal conception of the human by their Islamic beliefs or by their presumed militarism or connections with al-Qaeda: they are outside the *socius*, outside the human and outside the universal reach of the law. But if these people, these populations start speaking (conditions are set in which a 'voice' might be actively staged) and laying claim to rights, that kind of claim can expose the exclusionary basis on which universal rights have been extended (and not extended); it can also bust up the exclusionary conception of the human upon which that universality relies. In that sense they would stage a performative contradiction that opens up the field of the political. So, I think it can be quite radical for the so-called sub-human or the non-human to speak in the name of the human, to ventriloquize in ways that separate the voice of entitlement from the presumed subject or rights. This would be connected to your concern about local knowledges, since the one who is excluded from Western rationality and universality is nevertheless speaking within those terms. There is a scandal there that has to be sustained for the hegemonic notion of universality to be struggled against. I think if we seek recourse to the purely local without watching the way in which the local disrupts the operation of the universal then we are in trouble, because then local struggles can take place in a different relationship to the universal and the universal can continue in its hegemonic form, undisrupted.

NG   How is it possible in your 'restaging' of the universal to protect against the elevation of particular values into a position of universal hegemony (even if these values are in fact never universal)? The social may again be taken as an example, for it presents itself as a universal concept that is gender neutral and inclusive to all. But careful analysis of the presuppositions underlying this concept shows it to be highly particularized, not least because of its connection to specific forms of national citizenship or contract that emerged historically from the so-called Rights of *Man* (see, for example, Rousseau's *The Social Contract*). Could it be the case, then, that all claims to the universal are in fact highly particular, with the implication that there is no such thing, at least today, as universality?

JB I think we have to assume that there is no such thing as universality. But let us think about that carefully. There is no one thing we can say is universality. We cannot say that any view that puts itself forward as universal is in fact truly universal in the sense that it is not located, that it is not perspectival, that it is not culturally specific. So let us agree that every view that puts itself forward within the social or political domain as universal is in fact particular, local, culturally articulated, perspectival, situated in some sense. But if we take that as a presupposition, does it follow that we can no longer talk about the universal or that the universal is always a sham? It only follows that we can no longer talk about the universal if we think that the *only* way to talk about the universal is as some kind of foundational category or that for which we have a clear referent. You asked me earlier what this has to do with deconstruction, and I suppose I would say that universality is under erasure in the same way the social is – we do not have a single referent for it and cannot. It functions, however, discursively in ways that are highly consequential and diverse. For instance, one question we would have to ask is: under what conditions do particular kinds of social and political claims get formulated as universal? And if they get formulated as universal does that mean they understand themselves as universally applicable? I think these are two different things. I could have a position which I universalize without saying that it belongs to everyone or that it should belong to everyone. That does not mean that it is shared, but means only that the way in which I formulate it is in a universal idiom, or in an idiom which seeks to universalize the claim – make it general, non-specific, non-locatable. *Idioms of universality* – that would be a good title for a project that seeks to elaborate this point of view.

NG Could you give an example of this?

JB Say you walked into a meeting at a conference that the United Nations Committee on the status of women puts together, and you have one group of people who come forward and say that we need to put forward sexual autonomy as a universal right for women. There are lots of difficulties introduced with this claim. First of all, the idea that there might be a universal right for women suggests that there *is* a universal right that is very specific to one group and hence is not universal. It already knows that it is not universal in that sense and yet it wants it to be generally applicable to women, but it does not even tell us who a women is – we can't even get into that question. But the other problem, of course, is that there is another group that comes in and says: 'No, no, no! Sexual autonomy is a Western bourgeois notion, it presumes property of or in myself, but I don't belong to myself, my religion teaches me that my body is in fact sacred and it belongs to God, to the Church or to the bond I make with men or with a larger community, or that when I marry I give up those kinds of rights of autonomy, but what I would like to see are laws or conventions that would be established that protect me against violence in the home, or in the workplace or on the streets.' The first group is thinking that sexual autonomy will give the second group the protection against violence that they need, since if one is able to control what one does with one's sexuality that would mean that one would be able to protect oneself against sexual violence, or if one has bodily integrity, one would be able to say that one is protected against physical violence of some kind. The word autonomy, however, does not work cross-culturally; it opens up cross-cultural difference and becomes, as a result, a site for all kinds of debate within international forums. There may be ways of reconstruing the term that compel international consensus, or maybe not, or maybe those who want it will be willing to lose a certain number from their constituency by virtue of using it and they might even be willing to commit certain forms of cultural violence by using it.

What is interesting here is that it may be that the women who say they want general, even universal protection against violence articulate it through a notion that violence is wrong and should be condemned, but cannot articulate it through a notion of bodily or sexual autonomy because this conflicts with other conceptions of personhood that they live with that are highly relational or that are all about a certain dispossession of autonomy as essential to humanness. The first group may well also be seeking protection against violence but they may be also trying to espouse a certain notion of autonomy as a precondition of women's unanimity. There are going to be lots of struggles, but the question is: who is going to be able to hear whom? And how will the dominant have to yield, listen to or give up certain presuppositions of what they think a human is in order to understand why the form of universalization the second group wants to implement is not the same as theirs? And with this understanding, they will be broadening the possibility for coalition.

It is only when one starts universalizing the claim that the conflict comes into play, and it makes sense to assume that this is not an occasional or coincidental event, but one of the effects of universalization itself, one of the conditions for the rearticulation of the universal. If I am only making a claim for myself or for my group (if we could imagine a group that is somehow local and uncontested and monolithic) then there is not going to be a conflict but a kind of pluralism that houses all kinds of particularisms. We would then have a kind of liberal framework and we would say 'this group here can fight against violence through this means, and this group here can represent autonomy in this means'. However, this would diffuse the struggle between them precisely by producing a pluralist framework in which they would all remain local and particularistic. We would contain the potential antagonism and not let the rearticulation occur. We would also simply be invoking a formal procedure by which these various and particular groups become entitled to make their claims in their voices without ever coming into struggle with anyone else. The moment they start universalizing, however, that is where the conflict begins because the universal produces contradiction there. It engenders contradictions, and in the political field it always will. And that then produces a site for a kind of hegemonic struggle, and not just a hegemonic struggle around who will win but also an ethical task of cultural translation: 'What must I give up of my own localist conception in order to enter into coalition with someone whose epistemological framework is radically different from my own, but with whom I want to be able to make political community and articulate certain kinds of political demands in an international frame?' This, from a first-world perspective, is about dismantling a certain kind of localism, a localism that calls itself universality and exudes a smug satisfaction about what it already is. From a second- or third-world perspective, or even a perspective that falls outside of those categorizations (what Spivak means by subalternity), it means trying to speak in a dominant language that has for the most part effaced you, and trying to bring that effacement into view so that a challenge to dominant notions of universality can be registered. I'm not sure if this makes sense, but it would be my concrete way of understanding it.

NG   These arguments about 'the universal' seem to be tied to your pursuit of a 'radical democratic project' (Butler, Laclau and Žižek, 2000: 263). What type of democracy is at stake in such a project, and is it ever realizable?

JB   When I am referring to democracy I am talking about extending a certain participatory sphere of politics, that is to say, extending the possibility for participation in politics to populations who have been shut out of political discourse or have not found a way into a certain kind of political articulation for whatever reason. Beyond this, I would say that what makes a democratic vision radical is not just that it extends existing rights and entitlements to those who have not previously had them, but that the way in which we conceive of rights or entitlements or equality or justice more broadly is changed by virtue of new populations and demands entering into the sphere of politics. I see this as necessarily conflictual and agonistic, and I worry about consensus as an instrument of quietism or a way of trying to quell or pacify certain kinds of conflicts. I worry as well about the seamless extension of a hegemonic notion of what politics is or what counts as a political participant. When democracy does become monolithic and taken for granted, it forecloses from the political sphere whole populations and their demands as well as the idioms through which these make those demands. I think democracy has to be conflictual precisely because it has to disrupt that force of hegemony that produces a consensus that forecloses criticism.

NG   This reminds me of Lyotard, who tried to address the possibility of a theory of justice based upon dissensus (Lyotard and Thébaud, 1985), a task which, in turn, became the basis of his work *The Differend* (Lyotard, 1988).

JB   Yes, I think that is right. I think dissent now in the United States is especially important. It is not just that dissent is one value in a democratic project, dissent is that without which no democracy can exist. If Lyotard says that, then I agree. It is precisely this which is most under attack in the United States right now. And to go back to your earlier question about the social in relation to the literary, there are certain kinds of statements, pictures and media images that have become unrepresentable within the last year, certain kinds of political positions that cannot be heard, certain kinds of political views that, if spoken, will cost you your job, and certain images, say, of violence done to Afghan children and Iraqi civilians that cannot be shown in the press and, if shown, would entail radical punitive consequences. Right now, certain kinds of statements and representations have to be excluded in order for the social to constitute itself, and it is constituted in part through these exclusions. If people were to speak out publicly in ways that were critical of not just the 'War against Terrorism' but also of current Israeli policy in strong ways you would have a crisis for the *socius*. It is as if those kinds of utterances and representations have to be excluded for the *socius* to constitute itself in its current form. So, one needs a method for reading what is unspeakable and what is unrepresentable in order to understand the social. And I do think that literary reading is one that accepts that what is not spoken and not shown can constitute the field of what is. When I say that something like 'the capacity to read through ellipsis is crucial to any social theory' I am saying that what is erased or effaced is as crucial to understanding the social as anything that appears. This goes against the trend of American positivism in sociology to be sure, but it strikes me as the basis of an important critical function in social theory.

Going back to the question of radical democracy, I don't know whether it is realizable but I think there are disruptions, moments of extraordinary dissent and insurgent struggles. It is a dynamic situation. I think keeping it dynamic rather than foreclosed is the most important thing to do, especially now, and if one can keep the struggle dynamic then one is realizing something, but one is not realizing something in the sense of rendering it final or bringing it to a close.

NG   In a recent paper you extend this vision of a radical politics by looking at the connections between the body, subjectivity and power (Butler, 2002b). You do so by analysing the slippages in Foucault's work between *Discipline and Punish* (1979, orig. 1975) and his later essay 'The Subject and Power' (1982b, orig. 1981). The argument here is complex, but it seems to be that Foucault moves from a position which leaves the subject behind 'as the relation of power to the body' (Butler, 2002b: 13) to one in which 'the subject is not only produced by power, but objects to and counters the way in which it is produced by power' (Butler, 2002b: 17). Two questions might be asked in response to this. First, what happens to the body in this latter relation of subjectivity and power? And second, how does Foucault's work open up the possibility of political resistance or of becoming other? You say that 'he seems to find the seeds of transformation in the life of a passion which lives and thrives at the borders of recognizability, which still has the limited freedom of not yet being false or true' (Butler, 2002b: 19). What do you mean by this? Are you making an argument here for some kind of political vitalism?

JB   In his post-1978 work, Foucault is trying to understand how subjects perform or stylize themselves in relationship to certain norms or prescriptions, and he is trying to develop an ethic that is not based on repression and not on a simple notion of voluntarism either, since the norms that one has to conform to are also the norms that confer intelligibility on one's status as a subject. You cannot really just choose these norms; they confer being on you and constitute a certain kind of ontology. One is radically dependent on them, but at the same time there is a certain crafting or stylization of them that takes place. So, one question I have is: how is it for Foucault we are constrained in our intelligibility by these very norms at the same time that there is a possibility of crafting them or stylizing them? How do we understand the relationship between constraint and what seems to be a kind of agency or stylization? When one considers what he says about how one lives this situation of constraint, what is clear is that constraints are not just imposed unilaterally. They do not just deterministically decide us, but they are lived, and they are lived in a certain kind of ambivalence. One is constrained by norms, one's very intelligibility is determined by the norm, yet one can be critical of norms. The cost of being critical of those norms, however, is that one questions the very conditions by which intelligibility for oneself is wrought. As a result, the very ontological status of a subject becomes destabilized and the critic finds him or herself to become highly questionable.

Foucault makes this clear in his lecture 'What is Critique?' (1997), where he says that the practice of becoming critical involves not only criticizing the scheme of intelligibility through which subjects are constituted, but also risking a sense of self by not knowing who one is. This follows precisely because one has called into question those subject-constituting norms. There seem to be several ways he is implying a certain kind of affective structure here: one undergoes constraint and suffers it, but one is not fully determined by it and so struggles against it. So, when I use the word passion I am actually referring to a double sense of passion: passivity and suffering on the one hand, but also animation or even eroticism on the other. I would argue that Foucault's reflections on sexuality assume this double bind, for there is constraint and agency at once. And his descriptions of sado-masochism in his interviews suggest that to the extent that sexuality can be understood as a choreography it has to work with constraint and agency as simultaneous dimensions of bodily passion.

So, when I speak of a passion that is lived at the border of recognizability, I am trying to explain the affective structure of critique for Foucault. To be critical, for Foucault, is to call into question those norms that govern the ways in which subjects become recognizable, and to ask: 'why are those the norms by which recognizability is conferred?' If you ask that question, then you will to some degree become unrecognizable, and you will pose the question of your own unrecognizability since you are also a subject. But what is the affective or bodily experience of that question? It means that one is being critical, risking unrecognizability and even suffering the loss of recognizability at the same time as becoming animated by this very loss. Foucault is also working always from a position of a subject whose passions are not quite categorizable or ought not to be fully captured through existing social categories or existing norms of recognition. To an extent he savours this, and he says that part of the practice of being critical is to watch over the domain of the unregulatable. For him, some aspect of sexual life generally – and I do think sexual life is the issue – is to be non-recognizable and non-categorizable. This is part of the critical practice of risking the recognizability of the self. Foucault is watching over that part of passion which is not quite regulated by any norm of recognition.

NG Is this a vitalist strategy?

JB No, it is a form of resistance. It is through not being recognizable that it resists the normalizing effect of recognition. The formulation does not mean that sexuality is in itself something that is beyond recognition. It could be captured. It is not as if there is some kind of intrinsic wildness or an intrinsic domain of the unregulatable. It is not as if there is a part of the body that no structural power can reach. It could reach every damn part!

NG　And what happens to the body in this relation of subjectivity and power?

JB　The body is what suffers and desires. I think Foucault switches from thinking about the body as a surface on which power is inscribed to the body as that which undergoes the drama of being constrained by norms and struggling against that constraint. So, instead of the body as a surface which is inscribed by power we see it as a passion that is beset by the paradox of constraint and agency. Passion is my word not Foucault's. But I am suggesting that Foucault himself has a theory of passion which is consistent with the later writings and which would make sense of the paradox involved in becoming critical. And by the term passion, I mean the experience of undergoing constraint as at once difficult and animating.

NG　Beyond this, at the outset of *Bodies That Matter* you ask: 'is there a way to link the question of the materiality of the body to the performativity of gender?' (Butler, 1993: 1). To what extent do you find the answer in the work of Foucault? And in probing 'the discursive limits of sex' (the subtitle of *Bodies That Matter*), are you following Foucault in exploring potential sites of theoretical *and* practical transgression?

JB　Foucault let me down a little here, because when one looks to Foucault to understand what he means by materiality there are several inconsistencies. Sometimes in *Discipline and Punish* it seems as if the body is a kind of material surface that receives inscribed effects, while at other times he seems to have a different notion of materiality – he talks about the soul as being materialized as if it is being given a reality or rendered a certain ontological weight.

For me it is important to understand the body not as something that is simply materially given but as something that is always being materialized, as something that is always being framed and animated through its framing. This is a continual and repetitive process. We are not just embodied once: we don't become a body after which we *are* a body. The body is being reconstituted all the time (here is a place where the biological sciences concur). There is a social frame for understanding its embodiment and its gendering which has to be understood as temporal. To the extent that we all live our bodies in time and that bodies remain bodies through time, they are constantly being reconstituted through certain kinds of social frames, including gender. And they are also working on those frames, struggling against those frames, and even breaking them open. These frames become the condition of intelligibility for bodily life, but they are also that against which struggles sometimes take place at the risk of becoming unintelligible. Risking intelligibility is a critical practice, but I am not sure that it is the same as transgression.

In the domain of bodily morphology and presentation and sexual practice there may be ways of leading a life or engaging in forms of bodily practice which are not readily categorizable and which throw into question the categories we have. I think there is a great confusion, for instance, about what it means to be heterosexual or homosexual or bisexual, and many people despair in the face of these categories given the structure of their affective lives, the history of their sexual lives, the content of their fantasies and the practical organization of their personal worlds. I am not sure it should be a priority that we seize upon and find the appropriate category and live in it consistently. I think there is something to be said about not knowing what these categories finally describe and cultivating a practice of living in that not-knowing. For example, if we understand the degree to which gayness constitutes straightness or straightness constitutes gayness and we start getting into queer domains in which we see how deeply related these categories are, it becomes harder to grasp them as clear and fixed identities. I think that is a good thing, if only because it opens up more room for people to live and to breathe. And living and breathing are really very important. I also understand how sometimes these categories have to be consolidated, even in a contrary fashion to function politically and I am more than willing to do that. Just because we stabilize a term for political reasons, it does not mean that we should come to believe that that stabilization constitutes the exhaustive truth of what we are talking about.

NG   It seems to me that there is a limit-philosophy at play here, for you talk about the discursive limits of sex and of what might lie beyond such limits.

JB   Yes, but for me the limits are not Kantian limits; it is not as if there is the sublime on the other side or at the limit itself. The limits are variable. What sometimes seems like a limit of recognizability, for example in the sexual culture of the United States in the 1950s, might later become a kind of norm of recognition. It is important to understand what are conceived as limits of intelligibility and survivability in any given time. Right now, for instance, there is the rise of teenage suicides among gay, lesbian and transgendered youth in the United States, which is very worrisome because one would think that the movement has succeeded in such a way that young people can now understand that a plausible life is waiting for them. But we are living in the midst of a backlash and a reactionary movement. There is quite a bit of uncontested violence against queer and transgendered youth which suggests that there are young people who are experiencing the limits of survivability. I would want to underscore that these are contingent limits, and they have to be changed. But they will seem absolute to those kids who are up against them, and it is from this sense of the absoluteness of the limit that suicide takes place.

NG It still seems to me that practice like this is not only critical but also transgressive because it is not only exploring certain limits and historicizing them but also seeing how these limits might be changed in a political sense.

JB In that sense, yes. But transgression is only one model for thinking about political change.

NG Finally, you once said that 'what it means to function as a "critical intellectual" involves maintaining a certain distance not – as Marx would have it – between the ideality of philosophy and the actuality of the world, but between the actuality of the ideal and the givenness of any of its modes of instantiation' (Butler, Laclau and Žižek, 2000: 269). Could you explain what you mean here? For example, what type of critique emerges through such a practice? And how is such critique connected to *phronesis*, or rather to the idea that theory has 'action as its implicit end' (Butler, Laclau and Žižek, 2000: 266)?

JB Let's take this in two parts. The first part is: what does it mean to have some notion of ideality that cannot be fully or exhaustively realized in any of its given social instances? There I would say that there are certain concepts, like justice, freedom or equality, and I would even add universality, which have to remain ideals towards which, or in the name of which, people struggle, but which no political struggle can lay claim to as its own exclusive achievement. In other words, in order for such concepts to remain ideal and to function as aspirations, they can never be fully realized – and can't be in any case. But for me what is more important than a full realization of any of those ideals is a world in which the struggle for them is paramount. And that is dynamic. The notion of a full realization is a static notion; we would come to the end and achieve some finality. What would we have at that point? I don't know. It seems like we would have consensus or harmony or the end of politics itself, and I think that that is not only impossible, but de-animating, if not a figure for a final de-animation. So, I would say that the realization of those ideals is an impossible deadness that we should not even wish for, because it takes away what is dynamic and alive and crucial to the meaning of democracy.

Those very ideals, however, if understood as ideal, can function to instigate a certain kind of struggle and even a certain kind of progress that is most valuable, and that is the end value. It is not the realization of the ideal which is the practical end of political struggle or radical reflection, but rather the sustaining of an open and contestatory democratic struggle in which no single position gets to gain ultimate hegemony. That strikes me as more important, probably because I worry about the foreclosures of imperialism or the epistemological violence that certain kinds of dominant cultural views can pertain.

As for the second part, I would say that theory is a kind of action. It does not take place outside of social practice because *it is* a social practice. There are various social practices of theory and many ways of doing theory. But theory must be done, and it is done: it is practised, it is performed, it is acted. It has certain kinds of socially generalizable features but the terms of its operation are contested: who is doing theory and who is not, that is the right theory and that is the wrong one, that is not truly theoretical and that is too theoretical? I don't think theory should be applied. If it needs to be 'applied', then it is already divorced from the social, and something has gone wrong from the start. I don't really think that theory should be prescriptive in the sense that it should tell people what to do and to legislate action from on high. But I do think that the critical function of theory has to be there in any democratic politics. By that I mean that a radically democratic politics would be one that also questions what has constituted the political field, what has constituted the social and will ask those difficult questions not just from the armchair of the academy but ask them in practice and perform actions that challenge them. This kind of questioning is part of a certain embodied action.

I have had concern in the United States about versions of political culture that tend to define themselves over and against intellectuals or intellectualism. They sometimes paraphrase Marx and say that 'rather than theorizing the world we should be changing it' or that 'intellectuals ask too many questions and paralyse us with those questions when what we need to do is act'. I agree that we need to act, but to act in the mode of the question, and our actions should be embodied forms of questions. This would be a kind of action that keeps open-endedness as part of its constitutive definition. For example, when we speak our opposition to war, our speech needs to embody questions about the legitimacy of the government and its actions. When we speak out, we also risk ourselves and pose and test the questions, 'who may be a speaking being in public right now?' 'Who can speak and who cannot?' On the one hand, these are critical questions, intellectual questions. On the other hand, they are questions implicitly or explicitly posed by certain kinds of political actions. This is where I think the critical practice of the intellectual actually comes together with a certain kind of political action. Any political culture that refuses to question the basis or consequences of its own actions in the name of unity or action over and against the intellect is, I think, not only anti-intellectual but also dogmatic. Above all, democratic politics has to make room for critical questioning.

NOTES

1. Many thanks to Amy Jamgochian for her help in copy-editing this interview.

REFERENCES

Butler, J. (1993) *Bodies That Matter: On the Discursive Limits of 'Sex'*. London: Routledge.

Butler, J. (1997) *Excitable Speech: A Politics of the Performative*. London: Routledge.

Butler, J. (2002a) *Antigone's Claim: Kinship Between Life and Death*. New York: Columbia University Press.

Butler, J. (2002b) 'Bodies and Power, Revisited', *Radical Philosophy*, No. 114, July/August, pp.13–19.

Butler, J., Guillory, J. and Thomas, K. (eds) (2000) *What's Left of Theory?* London: Routledge.

Butler, J., Laclau, E. and Žižek, S. (2000) *Contingency, Hegemony, Universality: Contemporary Dialogues on the Left*. London: Verso.

Foucault, M. (1979) *Discipline and Punish: The Birth of the Prison*. New York: Vintage.

Foucault, M. (1980) *Herculine Barbin: Being the Recently Discovered Memoirs of a Nineteenth-Century French Hermaphrodite*. New York: Pantheon.

Foucault, M. (1982a) *I, Pierre Rivière, Having Slaughtered My Mother, My Sister, and My Brother: A Case of Parricide in the 19th Century*. New York: Pantheon.

Foucault, M. (1982b) 'The Subject and Power', in H. Dreyfus and P. Rabinow (eds) *Michel Foucault: Beyond Structuralism and Hermeneutics*. Chicago, IL: University of Chicago Press.

Foucault, M. (1997) 'What is Critique?', in S. Lotringer and L. Hochroth (eds) *The Politics of Truth*. New York: Semiotext(e).

Lévi-Strauss, C. (1969) *The Elementary Structures of Kinship*. Boston, MA: Beacon Press.

Lukacs, G. (1974) *The Theory of the Novel*. Cambridge, MA: MIT Press.

Lyotard, J.-F. (1988) *The Differend*. Manchester: Manchester University Press.

Lyotard, J.-F. and Thébaud, J.-L. (1985) *Just Gaming*. Minneapolis MN: University of Minnesota Press.

Said, E. (1995) *Orientalism: Western Conceptions of the Orient*. Harmondsworth: Penguin.

CHAPTER 4

Bruno Latour: The Social as Association

NG   You are widely known to be a critic of the idea of the social. This position seems closely tied to your refusal to be either modern or postmodern, and to your proposal that we have, in fact, never been modern. But how exactly is your rejection of the social tied to your rejection of 'the modern'? And beyond this, how might we conceive of the social sciences in general, and sociology in particular, without placing the social at the centre of our analysis?

BL   From very early on, since science studies started, I have not considered the social to be at the centre of sociology, and from this starting point I slowly developed an argument about the anthropology of modernity. So, it actually goes the other way: because I started in science studies I realized that the social was not at the centre of sociology but rather what I call *association*. The etymology of these two terms is the same – the word *socius* which gives rise to the word 'social' is the same as 'association' – but 'association' leads us in a very different direction. It was after realizing the difficulty of my arguments in science studies for sociologists and also for philosophers of science that I was led to dig further and further in the argument around the modern. So, it is because I think the social is the wrong focus for the social sciences that I have been led to anthropology.

NG   This position comes out very strongly in your book *We Have Never Been Modern* (Latour, 1993), which you call an 'anthropology of science'. Perhaps the key distinction made in this work is between purification (the act of constructing 'distinct ontological zones' of culture and nature or of humans and non-humans) and translation (the creation of hybrids of nature and culture and with this new types of beings, including objects). But it is hard to grasp the connection between these two practices. For example, you say that the work of purification led to the proliferation of hybrid objects, with the implication that the modern project, which is based upon the purification of different dualisms and categories, could never actually begin without destroying itself. But how is this so? How is it, to use your own words, that: 'the more we forbid ourselves to conceive of hybrids, the more possible their interbreeding becomes' (Latour, 1993: 12)? And conversely, why is it that in 'premodern' societies hybridization cannot begin without an accompanying belief in purification?

BL   The sentence you quote is a proposition I made for empirical research in comparative anthropology. It is still being investigated. But first you have to understand the difference between purification and hybridization. The best thing is to take an example, say of the bio-ethical discussion around stem or embryo cells. If you interview biologists they will talk about law, ethics, religion, molecular biology, computers, and so on. You will obtain a long, long list of heterogeneous elements that will be linked together in a sort of seamless web. But at the end of the interview the biologist might say 'I am just doing science and I am not concerned with ethics or politics'. And here lies the difference between purification and hybridization. The first proliferation of heterogeneous entities is what I call 'hybridization'. It is the number of things necessary to do any good research in embryo or in stem cells. The other one is a gesture of cutting, a gesture that covers, hides, ignores and externalizes the work of hybridization. Now it turns out – and this is a very difficult argument that I am not sure I can prove – that this is absolutely the opposite of the premodern attitude, which would be very worried about hybrids and very explicit about forbidding them. What is peculiar to the modern Constitution, as I call it, is that it gives a lot of freedom to those who are able to say simultaneously 'I do all these things with embryos, with marketing, ethics, religion' and also 'I am not concerned by this proliferation of linkages as I am just doing my little science in my laboratory'. What I have been interested in for all these years is the source of this freedom – its creativity, its energy, and its juvenile enthusiasm – which is provided by this built-in irresponsibility, so to speak. But this has a price. The price is that it is very difficult to do an anthropology of the modern because of this double-take. This is what is meant by the sentence you quoted, and it might not have been fully validated yet but I still think it is an interesting proposition: the basic linkage between the two processes is that the more you ignore hybridization, the more you multiply hybrids.

If you look at the work of Ulrich Beck it is interesting to see his plea for reflexive modernization as precisely a plea to get rid of this ignorance, of this double-take, and this is what he calls 'risk'. That is why I am so interested in Beck, because he points exactly to the point where risky objects, or what I would call 'dishevelled' or 'quasi-objects', are precisely what we have to portray explicitly. But, of course, his position as well as mine has a political price, which is just the opposite of the one not paid by the modernizers, which is that we have to slow down. We have to slow down innovation to obtain due processes in the political representation of innovation. I am not sure my proposition is validated anthropologically but it is validated politically, because, politically, it is perfectly clear that it is this double bind of the modern which forbids what we call 'reflexive modernity', or what I call 'non-modernity'.

NG   You say that because the quest for purification necessarily engenders acts of translation the modern can never actually begin. But why define the modern simply in terms of purification? What is the theoretical motivation for doing so?

BL   Purification is simply one of the many mechanisms making up the anthropology of ourselves. There are endless ways of defining modernity, but my take, because I was coming from science studies, was to use the position that science is a good tell-tale to decide who is modern and who is not: tell me what you think of science, and I will tell you who you are. Purification is one way to divide between natural, dead, mute matters of fact which are simultaneously real and meaningless, and, on the other hand, humans with intentions, subjectivity, intentionality, interests, who have many things in their heads but which are all unreal and meaningful. Strange system is it not? Of course, it is simply a Constitution because the world itself is not really made of boring matters of fact, on the one hand, and of acting intentional subjects, on the other. In the world these things do not exist, so they have to be made out of a political Constitution. It seems to me (although this is not really history but more of a proposition) that a good test to know how modern someone is is to see how much of a distinction he or she will accept between matters of fact and intentional humans. So far, it has worked very well for finding my way through the social sciences, which are massively modern. It is a good litmus test.

NG   It seems that one of the things you are particularly keen to do is to overcome all conceptual dualisms, particularly those relating to fictional divisions between nature and culture. But could it be that because you set up your initial problem in terms of certain dualisms (nature and culture, or purification and translation) you can never in fact free yourself from these oppositions? For example, in talking of nature-culture hybrids do you not in some sense lend credibility to the actual existence of nature and culture, thereby reinforcing rather than overcoming an underlying dualism?

BL   I have nothing against dualisms, it is just that as social scientists we must find interesting dualisms, not the ones that render our subject matter impossible to study. For instance, I am very interested in another dualism (which I have introduced in my book *Politiques de la nature* (Latour, 1999a)): the difference between the number of entities to be linked together (i.e. how many are we?) and the question of sharing a common world (i.e. can we live together?).

The dualism between these two absolutely essential questions is very important for me, so I do not take a position against duality *per se*. And if I say that a fact/ value or human/non-human dichotomy does not work, it does not mean to say that I am against all dichotomies. Rather, it is because I am trying to get rid of the ones that have been made to render the modern unstudiable, that is all.

But things change fast here, and there is now very good work by anthropologists like Philippe Descola on nature and culture, so that this dichotomy is no longer as powerful as it was when I was writing *We Have Never Been Modern*. And in playing with the association between humans and non-humans, I am trying to do something different from distinguishing between subject and object, but I agree it is difficult as people constantly come back to the old dichotomies. It is my readers who reinforce these dualisms not me, but maybe this is because I don't do enough work!

NG One key thing that comes out of this approach is a theory of the object. This theory has a distinctly political edge. For example, you talk of a 'parliament' or 'democracy of things'. Why is this?

BL First, because of the etymology of the word thing, which also means assembly or *Ding* in German and old English. All 'things', so to speak, have started in a political assembly of some sort, in a quasi-judiciary state of affairs. This is why I use the term 'state of affairs' rather than 'matter of fact', and also for the simple reason that objects have always been involved in politics under the aegis of Nature. Nature is not an obvious ontological category; it is a highly elaborated and controversial way of doing politics. When things were convoked or assembled as Nature, for instance the gene in socio-biology, they have always been part of a political process. The problem was that it was completely implicit and it was the peculiar political function of Nature to do the job outside of the political domain, which remained limited to human intentions and representations. What I have done is simply to ask: if they are political anyhow then what is the due process? Let us imagine the due process for these things. I am not politicizing these non-political matters of fact, for they are already political states of affairs; I am bringing them back into normal due process, which I think is the responsibility of intellectuals.

NG You have also spoken of quasi-objects, and more recently, recalcitrant objects. But is there necessarily anything new about seeing objects as hybrid social and a-social forms? In your conversations with Michel Serres (Serres and Latour, 1995: 200) you complain that social science has been 'obsessed by subjects alone, by people interacting among themselves, and never speaks of objects *per se*'. But is this exactly true? In the work of Karl Marx, for example, there is the idea that capitalist production fetishizes objects (in the form of commodities) by investing in them a particular set of social relations, while at the same time reifying humans by making them more object-like. In this way it would seem that sociology has spoken about objects since its inception. Would you disagree with this viewpoint?

BL Commodities, fetish, reification! The three words I have combated most . . . Yes, sociology has spoken about objects, but so badly! The notions of fetishism and commodities are among the worst things that have happened to sociology to understand economics, capitalism and objects. The notion of fetish is exactly the sort of illusion social scientists possess about the illusion of others and is exactly what has made the anthropological study of markets and goods so impossibly difficult.

Of course, in Marx there is an attention to materiality that is very important. But all the material elements are linked together to make an infrastructure. So the objects are there but they take the role of a vast infrastructure whose causal forces are largely exaggerated, because they are either too powerful – they cause social relations to happen – or far too weak – they are simply congealed, frozen or reified social relations. Objects have never had a chance in the social sciences because either they are too powerless (and this is exactly the notion of fetish where they are supposed to be just that onto which we project human ingenuity), or too powerful (and they make you do things causally). I don't know of any social scientist, except Simmel perhaps, who has done any interesting work on neither all-powerful nor powerless objects. They always count for too much or not enough.

Object agencies are never focused on, which is not surprising, of course, because social scientists had other tasks, especially emancipatory tasks that blinded them to the interest of the object, and it was not their priority. But in science studies, objects are everywhere, not as simply 'reified' but, on the contrary, as controversial states of affairs. And the traditions of technical determinism or technical push have offered no resistance to the fieldwork we have done in technical laboratories or technological projects. It is as simple as that. Yes, the social sciences have spoken of objects, but mainly as superficial screens on which to project the social.

NG Part of your approach to the study of objects has been to develop a physical sociology to sit alongside, or be incorporated into, what you call 'social sociology' (Latour, 2000). But what do you mean by 'physical' and 'social sociology'? And what is the new 'political situation' that you say is lending to the weakening of divisions between natural and social scientists?

BL That was partly a joke, of course. I was comparing sociology with anthropology, which has the chance, not in Britain but in the United States, of having physical and cultural elements side by side, just as there is physical and human geography, and in psychology neurobiologists and psychoanalysts sit on the same committees. But sociology is different because of what Zygmunt Bauman calls its 'legislative pretension' – to solve the social question by shortcutting political process – and so has never been very interested in having a physical part. This would not be much of a problem, after all sociologists can do all the things they want and I don't care much, if the situation had not changed quite a bit since the nineteenth century. Today the problems are with the state of affairs: the number of elements that are hybrids and in need of a political voice have multiplied. And it is extremely annoying to have sociologists of the social type saying 'well I'm just dealing in the symbolic dimension of the object but, of course, I don't touch the object and I let you, the biologist, economist, geneticist, physicist, do that part of the work', because it means that you deprive yourself of the entry into political processes with any sort of weight. And that is why I fight against this object-less sociology and against the disregard for science studies – especially in Britain, which is paradoxical because this is where it was invented – because I think it has become politically detrimental.

NG Recent theories of the object have also been tied to ideas of networks and flows. But you seem to have dropped this language from your writings. For example, you have objected to using the term 'network', saying that it now means 'transport *without* deformation' and 'instantaneous, unmediated access to every piece of information', or in other words the very opposite to what you originally meant (Latour, 1999b: 15). In place of this, you talk of the 'topology of the social', and of the transformation of 'the social from what was a surface, a territory, a province of reality, into a circulation' (Latour, 1999b: 19). What do you mean by the idea of this social as circulation?

BL I don't use the word network because of what you say, but I still think it is useful. I have changed my mind since this paper you quote, because now I am using the work of Gabriel Tarde. There were clearly two traditions at a beginning of sociology: one a sociology of the social, and the other one the sociology of mobilities, transfers and what Tarde called 'imitative rays' (which is not a very good term but is really the translation of the equally bad term 'actor-network'). So, there were already at the origin of sociology, at least in France, two traditions. One of them saw the social as a special part of reality, different from geology, biology, economics and so on, and another one saw very well that what counts in the social is the type of connections that are made.

In this view, the social is not a homogeneous domain of reality composed of social elements, but a movement between non-social elements – a piece of law, laboratory practice, etc. – connected in certain ways. What I have been doing together with Michel Callon and John Law around the word network is to revise or revive this second tradition. It turns out that network is also a term used for sewage, telephones and the Internet, so I tried to play at one point with the word work-net, but it didn't function very well. What is important in the word network is the word *work*. You need work in order to make the connection. It simply means that we designate what is not already there as a *sui generis* reserve of forces, while the sociologists of the social, the other guys, invoke it under the name of society. That is the difference between the two arguments. But I still think that the word network can be used.

NG   In view of this, how do you now approach concepts such as 'local' and 'global', which, you say, 'work well for surfaces and geometry, but very badly for networks and topology' (Latour, 1993: 119)?

BL   That is precisely the earliest and in my view the most important aspect of our social theory, and one dating from a 1981 paper I wrote on the Big Leviathan (see Latour and Callon, 1981). But I have never met any social scientist that has understood it. Scale is not one of the things that the sociologist should decide but what actors themselves produce in scaling or measuring up one another. This means that the 'local' and 'global' are two totally implausible departure points, not because they have to be 'dialectically reconciled' as in the notion of *habitus*, but because they simply don't exist. The social world is flat or, if you wish, dimensionless. I have tried to demonstrate this in a book I did on Paris, but there is nothing to be done: sociologists have the practice of zooming from macro to micro built in their skulls, it seems, and so the most important features of social theory – that scale is produced, sites are localized, and the global is always localized in highly connected loci – simply escape them.

NG   In addition to seeing the social as circulation, you have also defined the social as a part rather than as a whole. By this you seem to mean that the social does not exist at different levels of analysis (macro or micro), for 'the big is never more than the simplification of *one* element of the small' (Latour 2002: 123). This idea is developed from the work of Gabriel Tarde, in particular his writings on monadology (see Latour, 2002). What interests you in the work of Tarde, and how might his work lend to an analysis of the social?

BL   Tarde is the inventor of sociology just as much as Comte, Spencer and Durkheim, except he has been kicked out because he has been accused of psychologizing everything – which is the exact opposite of what he says. What he calls sociology is *interpsychology*, that is, the attention to all those circulating entities that for him are what the social is made of, and he never said a thing on *intra*psychology. Basically he was an associationist very early on. He has this extraordinary idea that what is blocking the whole interpretation of the social is the macro and micro distinction. I have made this argument for years but I found the same thing in Tarde and that is why I am so interested in him. The macro is just a slight amplification or standardization of the micro. Organizations are not a pyramid or a sphere but the slight provisional amplifications of the variations of the micro, and that is why doing a monadology, doing local fieldwork, is as interesting, or in view of Tarde more interesting, than gathering statistics. To make his point Tarde goes into Leibniz and develops a monadology – which influenced Deleuze very much by the way. It is hard to swallow for social scientists because what Tarde did not do was to break with philosophy, and, of course, for sociologists this is a sin because the idea is that you have to break with philosophy in order to be scientific. Tarde does not make this distinction, and nor do I.

NG   You have spoken of the revenge of Tarde over Durkheim, or the idea that 'society explains nothing but has to be explained' (Latour, 2002). Does this apply to the social too, or are 'the social' and 'society' two quite different things?

BL   Society does not exist – this is Tarde's position and is my position too, as well as Mrs Thatcher's ... You do not need to add society to anything to provide a social explanation. The social (as society) explains nothing. It seems to explain something only in the very perverse view of social scientists – the one held by Bourdieu especially – that it is a necessary illusion, that if we were to reveal the illusion behind market forces, art, science, etc., people would be so blinded by truth that you would need to cover it up with a veil of illusions. But as I have said many times, the ones who need the veil of illusions are the sociologists, not the actors themselves. It is like ether in physics at the end of the nineteenth century. Just as physicists at the turn of the last century learned to do without ether, social scientists can learn to do without the social understood as society, but not the social understood as association, of course, because that is our business. The notion of society is the remnant of transcendence in social sciences that do not care for religion. Society is their religion, their last transcendence, and plays the same role of God as in some forms of very bad theology.

NG   So society is a transcendental or quasi-religious concept?

BL   Yes, it is exactly that. It does nothing but reassures, gives moral comfort, and allows the sociologist to have an overview. It does moral things but has no empirical grasp. And that is why I am fighting it.

NG   But how is what you do so different?

BL   The responsibility of the social scientists, in their view, has always been to enlighten the actors, and to emancipate them. So, whenever it becomes a bit complicated philosophically because actors do all sorts of bizarre things – they define scale, they define time, they define subjectivities, they go into very bizarre, complex arguments about divinities, about market forces, etc. – what do the social scientists do? They ignore all these things because they want to free these actors from their ignorance. If someone believes in God, they say we know that God does not exist, and so belief must be projected onto something else. The actor might insist that he believes in God, but this would fall on deaf ears with the social scientist, and the ontology of God is thrown out of the picture. The sociologist would do the same thing with law (just a packaging of social forces), with technical objects (they are just there to project social forces), with scientific nature, and so on. Every time they have troubling data, they throw them out and replace them with the all-purpose social. It is the only discipline that does so, and all, of course, in the name of scientific method!

NG   How might we get around this problem?

BL   I am an empiricist. I am trying to follow what the actors do. And if they do and say complicated things, like if they say that God made them act, then I take God in the picture very seriously and I follow to the bitter end what sort of ontology *that* sort of God involves, rather than snugly bracketing out the 'real force of God' because 'obviously' we 'know' that 'He does not do a thing'. This method has been carried out recently in two marvellous studies by French scholars Albert Piette and Elizabeth Claverie, and in their hands God becomes a very important *actor*; yes, God does things and is no longer the sort of obvious illusion which the sociologist's task is to make evaporate. These two research programmes are very, very different.

NG   Further to this, you also make the distinction between collectives and societies (Latour, 1999c). What is the purpose of this distinction? And how might it connect to a theory of the monad?

BL The first assembly in the modern Constitution is that of Nature, considered as non-political, and the second is Society, with this one and this one only being explicitly political, legal and moral. If my argument is followed, and if incontrovertible matters of fact are becoming more and more controversial states of affairs, we are entering a risk society or second modernization, and so the divide between the two assemblies has become moot. The social, as I have just said, is not the right object to study because there is nothing in the world homogeneous enough to compose it. You cannot divide any object – a tape recorder, a gene, etc. – into its natural or symbolic components any more. So the question is: how do you assemble them again and anew? And this is what I call a 'collective'. But what is important in the collective is the verb *collect*. How do you *collect*?

I have elaborated this argument much further because I am interested in the task of collecting, and in the two questions I mentioned before: one of them being how many are we, and the other, how can we live together? In my view, it is this convocation of a collective that is now the duty of the social sciences and what I call politics: the progressive composition of the common world. This is a very different political duty from the past, which was a mixture of emancipation and scientism. I am trying to avoid these two things and imagine a destiny for the social sciences that breaks with the modern, because sociology is especially modernist. In fact, I am simply trying to understand why so much social science is pure trash. It is always a mystery to me: how do all these interesting people on interesting subjects manage to write all this absolutely boring, uninteresting stuff? It is not: why are the social sciences not 'really' sciences? That is the obsession of the epistemologists. I am simply trying to understand why they are just plain bad. Why are they empirically bad? Why are there so few empirical, first-hand field studies? That is what I am interested in. One possible solution, I don't claim it is the only one, is that whenever it becomes complicated philosophically, metaphysically or ontologically the social sciences simply stop and shift to their emancipation mode. They say: 'this is too complicated, let us be relevant'. In this way, they constantly thwart the effort of description because of an appeal for emancipation or a political relevance which, of course, they do not have because they are locked in their campuses, like everyone else. But I am trying to imagine another take, which would be, first, more scientific – actors would be allowed to deploy their metaphysics and their ontologies – and, second, more political: the collective has to be convoked. Like Isabelle Stengers, I portray the social scientists as the diplomats of this collective, and then ask: how do we do this?

NG As for the second half of my question, if we connect things or monads together do they not in some way lose their singularity?

BL   We don't know this before we have tried to assemble the collective and pay the full price of this convocation. If we wanted to get all the Gods together they might not want to lose their singularity. This is why the notion of diplomacy is so important: to record this singularity as far as possible and to avoid as much as possible the collection being made cheaply. For example, Nature was one way of making the collection cheaply, and so was Society.

NG   How might we proceed to collect things then?

BL   This is the object of my work on the politics of nature (Latour, 1999a). I did a whole book on the 'parliament of things' which asks how it is organized. It is pure political philosophy but it is a very important question. It is perhaps the most important question for the social sciences, one that was given too fast a solution at the turn of the last century by the Durkheimians through a mixture of emancipation and scientism. But these questions have, of course, become very interesting again and very difficult, and this is what I am concerned with now.

NG   Apart from this, you have also been involved in the *Iconoclash* exhibition at Karlsruhe. Does this mark a change of direction for you? In your accompanying piece to this exhibition – 'What is Iconoclash' – you say that the show aimed to present 'images, objects, statues, signs and documents in a way that demonstrates the connections they have with other images, objects, statues, signs and documents' (Latour and Weibel, 2002). This seems to follow on from your general interest in networks and quasi-objects, but what is your interest in images here? More specifically, why are you interested in the clashing rather than breaking of images (iconoclash rather than iconoclasm)?

BL   It was a very big undertaking. There is no fast link with the social science arguments we just made, it is linked rather to another interest of mine – doing an anthropology of a critical gesture. As I got into this argument about the social, I got more and more interested in why critique is the normal way to behave for Left social scientists, having read Marx and Benjamin. If they study so little it is because they are so busy debunking. So, I became interested in the destruction of images in the anthropology of this very gesture of breaking fetishes. And, of course, there is a long iconoclast tradition in religion: Protestantism, Byzantinism, Catholicism against the others, and so on. There is an absolutely enormous tradition which is extremely interesting and about which I know much more since this exhibition. There is also the case of modern art, which is also engaged in a very strong iconoclastic tradition. And finally, there is the argument in science about theory against intuition, and also the very powerful right science provides for 'debunking' beliefs. So, there is an enormous domain which we mapped out in this exhibition and the catalogue. This domain is a clash rather than a clasm.

I am not interested myself in being an iconoclast – although I have been accused by some scientists of being one! – but I am interested in using iconoclasm as a topic rather than a resource, and to try to say something *about* critique that is not critical. Luc Boltanski calls this 'a sociology of critique' instead of a 'critical sociology'. I think critique has emptied itself and its forces have been weakened. Again, this corresponded with a belief in emancipation, with a certain definition of the social sciences, a certain confidence in political processes, and a certain belief in inevitable modernization. But none of these things are still there, so all of these mental armaments of social science have to be retuned. This is what I tried to do in this exhibition with my colleagues, which was a marvellous experience of trying to spatialize complex arguments. And, by the way, I am doing another one in 2004 on the question of assembling the collecting of things. This is because the next question, after the question of critique, is 'how do we now do the work of assembling the collective?', which was exactly your previous question. How, for example, do you compare procedures in different domains, from scientific congresses to Palabres in Africa, at the very practical level?

NG   What do you think sociologists might learn from an exhibition such as *Iconoclash*?

BL   Sociologists have stopped learning from those sorts of places a long, long time ago! They have deprived themselves of philosophy, literature and art. There was one sociologist in the exhibition – Luc Boltanski – but he is the best and most innovative social scientist in France. Apart from him I do not think there was anyone else. The exhibition itself was thick with things and images and questions of theology (which, of course, social scientists despise or 'socially explain'), science (which they either worship or love to hate), and art (which they constantly 'socially explain'). But when you 'socially explain' things you are not interested in things anymore. This exhibition was not made for sociologists but for the general public who could reject the belief in belief they had been accused of holding! I wanted to call this exhibition at some point the 'revenge of the Philistines'! At last, a breathing space with no 'social explanation' . . .

NG   Finally, what continues to attract you to the discipline of sociology? And in which direction would you like to see the discipline move in the future?

BL   I like sociology, but I don't like sociologists! There is something deeply disheartening in the way sociologists think they have the right not to look at their data. My view of sociology is influenced, of course, by the fact that I live in France, which has been completely swamped by the worst possible Durkheimianism, which is Bourdieu's 'critical' sociology – that is, the least critical of all sociological *imperium*. But if you look at Boltanski's work (he used to work with Bourdieu) it is fabulously interesting sociology. Even in France there are very, very good sociologists, but they work on completely different paradigms from that of critical Durkheimianism. And this does not mean that they work in my little paradigm of the sociology of association. There are lots of domains of sociology that are very interesting.

So yes, in spite of all that I have said, I believe in the discipline. Like Comte I even believe it is the Queen of the sciences! I think the discipline as a collective has an essential role to play, exactly as important as Comte imagined – in a very different way but just as important. After all, what Comte wanted was for sociology to do this diplomatic work. Of course, he was a complete madman and the argument for sociology being the science overseeing all other science was ridiculous. But the idea he had of sociology being a master of ceremonies of the collective (to use my term) was right. So, I believe just as much in sociology as Comte did, but for very different reasons.

I think sociology is very important, but I don't understand why it is constantly limited. One of the limits, I know, is coming from its bizarre ideas about science, but this, I think, we have overcome to some extent through science studies. Another limit is coming from the idea of the social. I think that the sociology of associations is overcoming that defect as well. So I think we are making some progress. What is missing now might be the new type of numbers, the new type of data, because you cannot always stay at the limit of qualitative data. You have, at some point, to be able to get a different type of numbers for the same tasks that statistics used to give sociology at the beginning of the last century. This is the limiting factor now, but I believe a lot in digitalization, which highlights or materializes social connections in a way that may be very productive for giving qualitative sociology its quantitative arm. So, I am very positive for sociology, but it cannot remain stuck in the 1950s or in the deconstructed ruins of Marxism. It cannot continue to use a destitute repertoire which, while important at the beginning of the twentieth century, between the wars and for reconstruction after the war, has now used itself up.

REFERENCES

Latour, B. (1993) *We Have Never Been Modern*. Cambridge, MA: Harvard University Press.

Latour, B. (1999a) *Politiques de la nature*. Paris: La Découverte.

Latour, B. (1999b) 'On Recalling ANT', in J. Law and J. Hassard (eds) *Actor Network Theory and After*. Oxford: Blackwell.

Latour, B. (1999c) *Pandora's Hope*. Cambridge, MA: Harvard University Press.

Latour, B. (2000) 'When Things Strike Back – A Possible Contribution of Science Studies', *British Journal of Sociology*, Vol. 51, No. 1, pp. 105–23.

Latour, B. (2002) 'Gabriel Tarde and the End of the Social', in P. Joyce (ed.) *The Social in Question: New Bearings*. London: Routledge.

Latour, B. and Callon, M. (1981) 'Unscrewing the Big Leviathan; or How Actors Macrostructure Reality, and How Sociologists Help Them To Do So', in K. Knorr and A. Cicourel (eds) *Advances in Social Theory and Methodology*. London: Routledge and Kegan Paul.

Latour, B. and Weibel, P. (eds) (2002) *Iconoclash: Beyond the Image Wars in Science, Religion and Art*. Cambridge, MA: MIT Press.

Serres, M. and Latour, B. (1995) *Conversations on Science, Culture and Time*. Ann Arbor, MI: University of Michigan Press.

CHAPTER 5

Scott Lash: Information is Alive

NG Your writings on postmodernism, in particular your *Sociology of Postmodernism* (Lash, 1990), are well known. But in the early to mid-1990s you seemed to drop the idea of a postmodern sociology in favour of a theory of reflexive modernization. Why was this?

SL I never did really. I did a chapter of the reflexive modernization book with Ulrich Beck and Anthony Giddens, but I never dropped the idea of postmodernism. I was an author of *Reflexive Modernization* (Beck, Giddens and Lash, 1994), but I was always the odd man out. Now, I don't see myself so much as the odd man. I see a lot of similarities between Ulrich Beck and me, with Anthony Giddens being a bit different. I think Giddens has subsequently moved towards a neo-liberal position, and to a global consensus position on international relations. That is, Giddens would seem to share with David Held a sort of Habermasian position, which could justify military intervention in favour of democracy in very many instances. Beck's recent work, on the other hand, promotes Kantian perpetual peace. This goes against the sort of universalist consensus found in, say, Habermas to view nations instead as linked in a sort of nexus of treaties. Thus Giddens' and Held's position could be used to justify a Bush-Blair sort of foreign policy, while Beck's is closer to that of the 'old Europe'. In this context I agree with Beck.

But back then I saw Beck and Giddens as being very similar and me as the different one. They were the two 'modernists' and I was the 'postmodernist'. In a sense, they were more mainstream than me. Giddens' theory was that you could have the subsumption of irrationality by rationality somehow. Beck always had a strong notion of unintended consequences, and I think I criticized him for being too much like Giddens, which was wrong. We now know that in Giddens there are many unintended consequences, although I think that was partly Beck's influence. Meanwhile, I was interested in the aesthetic and the hermeneutic dimensions of reflexivity. But *Reflexive Modernization* wasn't exactly my main contribution then, as at the same time John Urry and I did *Economies of Signs and Space* (Lash and Urry, 1994). So, I didn't see myself as not being postmodernist at the time, although I don't particularly like the term that much.

NG So you didn't feel at the time that postmodern forms of thought – by which I mean the work of thinkers such as Lyotard and Baudrillard – had lost some of their intellectual purchase?

SL No, I didn't think they had lost their intellectual purchase. But I wouldn't call them postmodern *per se*. For me *Reflexive Modernization* wasn't that important a book. *Economies of Signs and Space* was much more important and was published at around the same time. There, you have a strong notion of information flows and other different kinds of flows. There is almost an informational idea in the notion of flow there that is really important. Some people would say it is postmodern but I don't think it necessarily is. From that book on, information or the information society would be as important to me as postmodernity. For me – maybe I am being reductive – postmodernity is identified with postmodern architecture and also certain kinds of pastiche. And those kinds of pastiche and those kinds of architecture are mish-mashes of dead forms. They don't connect to the intensity of desire, to lines of flight, to life and the way we live today.

But I wouldn't say that the writings of Baudrillard and Lyotard are like that, as they are much more in tune with what is going on. Lyotard for me was much more important for his *Discours, Figure* (Lyotard, 1971) and his work on the 'libidinal economy' (Lyotard, 1993) than his ethics. The idea of figural signification and perhaps figural power in my *Sociology of Postmodernism* was from Lyotard. Baudrillard, for his part, was taken up in a major way by 1990s' media theory and media artists, but now their loyalty has very much transferred to Deleuze and Guattari. Surely Deleuze is a major thinker and Baudrillard more a very creative cultural critic. But though he is out of fashion at the moment, I think Baudrillard still has lots of important things to say about consumer culture, brands, and the media. His ideas of 'sign value', of things (i.e. not representations) that signify, of hyperreality continue to be amazingly rich in their implications. But what is called – on the Continent and especially in Germany and Holland – 'media theory' or non-linear theory is now very much a revival of vitalism. It is, of course, Deleuzian, and has brought Bergson back to centre stage. It would not refer to itself as postmodern. 'Postmodern' is a term that has left academic discourse to enter everyday talk. In the past two weeks (March 2003), for example, journalists have referred to Daniel Libeskind's design for the World Trade Center site and his Jewish Museum as 'postmodern', in that it is historical and tells a story. Robert Kagan has referred to European foreign policies and their general 'Kantian' assumptions of perpetual peace as postmodern, in comparison to the modernist, Hobbesian United States. Where, however, does this leave an architecture and urbanism of information flows and as it were non-linear 'stoppages' (i.e. an architecture similar to the flows assumptions of Urry's and my *Economies of Signs and Space* and, later, my *Critique of Information* (Lash, 2002))? This is not a narrative notion *à la* Libeskind, and is surely not the classical modernism of Norman Foster and Richard Rogers. I would not call it postmodern, but would instead use terms like 'informational', 'non-linear', or 'vitalist'. Indeed, most recently I have been using the term 'vitalism' and not 'postmodern'. I am not anti-postmodern at all, but concepts like 'communication', 'information', 'life' and 'media' now do the same sort of work that postmodernism did for me in the late 1980s.

NG You say that *Economies of Signs and Space* was a more important book for you than *Reflexive Modernization*. What was the connection between this work and the earlier *End of Organized Capitalism* (Lash and Urry, 1987)?

SL *The End of Organized Capitalism* was about fragmentation. It was, in a sense, connected to the problematic of flexible specialization, of the transition from 'fordism' to 'post-fordism'. Flexible specialization focused on the vertical disintegration, the outsourcing of the bureaucratic, hierarchical firm. We saw that as one instance of fragmentation: the disintegration of institutions and organizations – from trade unions to the welfare state to mass political parties to the family. *Economies of Signs and Space*, meanwhile, is about flows. It is about the flows that result from the disintegration of institutions and structures. Its problematic would connect more with the writings of Manuel Castells, with David Harvey's *Condition of Postmodernity* (Harvey, 1989), or the work of Arjun Appadurai. It is interesting that Harvey (in that book) and Appadurai (in his famous article about the media scape, the technoscape, etc. (Appadurai, 1990)) drew on our *End of Organized Capitalism*. Flows, it seems, follow from fragmentation. The most important connection, for me, is probably the chapter on the culture industries in *Economies of Signs and Space*, which a lot of people really plugged into and liked. We did a Nuffield Foundation study of culture industries in London and looked at the vertical disintegration, or flexible specialization, of the culture industries – outsourcing and that sort of thing. Then, somehow in doing it, we focused on, first, the brand-value of commodities, which is a bit like Baudrillardian sign-value, and secondly, on the way they flowed. We went from a kind of 'productivist' problematic – concerned with small firms resulting from vertical disintegration – to, in the same little piece, a problematic of brands, sign-value and flows. And this second problematic was closer to the central ideas of *Economies of Signs and Space*, although maybe not fully developed.

Beyond this, my work has been about two logics that have been ongoing for the past few decades: one of fragmentation, the other of de-differentiation. Fragmentation was the theme of *The End of Organized Capitalism*. The de-differentiation theme was established in *Sociology of Postmodernism*, which understands modernization as a process of differentiation, and post-modernization as a process of de-differentiation. Of course, we get de-differentiation in Baudrillard's 'implosion'. But Deleuze's (and Bergson's) 'movement-image' is about the de-differentiation of what was originally in the sphere of spirit, 'image', and what was in the sphere of matter, 'movement'. This idea of movement as de-differentiated flow is central to *Economies of Signs and Space*, and, I think, to ideas of the network society and even actor-network theory. It is part and parcel of a *vitalist* problematic. This is the important step that Hardt and Negri (2001) made in *Empire*. They took this problematic of flows – via Deleuze – into a fully fledged vitalism, in which flows of life (desire) become the central and governing flow. More recently, I have written about fragmentation in a certain 'outsourcing' of subjectivity itself. This is an out-sourcing onto experts such as psychoanalysts, personal trainers and plastic surgeons. It is also an outsourcing of the subject onto the flows: it is where the 'flux' of subjectivity becomes externalized as flow. This connects, of course, importantly to McLuhan's externalization of the nervous system onto the neural networks of the global village. In this context, Celia Lury (1997) speaks of a 'prosthetic culture'. But for me, the outsourcing (fragmentation) of sub-jectivity becomes at the same time a new indifference of the subject, a collapse of the subject into the flows. This, of course, does not mean that all is flow and nothing is structure. New global flows solidify, as it were, into the formation of emergent global 'microstructures' (Karin Knorr Cetina), or more macro 'eigenstructures', but this is within a much more general plane of immanence. My initial understanding of the idea of immanence was in contradistinction to transcendence. I encountered this as a Ph.D. student in reading Talcott Par-sons' *Structure of Social Action* (Parsons, 1967), but now I would speak of immanence via Deleuze.

NG   I would like to go back to the *Reflexive Modernization* book for a moment to help situate the development of your thought. At the conclusion of this work (Beck, Giddens and Lash, 1994: 199) you argue that the debates between Left and Right which characterized social theory of the 1960s and 1970s have been overtaken by a new opposition between rationalistic or scientist under-standing on one hand (for example, Althusserian Marxism), and culturalist or hermeneutic views (of, you say, Mary Douglas and Jacques Derrida) on the other. Where would you locate your own writings within this opposition?

SL My own work is a funny combination of flows and non-linear systems on the one hand, and, on the other, a certain kind of hermeneutics of retrieval (from Ricoeur), and so I would locate most of my work probably in neither camp to be honest. There is a hermeneutics of retrieval in *Another Modernity, A Different Rationality* (Lash, 1999), but I think most of my stuff is much more about flows, disorganization, immanence, collapse and de-differentiation. So it doesn't quite fit into that juxtaposition, except that I am interested, to a certain extent, in the hermeneutics of retrieval and memory. Indeed, this is where I cannot go along with vitalism. There is an absence of a grounded notion of memory.

NG But a framework of scientistic and interpretive understanding seems to underpin your reading of the sociological tradition. More specifically, this seems to hang on a reading of the critical philosophy of Kant. In *Another Modernity, A Different Rationality* (1999: 116–17, 167), you draw out two lineages of social thought from Kant's division between *Verstand* (what is called understanding, although not in the interpretive sense) and *Vernunft* or reason (the ideas or value of reason). From the former (although mediated by neo-Kantianism) you say comes the positivistic thought of Durkheim, while from the latter comes interpretive sociology and the *Lebensphilosophie* of say Dilthey and Simmel. Weber, meanwhile, seems to hang somewhere in between. Is this a correct reading of your position?

SL I wouldn't say it is a position but I think you have understood it very well. *Verstand* is the understanding and *Vernunft* is reason – God, freedom, the thing-in-itself. Surely, hermeneutics and phenomenology come from the latter. Hermeneutics is part and parcel of phenomenology. Phenomenologists find the thing-in-itself through some sort of transcendental reduction, one way or another. This starts with Husserl. It is also true of Heidegger's much more in-the-world reduction, and Derrida and Levinas have their roots in phenomenology. The idea of difference in deconstruction is phenomenological basically, and it is vastly other than the idea of difference in Deleuze's vitalism. There was an absolute fascination and obsession with the thing-in-itself, even in Schopenhauer, about which Georg Simmel writes at length, and now I am convinced that vitalism or *Lebensphilosophie* is in neither camp. But in *Another Modernity, A Different Rationality* I did put *Lebensphilosophie* way onto the hermeneutic side. I made the distinction between *Lebensphilosophie* (vitalism) on one side, postivism on the other, with Weber in the middle and Simmel with the *Lebensphilosophen*, which was probably right, and Durkheim with the positivists, which is partly right. Phenomenology and hermeneutics, from Heidegger, Gadamer or Ricoeur, do come from *Vernunft* because they try to get an angle on the thing-in-itself. And they are fascinated and obsessed, as is Romanticism, with this. But I think that *Lebensphilosophie* entails a heavy monism. Both positivism and hermeneutics have dualist assumptions, and each disagrees with the other to a certain extent. But *Lebensphilosophie* won't accept the *Verstand/Vernunft* distinction, whereas both main traditions will. Hence, what comes from *Lebensphilosophie* is, for example, media theory, but also some of the network theory, and some of Latour and Negri. This involves a bit of a revolution in sociology, which has to happen now (or else sociology becomes increasingly irrelevant). The last three chapters of my *Another Modernity, A Different Rationality* wind up collapsing the *Verstand/Vernunft* distinction, where I talk about informational stuff, with Virilio and Benjamin. But I think it is still a useful distinction.

NG Another problem you have tackled is the interplay between social and cultural theory. You present *Another Modernity, A Different Rationality* as a book in cultural theory just as much as a book in sociology. You are also both a Professor of Sociology and the Director of The Centre for Cultural Studies at Goldsmiths' College, University of London. Do you find any tension between the interests of social and cultural theory? And how do you think we might proceed today to distinguish the social from the cultural if this is still possible or desirable?

SL Probably the most interesting thing I can do is to not quite answer the question but approach it from the side. The introduction to *Another Modernity, A Different Rationality* was partly a ploy. It tried to bring in readers from everywhere, but it didn't help that much as people read the book who wanted to. But I suppose I do think of myself as a sociologist, and I am considered one. If I work with architects or media theorists then I am the sociologist they bring in, and my books are in the sociology or sociological theory sections in book-shops. I have stopped dis-identifying myself with sociology, which I previously had done a bit. I have been interested, again, in Georg Simmel and Gabriel Tarde for the last year or so, which has brought me back to sociology. Further, Bruno Latour and Maurizio Lazzarato make me think that there can be some kind of monist sociology that doesn't have to be just mediology. And as for the tension between social and cultural theory, I am not really worried about this. I am just trying to build a Centre at Goldsmiths' without too many sociologists in it, otherwise it wouldn't be a centre for cultural studies. But I am happy to be a sociologist. I'm not in denial!

NG   But what is the continued appeal of sociology for you? Do you still feel you are working within the realm of social theory?

SL   I suppose I am, even if I don't feel I am. In a funny way you are talking about social theory without a classical notion of the social. It has changed. There is a vast mediation of everything. I suppose the two words I would use to describe what is going on are media (or general mediatization) and communication. Everything has become communication in some way, including non-linear theory with its communicating monads or whatever you want to call them. I would have said sociology wasn't coping with this, but now a lot of sociologists are. For me, it is about creative rereading – for example, I now read Beck much more in terms of non-linear systems, or Latour in terms of a general plane of immanence and actor-networks. I think society has become networked in a vast way, and these networks are largely of mediated relations where you have technological media connecting people, even if they be of transport. There really isn't a way out from this. We cannot talk about the media and society any more because the media is in society. Maybe it is a media or mediated society where classical social relations have been commuted into much more communicational relations. But it seems that sociologists very often are the ones that understand this, even today. My reading of Beck and Latour is that they are very on the spot. And Castells (2000) too, by accident, with his *Rise of the Network Society*, which he doesn't really theorize. But we must also be careful not to understand society as a general network of flows. As Karin Knorr Cetina stresses, there are emergent global microstructures – like new markets – that are not at all networks. There are, instead, branded global hierarchies – like, say, Nike or Disney – that expand through global horizontal integration and even vertical integration to the point of sale. These are not networks.

NG   You yourself talk of another modernity and a different rationality (Lash, 1999). What might this modernity and this rationality look like?

SL   That was a provocative title that I worked out with the then editor of Blackwells. It came from an Alasdair MacIntyre book, which I think was called *Whose Justice? Which Rationality?* (1988). By the other modernity, I meant a modernity that was different to rationalism and cognitivism. I also meant something that was different from aesthetic modernity, which itself is often quite abstract. What I meant instead was some idea of the ground: something that grew out of the romantic critique of rationalism. For me the key theorists were probably Heidegger, Hegel and Gadamer. There was something of the ground, of the 'being-in-the-world' of these thinkers that was part and parcel of modernity. I wanted to help retrieve this in the book. Today – and at the end of the book in my discussion of Walter Benjamin – the other modernity is most present to me in the notion of memory, whether individual or collective. This memory for me is human. The 'different rationality' in the title is not an irrationality and has its own logic, though this might be the logic of analogy.

NG Is there a Hegelian position underpinning this project? For throughout *Another Modernity, A Different Rationality* you seem concerned with the opening of a third space, for example: between or beyond *Verstand* or *Vernunft* towards what might be called the aesthetic, or between or beyond discourse and figure towards sensation. You talk in the introduction to this work of the 'broken middle'; are you in some way trying to reclaim this ground?

SL Two different things are going on there. A lot of the book is about something like the broken middle, but the broken middle is different to sensation. The first nine or ten chapters are about that, where I am looking for this ground. Gillian Rose's *Broken Middle* (1992) is that ground. It is a ground that has to do with hermeneutics of retrieval – it can be tradition, an urban fabric, it can be the semiotic index that is connected directly with concrete reality. And yes, some of that is quite Hegelian. In a Kant versus Hegel argument I am with Hegel. So that is true, and that way I have had a lot of use for Gadamer, who I think is profoundly Hegelian. I would also want to understand Heidegger as not anti- but relatively pro-Hegelian. There, I am very much with Gillian Rose, although she always grounds everything in something like law, which I don't think is very grounded. I am trying to move to the much more concrete. In some chapters, it is the urban fabric; in others, it is memory or tradition. Gillian does this too but by formulating the ground as law, which is often abstract. But she does it brilliantly: she is a fantastic writer and a wonderfully original thinker.

Meanwhile, the sensation thing is different. In *Another Modernity, A Different Rationality* – before the speed chapters on Latour, Virilio and Benjamin – I wrote a chapter called 'Discourse, Figure, Sensation'. I work through Lyotard's seminal piece 'Figure Foreclosed', which addresses the anti-figural nature of Judaism. I try to develop an argument that moves from figure to sensation. Here, discourse is like semiosis, whereas figure is like iconic representation, and sensation works through an immediacy that is much closer to the semiotic index. Sensation is something that is much more immediate than figure. For me, discourse, figure, sensation also map out as Lacan's symbolic, imaginary and real. In Kant's Third Critique (*Critique of Judgement*) you have the beautiful and sublime, and the imagination and understanding. And with the clash of the categories in the Third Critique, Kant's imagination maps very well onto the Lacanian imaginary which for me is the figural. The understanding maps rather onto the Lacanian symbolic. But I wanted to undercut all that and get right onto sensation, onto the real. And that is different, that is moving to a *Lebensphilosophie* position, a kind of Deleuze-Nietzsche position that is vastly different to the Hegelian stuff. And this, in turn, is a sort of transitional chapter leading to the much more vitalist final three chapters on Virilio, Latour and Benjamin.

NG How do these parts of the book hang together then?

SL They don't hang together as well as they should. Two-thirds of the book is a quasi-Hegelian position, and the rest says that all this is collapsing into sensation, into flows. So, in the end, the other modernity in the book becomes the ground, which comes from Romanticism: a much more Hegelian grounded modernity of memory and tradition (which only comes with modernity because you are looking backwards). And in the last part of the book the title doesn't fit terribly well. You move into a much more global, information-flows world. The transition to this is the chapter on sensation. But this contradiction is the very contradiction or tension in which we irrevocably live. On the one hand, we live in the immanence of the information flows (Chapters 11–13 of the book). On the other, we mourn the disappearance of the ground: we mourn the loss of individual and collective memory. We need to retrieve this but we cannot, and yet it is still an integral part of us. In this sense, to be post-human is also very much to be human. It is in this way that we are melancholic.

NG You also say in the introduction to *Another Modernity, A Different Rationality* that it is 'a work in the spirit of affirmation of technological culture' while 'at the same time a work of mourning' (Lash, 1999: 15). This brings us to your recent work on information and media theory. Would you also describe *Critique of Information* (Lash, 2002) as a 'work of mourning'?

SL *Another Modernity, A Different Rationality* did foreground mourning. What is being mourned is the ground. What is being mourned is memory or tradition or what is being *emptied out*: what is being mourned is the symbolic in fragments. Contemporary politics in the age of information, in this age of immanent collapse into flows and non-linear systems, must also somehow be a politics of melancholy. That is the connection, and I still somehow think that. We are fated to be affirmative in the Nietzschean sense, yet we mourn the now largely spectral individual and collective identity.

NG But how does that sit alongside an affirmation of technological culture?

SL Well, I think that we can't go backwards. We are living in a technological culture and this means affirming it and using it. We are positive in terms of excitement with its possibilities, but we understand also that this has to do with the death of the human.

NG Would you describe *Critique of Information* as a work of mourning then?

SL No, not at all. There is no mourning in that book at all. It is part of my contradictory personality. Even in *Sociology of Postmodernism* I had post-modernism 1 and postmodernism 2: one was the more romantic, grounded, hermeneutic one, and the other one was very informational and post-post-. But *Critique of Information*, like *Economies of Signs and Space*, only has the one side, which is the *hyper-modern*. There is a possible way out from this (but I am not sure I want it) through an idea of memory. The thing that worries me about leaving the ground and mourning is the loss of a meaningful notion of memory. Not tradition so much as memory. The way I always understood it was that you needed some kind of dualism, for surely when you are even mourning the lost ground there is an implicit dualism, even if it is the dualism of a 'spectre' that is a figure that isn't there any more. But there are other ways of thinking about memory, and surely Michel Serres and Daniel Libeskind do so by seeing memory itself in technology. So, it may be possible to remain within a tech-nological monism and still retain a notion of memory within that monism. I am not sure I want it, but perhaps you can do it.

NG Your understanding of contemporary information culture, particularly in *Critique of Information*, seems to rest on a theory of 'technological forms of life'. What are these forms?

SL The 'Technological Forms of Life' chapter is an important one in the book, but now I see it completely differently. The funny thing is that this wasn't a vitalist chapter. It starts out with a Wittgensteinian idea of forms of life and then works them through as technologically mediated. 'Forms of life' are here based in what French theorists – from Mauss through Lyotard – call the social bond (*lien social*). But technological mediation makes the forms of life (and forms of life are ways of life, are culture) become culture-at-a-distance. It makes relations more sporadic, intense and stretched: compressed and dis-tanciated simultaneously. Thus, the time-honoured social bond of forms of life becomes the *communicational* bond of technological forms of life. By commu-nication I mean again something that is non-narrative: it is more temporally compressed (hence briefer and more intense) and spatially 'stretched' than a narrative. Such temporal and now also morphological compression and spatial stretching is possible only through technological mediation. This technological mediation is no longer through the means of production, but through the means of communication, and these include means of transport. This stands in contrast to the classical social bond, whether the classical bond is that of *Gemeinschaft* (tradition) or *Gesellschaft* (modernity). The rise of technological forms of life corresponds to the fragmentation of *gesellschaftlich* institutions, and indeed supersedes or largely takes over the social bond of the capital relation. And this is the social bond – based in institutions and organizations (including the factory) – becoming largely displaced by the *communicational* bond.

NG What concept of life are you working with here if it is not a vitalist one?

SL It is not a vitalist one, but I want it to be a vitalist one now. It should have been but it wasn't and it is now. A vitalist notion of life is much different to this Wittgensteinian one. The Wittgensteinian one is essentially phenomenological and humanist. A vitalist idea of life, meanwhile, starts with far simpler sorts of matter than us human beings. Indeed, it begins with inorganic matter, and here is where we can start with most vitalists. It can be Friedrich Nietzsche in *The Will to Power* (Nietzsche, 1968), or Gabriel Tarde, especially in his writings on monadology, or Bergson in *Matter and Memory* (Bergson, 1991), or in Deleuze and Guattari. Vitalism is the opposite of mechanism. In vitalism, matter is self-organizing or self-causing. In mechanism, causation is external. But usually there is a vitalist hierarchy of self-causation in the Aristotelian sense. Thus, inorganic matter has the weakest powers of self-organization, organic matter has more such powers, animals are yet more self-causing, and God or Nietzsche's *Übermensch* the most self-organizing.

Vitalism starts with the assumption, from Tarde, of fundamental difference. This is Leibnizian monadology as distinct from Cartesian atomism. In monadology, simple substance is difference, whereas in atomism, simple substance is identity. So, you start out with two monads standing in a relation of, as it were, inter-objectivity. These monads are, from the start, in a relation of affect and communication, and thus more than one of causation with respect to one another. Each monad also perceives the other. This is already Bergson in *Matter and Memory*. Each monad perceives only that aspect of the other that accords with its interests. Each monad exerts a certain action, it imparts a certain movement via a certain vibration or resonance to the other, again according to the particular monad's interests. So, the first monad exerts an action on the second. The second will, of course, react towards the first in connection with the second monad's interests, and when there is an interval between the action and reaction there is, for Bergson, memory. Only with this interval is there life. This interval is also the reflexive moment of self-organization. But this idea of life is vastly different to Wittgenstein's phenomenological and humanist idea of forms of life. This second may be derivative of the first, but this idea of life, in which, for example, information itself is alive, is the vitalist one. And it makes a lot of sense in the contemporary social world. I formulated a non-linear take on reflexivity in my contribution to a recent *Theory, Culture & Society* debate about reflexive modernization (Lash, 2003), to which also Bruno Latour contributed. But I wrote this piece about two years ago, and more recently I have given reflexivity the sort of properly vitalist reading outlined above.

NG   What notion of life did you have back in *Critique of Information*? And what was your interest in Wittgenstein?

SL   I wasn't obsessed with Wittgenstein. I gave a paper to the American Anthropological Association called 'Technological Forms of Life' and it wasn't worked out. But by the time I gave it for my Inaugural Lecture it was quite good. I published it almost completely and everybody has really gotten into it. It occurred to me that 'forms of life' is one way of understanding culture: culture can be called forms of life. The two classic definitions of culture are culture as a form of life (e.g. British culture, British form of life, British way of life), or culture as representation. But I wanted to look at culture as 'forms of life', and I wanted to see what happens when these become technological. So it wasn't literally Wittgenstein, but was a way of understanding culture. I wasn't into vitalism then, but now I like to see culture as a form of life. And I like to see life as substance, life as drive, life as lines of flight, life as some kind of energetics, and these things take forms more or less. Georg Simmel wrote extensively on 'life' in such a vein, so I would take a much more Simmelian point of view right now.

NG   And what about Tarde and Bergson? What do you get from these writers?

SL   Simmel, of course, was very influenced by Bergson. And, Maurizio Lazzarato told me, Bergson did the oration at Tarde's funeral. Tarde was the predecessor of Bergson and Simmel, and Durkheim, of course, was fundamentally opposed to Tarde. The Tarde-Durkheim counter-position is a major source of the birth of sociology. And Bergson was the biggest thing around at the time, but I know Simmel somewhat better than I do Bergson. Bergson appeals to me, as he does for a whole contemporary generation of cultural theorists, through the Deleuze connection. Bergson was also fundamentally influential to Prigogine and Stengers, who have been seminal for non-linear and complexity theory. Bergson is read as a monist and a vitalist, and in his work you find pre-human kinds of entities that are communicating, that are reflexive, that are not quite 'thinking' but are getting close, and that somehow have certain amounts of intelligence and have perception. I think this helps us think about post-human things, like camera lenses having perception. In this way, vitalism is at the same time pre-human and post-human, and it tends to presume a monism, a certain de-differentiation into a 'plane of immanence'.

NG   So how do you think that such vitalist thinking might inform a social theory?

SL   One way in is through Georg Simmel. Notions of flow and flux are paradigmatically vitalist. In Simmel (and others) there are flux and flows of consciousness. But now you have a general externalization of flux and flow – as in David Cronenberg's *Scanners*, where the head explodes and flux and flows come out – and you get global villages and networks: nodes and stoppages and non-linear *forms*. I think flow and form are the right words. I do not want to break with the notion of form, though it has been so often criticized. Simmel had a strong notion of form and a strong notion of life. Flow is life somehow, but not all life. Flux is life, whereas flow can be less life-like, for flux has an intensity to it that flow doesn't necessarily have.

I think that what sociology has to deal with is a contemporary *Weltanschauung* which is vitalist and which is complex. The contemporary *Weltanschauung* builds in assumptions of complexity from chemistry to biology to physics to computer science to our everyday understandings of interactivity – from Alan Turing through Norbert Wiener to now. Sociology has to deal with this and with the various collapses into the immanence of the contemporary order, for example: the emerging indifference of culture and economy, of image and movement, of spirit and matter. Baudrillard, with his theory of hyperreality, gets us part way there. For Baudrillard, hyperreality was understood as a form of emergent non-linear power that would make us long for the old days of simple domination by the (linear) commodity. You are aware of this in your own distinguished work on value and the orders of the simulacra. But sociology needs more generally to take on these ideas of immanence, of flow, of reflexivity in the sense of open systems that are self-causing and self-creating. Thus, Lazzarato and Latour, have (re-)turned to Gabriel Tarde, because Tarde had an idea of monads, almost from Leibniz, as communicating and more or less open. I think that communication works like that, and even our psyches have bits that are almost communicating monads that can fall apart or come together and be more or less coherent. It is almost that in the sea of chaos there are islands of order, and those islands of order are more or less coherently communicating monads. All this is in complexity theory and vitalism right through. The key book here is Maurizio Lazzarato's *Puissances de l'invention: La psychologie économique de Gabriel Tarde contre l'économie politique* (2002).

Let me also approach this from a different angle, and this is the central point made by Antonio Negri and the writers associated with the Paris journal *Multitudes*, such as Lazzarato, Yann Moulier Boutang, Eric Alliez and Paolo Virno. For Negri and *Multitudes*, life displaces labour as the governing principle of the contemporary global order. This is also, I think, the major contribution of Hardt and Negri's *Empire*. For the national, manufacturing society there was the principle of labour, but for the global information order there is life. These theorists, influenced by Spinoza, speak of power in terms of *puissance and pouvoir*. 'Puissance' is life; it is an energetics. The multitudes are such puissance, and they stand in contrast to the earlier *'peuple'* (people). The people – including the classical proletariat – operate from a principle of identity, whereas the multitudes operate from a logic of difference: the *peuple* as proletariat in regard to labour, the multitudes in regard to life. This is the politics of life as *puissance*. It works less through struggle than through flow, through escape, through something like the Situationists *dérive*, through Deleuzo-Guattarian 'lines of flight'. But power as *pouvoir* also works through life. This bio-power is *bio-pouvoir* (not *bio-puissance*). Power had to do with labour, but now it connects to life. Power once had to do with the appropriation of abstract labour, but now it has to do with the appropriation of concrete life. Deleuze is here the theorist of *puissance*, Foucault of *pouvoir*. In this sense, as I argued in a very early piece on Foucault and Nietzsche ('Geneaology and the Body' (Lash, 1983, and republished in Lash, 1990)), Foucault too is a vitalist, but only from the point of view of *pouvoir*. His idea of *bio-pouvoir* is stronger than Deleuze's idea of 'control'. But this is not surveillance. Power through surveillance is abstract and from above. This is old power. It is the opposite to the newer *bio-pouvoir*, and Foucault (2001) was clear about this in *The Order of Things (Les mots et les choses)*. Here, in the Classical Age, words related to things from above and abstractly through classifications, the general grammar, etc. Then, more recently, words began to enter into the very heart, the very physiology of things. The Classical Age has to do with surveillance, the more contemporary age with *bio-power*. I disagree with Foucault in terms of his over-emphasis on the discursive nature of power: for me it is more figural and through things. But I fully agree with his idea of bio-power. My Ph.D. student, Sebastian Olma seeks of it as ontological power. I agree: power was once epistemological and abstract, but now with the appropriation of concrete life it becomes ontological.

NG You are also quite insistent in *Critique of Information* that theory be critical theory. You say that there is no outside to the information order, but given the speed, complexity and exorbitance of this order, how might critique come from within it?

SL I got this idea from a Japanese scholar named Kyoshi Abé who was a post-doctoral fellow at Goldsmiths' when I first starting teaching there. He was really interested in critical theory in the classical sense and was obsessed by Japanese information science. Then, I gave a paper in Japan about four years ago that was about critique. And I thought: how can we have immanent critique? How can we have critique without a transcendent? How can we have critique with a monist set of flows? The answer is that it has got to be an immanentist critique. I say in the book, and I partly agree – I am not completely there – that it works for a kind of 'and': that conjunction that keeps adding on. Maybe this is all we can do: critique takes place through reflexivity, through self-organization, not through a transcendent, i.e. giving a goal or anything to it. What we can do as thinkers and sociologists is not to give a decisive 'and', but perhaps contribute a little bit of an 'and' or conjunction which helps whatever more or less open system we are in become more open and more reflexive.

NG Is there not a danger, given the unprecedented acceleration of the information order, that this critique might never take place, and that if it does it might never be heard due to the growing mass of information in the system?

SL I take your point, but I am not sure. First, it still takes, say, four years to write a book. And there are a lot of places in which there is still a lot of slowness around, so slowness is still possible. Second, critical interventions can perhaps now be more event-like, more like art events, installations and performances. The intervention of theory itself could well be more event-like. Hence, what I like to do often is to work with teams of designers and architects on a project, or to make a critical textual intervention in an exhibition, or something like that. For like information, events are short-lasting. Transcendental critique takes place through an instance of far greater duration than the empirical processes it criticizes, but *immanent* critique is a piece of what is criticized: that which is criticized is often fleeting, intense, byte-like, but so may be the critique. Critical theory may take place less through the long book than through, for instance, theoretical interventions in political events, art events, media events, or in urban planning.

NG Following up on this, your book is called *Critique of Information*. What, exactly, is the object of this critique? What is under attack?

SL   First, I would say that the book only works with the breaking to bits of subject-object thinking. This means there is not an object of critique as it were: it is much more reflexive in the sense that it is taking place in an immanent networked plane. Hence, I wouldn't say it is a critique of *something*. It is not like a straightforward critique of capitalism or of pure reason. It is not like that at all, because those kinds of critique presume a transcendental and that you are outside of the information. Mine is an immanent critique, a reflexive critique: it is a critique of something that is lived so much by whatever is critical that that which is critical can never get the distance on it, and so whatever is being critiqued is never an object at all. In classical critique, the criticism is from a distance. This might be the critique of the particular by the universal, or the critique, as I mentioned before, of the understanding by 'reason'. This critique of the understanding by reason, or of necessity by freedom, grew largely out of Romanticism. It is the basis of the critique of exchange value from the viewpoint of use-value. What I am trying to say in *Critique of Information* is that we can no longer get this sort of distance on the empirical ubiquity of information flows. Critique may be a question of mapping, of cartography, of a certain sort of sense-making interior to the information. But it cannot get the distance of classical critique.

NG   In pursuing such a critique, why do you say that writing, and beyond this theory, must take a presentational rather than representational form? Does this, in turn, mean that social theory is destined to become media theory?

SL   The first part of the question I have almost answered by saying that we can think of things in terms of theoretical interventions. My friend and colleague Sarat Maharaj does just that as an art theorist in various Documentas and postcolonial spaces. And he often does it through verbal and catalogue interventions – through things that are a lot more ephemeral than the writing of long books. This means that social theory winds up becoming more like what people conceive of as being media theory, because media theory is probably seen as being much more performative. But I think that there is still a big difference between, on the one hand, social theory and cultural studies (which I'll put together for the moment), and media theory on the other, because media theory does not care about duration, memory or other notions of culture. There is almost a veneer of hype in media theory in which nothing outside of non-linear systems and flows is allowed in, and a belief that there is nothing outside of Deleuze and Baudrillard. I think there is a lot more to culture than just media and there always will be, and media theorists tend to miss out important dimensions of social relations, especially individual and collective memory. It is almost like you have to turn to a sociologist like Nikolas

Luhmann – who I think writes very much in a non-linear communicational mode – to start understanding the social basis of communications. And I do think sociologists have cottoned on to this well, another example being Tarde at the beginning of sociology. So, I have ended up being a dogmatic sociologist at the end of this interview!

NG   But in *Critique of Information* you say that media theory is perhaps our fate 'in the global information order'. Does this mean that social theory, because of its tendency to be patient and slow, is in some way destined to failure?

SL   I wrote that a while back, about three years ago. Subsequently, I have realized that a book that we write can be more or less a 'virtuality' that can be activated performatively in certain spaces and at different times – whether it be a teaching situation or a political event or whatever. This is Bergson's idea of the virtual, as developed in, for example, Sanford Kwinter's *Architectures of Time* (2001) or Brian Massumi's *Parables for the Virtual* (2002). I think that is the way an archive should be seen: it can almost be brought to life after the death of the author.[1] You could even work on it so that it created new things, for example: a Georg Simmel archive that could keep creating new things and could be performative. I am very positive about the way social theory and sociological theory can work in all sorts of performative spaces and media spaces.

NOTES

1. This idea is Hans Ulrich Obrist's.

REFERENCES

Appadurai, A. (1990) 'Disjuncture and Difference in the Global Cultural Economy', in M. Featherstone (ed.) *Global Culture: Nationalism, Globalization and Modernity*. London: Sage.

Beck, U., Giddens, A. and Lash, S. (1994) *Reflexive Modernization*. Cambridge: Polity.

Bergson, H. (1991) *Matter and Memory*. New York: Zone.

Castells, M. (2000) *The Rise of the Network Society* (2nd ed). Oxford: Blackwell.

Foucault, M. (2001) *The Order of Things*. London: Routledge.

Hardt, M. and Negri, A. (2001) *Empire*. Cambridge, MA: Harvard University Press.

Harvey, D. (1989) *The Condition of Postmodernity*. Oxford: Blackwell.

Kwinter, S. (2001) *Architectures of Time: Toward a Theory of the Event in Modernist Culture*. Cambridge, MA: MIT Press.

Lash, S. (1983) 'Genealogy and the Body: Foucault/Deleuze/Nietzsche', *Theory, Culture & Society*, Vol. 2, No. 2, pp.1–17.

Lash, S. (1990) *Sociology of Postmodernism*. London: Routledge.

Lash, S. (1999) *Another Modernity, A Different Rationality*. Oxford: Blackwell.

Lash, S. (2002) *Critique of Information*. London: Sage.

Lash, S. (2003) 'Reflexivity as Non-Linearity', *Theory, Culture & Society*, Vol. 20, No. 2, pp. 49–58.

Lash, S. and Urry, J. (1987) *The End of Organized Capitalism*. Cambridge: Polity.

Lash, S. and Urry, J. (1994) *Economies of Signs and Space*. London: Sage.

Lazzarato, M. (2002) *La Puissances de l'invention: La psychologie économique de Gabriel Tarde contre l'économie politique*. Paris: Les empêcheurs de penser en rond.

Lury, C. (1997) *Prosthetic Culture*. London: Routledge.

Lyotard, J.-F. (1971) *Discours, Figure*. Paris: Klickseick.

Lyotard, J.-F. (1993) *Libidinal Economy*. London: Athlone.

MacIntyre, A. (1988) *Whose Justice? Which Rationality?* London: Duckworth.

Massumi, B. (2002) *Parables for the Virtual: Movement, Affect, Sensation*. Durham, NC: Duke University Press.

Nietzsche, F. (1968) *The Will To Power*. New York: Vintage.

Parsons, T. (1967) *The Structure of Social Action*. New York: The Free Press.

Rose, G. (1992) *The Broken Middle*. Oxford: Blackwell.

CHAPTER 6

John Urry: Complex Mobilities

NG   Your recent work declares a shift in the basic subject matter of sociology: from the social as society to the social as mobility. With this, you say the discipline should shift its focus from the analysis of societies, nation-states and social structures to the study of 'networks, mobility and horizontal fluidities' (Urry, 2000: 3). You also propose 13 new rules of sociological method to facilitate such a change. But, to reflect on this proposed shift for a moment: are societies necessarily tied to nation-states? Is it possible to talk of network, transnational or world society, and, if not, what does this mean for thinking about 'the social'?

JU   What is important is to try to shift sociology from the study of society to the study of mobility. I am very keen to emphasize how societies, for a century or two, were tied to, or embedded within, nation-states, and that this society/nation-state configuration provided the context within which sociology emerged historically. I am not saying that somehow societies or nation-states have now simply disappeared. That would obviously be false. But that something of this tying together, this sort of connectivity, of society with nation-state, has come to be significantly weakened. And through the weakening of this relationship, the context within which sociology emerged has very substantially shifted. Yet much sociological work still takes 'society' for granted and presumes by this that there is an integrated nation-state society. This seems quite odd to me because at the very same time there is almost a new sociology – the sociology of globalization – but somehow there has not been much connecting together of these two trends.

Thus, one of the things I am keen to show is the importance of networked relationships across the globe, not that these networked relationships are remotely similar or patterned in the same way for different domains of activity. This has big implications for the so-called social because of the way in which patterns of sociality are now hugely dependent upon all sorts of networked relationships: networks of physical and virtual travel, of imaginative travel, and so on. These patterns of networked movement come to constitute the patterning of social life. Social life becomes very significantly interwoven with a set of material processes that form, constitute and extend the networked character of social relationships, which, in turn, are not simply isomorphic with the boundaries of nation-states.

NG   A key part of your approach has been to assert the metaphorical basis of sociological thought. In *Sociology Beyond Societies* (Urry, 2000), for example, you talk of the organic analogy and of later metaphors of exchange, vision, structure and body, and go on to develop new metaphors of mobility and the global. But at what point does a theory or concept cease to be a metaphor? You say, against Durkheim, that some metaphors are 'scientifically useful and not the consequence of a mere sensuousness', and go on to add that '*contra* post-structuralism ... it is possible to evaluate metaphors for their scientific pro-ductivity' (Urry, 2000: 27). Is this a basic task of social theory? If so, how might we proceed to evaluate one metaphor against another in regards to their sci-entific functions or uses? What criteria of judgement might we use?

JU   One thing I emphasized in *Sociology Beyond Societies*, something which is quite well known, is that social thought and social research rests upon various sorts of metaphors, such as the metaphors of exchange, vision, structure, body, networks, and so on. I also wanted to bring out how a lot of social theory and research is really a contestation around or over metaphors, and that these metaphors do not disappear or hide themselves but remain of enduring power and significance. I also show that this is not simply a matter of contested metaphors that are all equivalent to each other. I argue that different metaphors are of varying scientific fruitfulness, that they have different sorts of perfor-mative powers to characterize dimensions of social life, and that social theory and social research is concerned with the systematic evaluation of different metaphors. But I do not mean by this that one can, in a more or less empiricist frame, simply or merely deduce from any such metaphor empirically testable consequences which then provide quick, unambiguous evidence for or against a theory or metaphor. But rather, there are ways in which social science produces outcomes through deploying different kinds of methods, and some of these can lead to a greater plausibility of certain metaphors over others. I would want now to express this through the language of falsification. That is, that the metaphors and theories that remain are to a significant extent to be understood as those for which, or as yet, there have not been systematic and sustained refutations. Those that remain have this kind of status. Of course, there are all kinds of problems about the historical specificity of procedures, methods and techniques by which different metaphors/theories might or might not be 'tes-ted'. But, where there has been some attempt at falsification or testing, the

metaphors or theories that remain are those that have survived relatively
unscathed from these processes.

NG   You say that 'globalization involves replacing the metaphor of society as
region with the metaphor of the global conceived of as *network* and *fluid*' (Urry,
2000: 33; original emphasis). Does this mean that you treat globalization as a
metaphor or an empirical process, or as both? And from where do you draw
your metaphors of the global, network and fluid?

JU   There are various metaphors implicit in the idea of 'the global'. The
global is not simply a series of empirical processes as there are also different
metaphors at play here, even if they have not been very well distinguished from
each other. I separate the metaphor of region from the metaphor of network
from the metaphor of fluid (which are distinctions made by Annemarie Mol
and John Law) to then think through what these metaphors mean for the global
in a more substantial way. In a simple sense, these metaphors are drawn from
the sociology of science and technology. I believe this is a fruitful area because
this domain of enquiry has very much been interested in movement: the
movement of scientific findings, of test procedures, and of notions of, say,
health and illness moving across different borders. I thought it helpful to draw
on the distinctions being made within these analyses in science and technology
as a way of thinking about the mobility of all sorts of other entities in and across
borders, such as the mobility of people or ideas or information or money, and
so on.

NG   A further metaphor you use is that of 'scapes'. What is the difference
between a scape and a network? Are scapes networks of networks? Are they to
be treated as fluid forms of social structure?

JU   I, like a number of other people, was quite influenced by Arjun Appadurai's formulation of various scapes. This formulation made a distinction
between a notion of social structure through space and time or *scapes*, and the
empirical flows of different entities through and across these scapes. This
seemed a helpful formulation, and indeed Scott Lash and I used this distinction
in our *Economies of Signs and Space* book (see Lash and Urry, 1994). Scapes are
networks of networks that connect together certain relationships and not others. They connect together sets of nodes in ways that are not simply or
straightforwardly ismorphic with the boundaries of nation-states or even with
the boundaries of activities that corporations engage in, or of the boundaries of
the ways in which information is organized through time and space. But, more
recently, I have seen this scapes–flows distinction as a static distinction, and

although the idea of scape brings out how connections occur structurally in important ways, it does so separately from the precise flows. So, I now want to reformulate this through various notions of system, and by thinking of networks as dynamic open systems that partly are reproduced through the very processes through which the flows take place. A very rigid distinction between scapes and flows is therefore one I now find less productive.

NG In your analysis of networks, you propose, following Castells, that they 'are to be viewed as dynamic open structures' (Urry, 2002: 34) that have no centre and that promote horizontal forms of mobility (a point you re-emphasize in relation to global systems in *Global Complexity* (2002: 38)). At the same time, however, you say that 'flows', be they of people, images, information, 'create new inequalities of access/non-access which do not map onto the jurisdictions of particular societies' (Urry, 2000: 36). But is there not an implicit contra-diction in this position? Are not flows structured by the networks through which they travel, and are not all networks, including the Internet, in some way hierarchical? My basic question, then, is: are not networks a mix of open *and* closed associations (to use a Weberian vocabulary)?

JU I think maybe the term 'open', in thinking of networks as dynamic open systems, is the problem here. It is clearly the case that there are hierarchies of access and inequalities of flow, for example between those people, institutions or organizations that are closer to the centre or particular nodes of networks (depending on the topology of networks, as different networks have different sets of topologies). But I want to bring out the ways in which movements and activities within networks are both horizontal *and* hierarchical. There is a very high ratio of flows that take place within the constraints of a network, which, of course, separate that network from the non-network. And although these flows are structured, organized and full of inequalities, clearly there is a rich, com-plex, overlapping, diversity of flows taking place within the constraints of a given network. But perhaps I was trying to make the point too starkly against conventional notions of structure that are predominantly of hierarchy. It was to offset this view that I was keen to bring out the way in which a lot of writing about mobility has been predominantly hierarchical – that is, to do with social mobility up and down various sorts of hierarchies. In view of this, I was seeking to emphasize, in particular, the horizontal character of lots of networked relationships, which is not to say that there are not vertical components as well.

NG Can we talk of networks in terms of blockages as well as flows, and thus, like Zygmunt Bauman, of the emergence of new hierarchies of access and mobility, and, with this, the emergence of new forms of class relations?

JU   I am much taken with some of Zygmunt Bauman's formulations of fluid modernity. The way I would put this is that to talk of flows is to talk about non-flows, to talk of mobilities is to talk of those who are not accessing those mobilities, and also for there to be connections between two people or places through one network is, of course, to make those who are not connected more deprived by, separated from or excluded from participation in the particular set of social practices we are examining. This produces new hierarchies of access and mobility, but these new hierarchies have to be seen through analysis of scapes and flows, or through the distinction between regions, networks and fluids.

NG   You mention briefly in your discussion of networks and mobility that power is diffused through fluids into 'capillary-like relations of domination/subordination' and 'exercised through the intersection of various fluids working on diverse senses' (2000: 39). What do you mean by this?

JU   There are two separate points being made here. First, if this language of networks and fluids is productive then it implies that important inequalities of power are formed and re-formed in ways that involve networked and fluid relationships. And this seems to give an account of power that is much like the notion of power that Foucault talked about, although I have always found what he said about the social structure or bases of power to be underdeveloped. But the relatively newer language of networks and flows gives an explanation of the processes that Foucault interestingly examined, such as the 'capillary-like relations of domination/subordination'. Second, of course, Foucault brings out the embodied, bodily character of power relations. He demonstrates the importance of the visual sense in the operations of power through his analysis of the Panopticon, which is an exemplary paradigmatic analysis. I want to suggest, however, that networks and fluids also work through different senses, not just the visual one, although, as I have written in relation to travel and tourism, the visual sense plays a hegemonic organizing role. My point is, though, that the other senses are important, including obviously touch and sound and smell and also the kinaesthetic sense of movement. This is because the operation of power and the experience of power involve the interlayering of multiple senses.

NG   Following on from this, how has the nature or metaphor of power changed with the shift to global complexity? You say that 'Informational and mediated power is mobile, performed and unbounded. This is its strength and vulnerability' (Urry, 2002: 113). What is new here? And how might the power of the global system be explained through the idea of a strange attractor (Urry, 2002: 86)?

JU   One of the aims of *Global Complexity* is to try to be a little bit more precise about some of the new modes in which power operates, especially power operating within and through the analysis of various kinds of systems. In thinking about this, I wanted to bring out – and this was related to the analysis of complex scandals (a complexity of those processes which in the contemporary world generate scandal) – the role of informational and mediated power, which seemed to be particularly characterized by an intense mobility: it is performed, it can jump unpredictably from place to place, but having jumped from place to place it then exerts some irreversible consequences for those who are bound up with, and implicated within, scandalizing processes. I think this is an example of how there is an unpredictablity of where and when power is going to have its impact. Informational and mediated power is mobile, performed and unpredictable in its consequences, but having set up such consequences – often for quite small-scale reasons – it sets certain irreversible processes working through the system.

Also in *Global Complexity*, I draw on the mathematics of strange attractors. Over time, again through irreversible processes that are often set up in terms of relatively small causes, systems generate sets of consequences in which they move through iterative processes to produce new and unpredictable patterns. I talk, for example, about the attractor of glocalization. I show how all sorts of putative global relationships are drawn in and remade through these relationships moving between the global and local. So, rather than thinking of the global and the local as a fixed dichotomy, I tried to bring out the unending, irreversible, dynamic processes of globalization reinforcing localization reinforcing globalization, and so on. Each is bound up with the other and is in effect part of the same set of systemic processes, and many processes otherwise outside the system get drawn in and come to be remade as a consequence. Benjamin Barber's (1996) apocalyptic account of the Jihad versus McWorld, for example, contains in effect an analysis of how iteration produces new emergent topologies in the evolving relationship of Islam and the 'West'.

NG   How would you talk about power in this context?

JU   I am clearly not using power in any sense as the originator of outcomes, as being in itself productive. Power relations get made and remade in the very workings of system developments occurring irreversibly and dynamically over time, so that power is produced and performed but within the interstices of these kinds of strange attractor relationships. So power is not fixed, not a quantum. It is emergent and evolving, mobile and complex, unpredictable and irreversible.

NG   Globalization has been accompanied not only by the emergence of new forms of power, but also by new demands for human rights and citizenship. At the conclusion to your chapter on citizenship in *Sociology Beyond Societies* you say the following: 'Given the extraordinarily heterogeneous character of most national societies, and especially their capital cities, then some "uniting into a single civilization" through the power of the global mass media may be para- doxically necessary for the peculiar character of contemporary citizenship' (Urry, 2000: 187). What do you mean by this?

JU   This chapter of the book explored the making and remaking of con- temporary citizenship, particularly trying to think what this citizenship might be in relationship to a variety of global processes. I rather formalistically set out what we might imagine to be global rights and the global duties in relationship to a variety of global risks (which, of course, many other people have elabo- rated). And then I tried to think about where and how the processes simplis- tically referred to as 'global media' might fit in. I make some slightly paradoxical proposals, namely that there are certain ways in which the global media – the development of images of the globe, images of people and all sorts of activities, animals, places and environments that somehow stand for the globe – provide at least some of the preconditions for a putative global citi- zenship. In the book, I referred to various sorts of research on this issue to suggest that this is a reasonably plausible account. Partly, I drew on literature that looks at the development of national citizenship and the role of the mass media, especially print, radio and then TV in the development of national citizenship. Obviously, from Benedict Andersen onwards, 'Imagined Com- munities' have been seen as absolutely key preconditions for citizenship. But I was also trying to make some reference to the classic writings of T. H. Marshall on the nature of citizenship, in which the phrase 'the necessity for uniting into a single civilization' is used (again obviously only talking about national citi- zenship). Marshall sees this as something necessary for national citizenship, and I was trying to suggest that, oddly, global media may, through processes which people often hugely criticize as homogenizing, actually provide some limited basis for uniting into a single civilization (to requote T. H. Marshall). This, paradoxically, may be necessary for some notion of a post-national citizenship.

NG   Ideas of citizenship, more often than not, are tied to arguments about 'human rights'. In your account of the classical sociological tradition, you see an intrinsic connection between the social (as society) and the 'human': 'To be human meant that one is a member or citizen of a particular society' (Urry, 2000: 9). But now, you say, things are different, not simply because the social is no longer bounded by the nation-state but because social relations emerge through the intersection of human agency and 'inhuman' technologies or objects. To quote from *Sociology Beyond Societies*: 'Human powers increasingly derive from the complex *interconnections* of humans with material objects, including signs, machines, technologies, texts, physical environments, animals, plants, and waste products. People possess few powers which are uniquely human, while most can only be realized because of their connections with these inhuman components' (Urry, 2000: 14; original emphasis). From this, you argue, like Latour, that there are no longer 'uniquely human societies', only networks of connections between humans and objects, leading to the emergence of what might be called 'hybrid' societies. In response, you propose that sociology should change its focus, so that the concept of agency is *embodied*, and that theory shifts accordingly to address the ways objects or humans sensuously experience technologies. A number of questions might follow from this. For example: when you speak of 'the human', what exactly do you mean? In analysing the intersection between humans and objects, do you lend primacy to the study of the former? Is it indeed possible, if it ever was, to separate the human from the inhuman? Are we not all hybrid beings now? And if so, what would the loss of a discrete human subject mean for social theory?

JU   In both *Sociology Beyond Societies* and *Global Complexity*, I examine many interconnections of 'humans' with various 'objects'. These include signs, machines, technologies, texts, environments, animals, plants, waste products and so on. First, then, it is hard to think of human practices which are in any way separate from these interconnections, separate from the relationality between human powers and the properties and characteristics of material objects (I use 'material objects' as a generic term here, but, of course, all of these different objects have different kinds of powers). Second, thinking about these interconnections requires thinking about the sensed relations between humans and these objects, and characterizing this relationality involves examining the hierarchy of senses deployed in the relationship with one or more objects. Of course, it should be noted that often so-called humans are interdependent with more than one object simultaneously. Third, therefore, we can talk about a performance of human activity through working on and with these different objects, and the language of affordances of such objects is one that I have found very productive to characterize this relationality. So, in terms of developing a social science, I think there is no social science that is a science of the purely social. I think it may well have been always the case, but clearly the emergence of many kinds of new objects has brought this much more startlingly to our attention, and I would emphasize especially the significance of objects of movement. The sorts of entities I am thinking of here include various machines which *move* humans so that they can literally go further, faster and higher than previously. I think, for example, that the innovation of the motorcar was probably one of the most profound transformations of 'human' powers. The twentieth century involved what I call 'the car-driver hybrid', which transformed human powers to remake the nature of movement, city life, family life, the interconnections between the array of human practices which typically were thought to characterize social life, and so on. And there are, of course, a variety of other kinds of what I call 'mobile machines': earlier the bike and the train, and later the plane and space travel, and then, of course, those extraordinary new machines that move information and images more or less instantaneously, and which in part reconfigure 'humans'.

NG   You have a tendency to use the terms 'sense' and 'experience'. These are very loaded terms. Do you draw these terms from the critical philosophy of Kant, or rather from later thinkers such as Simmel? And to what extent has the basis of sense and experience changed with the advent of 'hybrid societies'?

JU   One thing I am especially interested in bringing to the fore is the nature of humans and their movement. I suppose Simmel's account of the city, more indeed than other accounts, captured the character of city life constituted through often-restless movement. I think it fruitful to deploy some of these notions to the connections between the nature of humans, not only when they are walking the city, but also when they are moving in and through the city and more generally through social life, especially in their deployment of a variety of different 'mobile machines'. The movement that the car allows, and yet simultaneously coerces us into, illustrates how it fundamentally alters the sensing of the city. This sensing is achieved by blocking out many of the smells, sounds and the temperature outside, as people move in their 'iron cages' of modernity through its streets. And yet for those outside, those not located in these cocooned iron cages, the experience of the street is made noisy, polluting, dangerous and insecure as these faceless 'monsters' transform the sensed experience of the city.

NG   In your outline of 'more new rules of sociological method', you propose two ways of dealing with the emergence of new hybrid social forms. The first is 'to consider things as social facts – and to see agency as stemming from the mutual intersections of objects and people'. The second is 'to embody one's analysis through investigating the sensuous constitution of humans and objects' (Urry, 2000: 18). These proposals assert the need for sociology to take ser-iously a theory of the object. But beyond this, how might these rules be put into practice? Do we need new methodological procedures and concepts alongside new metaphors? If so, what might they look like?

JU   One thing I have been thinking about recently is formulating some of this through what I call 'mobile methods'. In some way, the methods of research, and to some extent the methods of developing theory, should simulate the kinds of mobilities that the new rules of sociological method tried to reveal. More prosaically, it means developing methods of social research that are themselves mobile. For example, studying patterns of travel should almost certainly involve travelling along with the people, the objects or the informational or cultural flows. The significance of different temporalities necessitates methods that also simulate the temporal character of the entities, processes and so on. Another way of formulating this would be to follow the flows and to see where it is that people, objects or information flow. But this is, of course, an extraordinarily difficult thing to do because of the ways in which objects flow – they transform and are transformed as they move through different sorts of networks. But, still, that is the vision: a set of mobile methods simulating the movements of people, objects and information through time and space.

NG   A further aspect of your work on globalization is the analysis of different concepts and metaphors of time: social time, 'natural' time, 'glacial' time, 'instantaneous' time, and so on. In short, you say that 'a reconfigured sociology must place time at its very centre' (Urry, 2000: 105). But what does this mean for social theory? How can theory (a notoriously slow and patient endeavour) keep pace with events taking place in instantaneous time? Should it attempt to do so, and if so how?

JU   Through a number of different formulations I have tried to demonstrate that the notion of clock time is only one mode of time, albeit an extraordinarily powerful temporal regime. And indeed, in the history of modernity the emergence and extended power and reach of clock time has been exceptionally powerful. But I have tried to suggest, as indeed some of Castells' writings also suggest, that there are a multitude of different times, and that clock time is not the only kind of time. One can draw on certain metaphors of time to examine the most important characteristics of time in the 'social world'. And there are two in particular that I have been interested in. One is what I call *instantaneous time*, or what Castells calls 'timeless time'. There are many processes that appear to involve exceptional accelerations of time, and when we are chasing or following the flows, as described earlier, we find that many are moving at accelerated rates. One can see this in travel to the other side of the world, flows through the Internet, through the billions of TV screens across the world, and in the real-time reporting of major global events. This has dramatically and pretty well instantaneously brought all sorts of events, processes, information and people onto one's screens or into one's living room. Secondly, but at the same moment as this, the science of the environment and ecology has brought out the incredibly slow and long-term nature of many physical and biological processes. I like to call this *glacial time*. This seems to characterize quite a diversity of processes and responses to those forms of accelerated change that have developed within various sorts of social groups and social movements. So, I talk increasingly of the intersections of instantaneous and glacial time – and it is analysis of this relationship, rather than clock time, that would seem to be crucial to a reconfigured sociology.

But how can theory keep pace with events in instantaneous time? I think theories, because they are based in the academy, have much difficulty in keeping pace, precisely because of the various time regimes that characterize academic life and, indeed, processes of publication. These are still clock-time based. And this means that theory and theoretical work is often rather in the slipstream. A special example of this would be the relative failure, until very recently, to be able to capture the time of the Internet, and embed it adequately and systematically in thinking about social theory. But I think there are lots of other ways in which theories, and more generally social science, embedded in the time regimes and structural processes that characterize the university system have big problems. They are sometimes out of time or left in the slow lane. I suppose that is one of the reasons for the proliferation of electronic journals, and for the tendency for some social theorists (such as Anthony Giddens) to seek to articulate their views through more instantaneous mass media.

NG This idea of an intersection of instantaneous and glacial time underpins your work on globalization, but at the conclusion to *Sociology Beyond Societies* you also say that globalization involves a 'return' from the ordered world of the 'gardening state' (characteristic of modern societies) to the chaotic world of the 'gamekeeper state' (in which mobilities can no longer be easily regulated). This shift is the subject of your most recent book *Global Complexity*, which seeks to understand 'the global' through 'mobile' concepts, metaphors and ideas drawn from complexity theory. But how does this complexity approach lend to ana-lysis of 'the social'. You say that 'there are "societies", but ... their societal capacity has been transformed through becoming elements within systems of global complexity' (Urry, 2002: 106–7). What do you mean by this?

JU The key thing I am trying to bring out is that the analysis should shift to systems, and that systems are made up of some exceptionally mobile elements as well as immobile elements. Each system, as I see it, is characterized by a specific configuration of the mobile and immobile. Indeed, it is precisely because of such immobilities that systems possess complex characteristics. If all relationships were completely mobile or, indeed, completely immobile then there would be no complexity. These systems are not simply or necessarily to do with societal capacity, although there are clearly elements of societal systems involved here. Societal capacity has become effected by, and drawn into, those relationships or systems of global complexity. And furthermore, systems of global complexity involve always a combination of the physical and the social – they are hybridized, brought together, and they involve a rejection of the characteristic distinction between the social and the physical, or the social and nature. The social world is therefore a set of complex living systems which are neither natural nor social but hybridized, also demonstrating emergent characteristics and properties.

NG So, in using complexity theory you seek to theorize the social world in terms of complex living systems, and with this you attempt to transcend 'outdated divisions between nature *and* society, between the physical sciences and the social sciences' (Urry, 2002: 18; original emphasis). But what is achieved by dissolving the distinction between 'the physical' and 'the social'?

JU I am making three separate points here. First, the very distinction upon which the academy is founded is historically rooted in the nineteenth-century hubris that the social world is separate from, and superior to, the physical world, and that there should be developed sciences of that social world. Second, dissolving the distinction between the two is to promote analyses of those complex hybrid systems – such as the Internet, automobility, information, global flows of waste products, international terrorism – that seem to populate the current world. Third, these hybrids balance on the edge of order *and* chaos, they are not anarchic, not without ordering, but at the same time they are not ordered and moving towards equilibrium.

NG A key idea you draw on from complexity theory is that of 'iteration'. You say: 'It is iteration that means that the tiniest of "local" changes can generate, over billions of repeated actions, unexpected, unpredictable and chaotic outcomes, sometimes the opposite of what agents thought they were trying to bring about' (Urry, 2002: 47). Beyond this, you outline three core ideas of complex change: first, that 'there is no necessary proportionality between "causes" and "effects" of events or phenomena'; second, that 'there is no necessary equivalence between the individual and statistical levels of analysis; and third, that 'the statistical or system effects are not the result of adding together the individual components. There is something else involved, normally known as emergence' (Urry, 2002: 24). Such ideas stand in opposition to the structure-agency formulations that underpin most existing theories of social change. Given this, how do you suggest sociologists study such complex, non-linear forms of change or what might be called 'emergent properties', especially given the chaotic and unexpected nature of iteration?

JU One thing to do would be to see these relationships as occurring over time, often over long stretches of time, and obviously having consequences over substantial distances, but where the effects may arise unexpectedly or unpredictably in diverse locations. One would not necessarily expect to be able to comprehend these processes through typical methods of research. They certainly involve longitudinal study, but they require longitudinal study that does not presume that there are fixed entities with variable attributes. The entities are various components of the processes themselves, and they will be transformed over time through these long-term iterative processes, rather as Andrew Abbott describes. To some degree what is involved here are systems that partly remake themselves through relatively small sets of events occurring in a particular order and with long-term consequences. One of the areas I have been particularly interested in thinking about is the car, and the pattern of path dependency which was laid down in the 1890s. For a pretty contingent set of reasons which happened to occur in a particular order, the petroleum car became the dominant system, although probably at the time it was less efficient than steam or electric powered cars. There were certain contingent effects, certain unpredictabilities early on, and it is a question of tracing iterations that had the effect of stabilizing the car system as relatively unchanging while everything else around, its 'environment', was rapidly changing. This is interesting because it produces a long-term stability where the car system has gone on, expanded and proliferated itself across the globe – it is the most significant example of a globalizing industry and a global set of social practices – even though its causes were small-scale (such as the 1896 race held in which only two vehicles finished, one of which was a petrol powered car). Temporality is very much involved here, and implicit in this is a rejection of the so-called structure and agency formulation. The emphasis is instead on systems. These systems can have non-linear properties, consequences and emergent effects. Emergent effects may emerge through extremely tiny changes that get magnified through iterative processes, and these tiny changes can be absolutely infinitesimal – it looks like the same attitude, or the same car or system, or the same political process – but the minutest of changes can produce significant emergent properties.

NG   Within this theory of complexity there still seems to be a place for an idea of structure or system. 'Systems', you say, 'are . . . seen by complexity as being "on the edge of chaos" '. Beyond this: 'Order and chaos are in a kind of balance where the components are neither fully locked into place but yet do not fully dissolve into anarchy. Chaos is not complete anarchic randomness but there is a kind of "orderly disorder" present within all such dynamic systems' (Urry, 2002: 22). Is capitalism one such system?

JU   There are some stable systems which get set up for contingent reasons but then have profound irreversible consequences, and as I said I am particularly interested in the character of the car system. But such systems have a curious balance of order and chaos. They are not well ordered, and neither do they simply reproduce themselves, nor are they anarchic. I take the way that Ilya Prigogine captures, describes and characterizes these systems, which are almost balanced on a knife-edge, almost ordered and yet about to move off into a state of chaos. This is my general view of the character of the social systems that populate the contemporary world: there is an orderly disorder present within dynamic systems. And I would see a variety of such systems. There is not a single capitalist system but there is an array of systems governed by capitalist principles, and in some ways Marx was an early systems theorist. He brilliantly brings out how capitalist relations both produce massive increases in pro-ductivity, growth, income and so on, and also a tendency for the rate of profit to fall, with increased contradictions, and so on. So it is an ordered system on the edge of chaos, and Prigogine's notion of orderly disorder in many ways perfectly captures the way that Marx was seeking to characterize capitalist relations. There is not a single capitalist system but a whole array of systems characterized by capitalist processes, and each of these can be seen through this dynamic systems thinking, just as some people have also begun to talk about the development of various kinds of social movements – the way that resistance systems get set up is also characterized by similar processes of self-making, but in which the system is also on the edge of chaos.

NG   Further to this, you propose that while the global is to some extent 'self-making', the global system 'as a whole should not be seen as autopoeitic' (Urry, 2002: 101). How do these two arguments fit together?

JU   I would quote Prigogine again here when he describes the non-linear dynamic world as consisting of islands of order floating within an increasing sea of disorder. The islands of order make the larger sea more disordered: there are many hybrid systems self-making themselves across the world, as putatively global, but overall there is no global system that is self-making and autopoeitic.

NG   You also talk of 'cosmopolitan global fluids' (Urry, 2002: 133). What are these? And how can you use complexity theory to explain the emergence of 'global standards by which other places, cultures and people are positioned and can be judged'.

JU   In *Global Complexity* I discuss a wide array of globally integrated networks and global fluids that are making themselves across the world as just described. One such global fluid is what I call 'cosmopolitanism', which seems to be an increasingly powerful self-making entity that is spreading, albeit hesitantly and uncertainly, certain global standards. Its increasing scale and complex impact will irreversibly transform each civil society, altering the conditions under which social actors assemble, organize, and mobilize. And as they assemble, organize and mobilize differently, so new, unpredictable and emergent cosmopolitan identities, practices and cognitive praxes will emerge. But this is not to say, of course, that the world is 'cosmopolitan', more that this is an emergent pool of order, competing with and intersecting with a wide array of other global fluids.

NG   In the concluding pages of *Global Complexity* you attempt to connect ideas of global complexity and cosmopolitanism to a theory of reflexive modernity. Indeed, you say that 'The form now taken by reflexive modernization is the global fluid of cosmopolitanism' (Urry, 2002: 139). Why is this?

JU   I suggest that processes of reflexive modernization are to be seen as stemming from this emergent global fluid of the cosmopolitan. Cosmopolitanism provides dispositions of an appropriate cultural reflexivity within emergent global complexities. Such a cosmopolitan fluid involves redrawing the speed of the global *and* the slowness of the ontologically grounded. It transforms the conditions under which other networks and fluids operate as well as what have been understood historically as 'societies'. And accompanying this, there is a corresponding shift from national society to the increasing power of a cosmopolitan global fluid, or from modernity to reflexive modernization as others have expressed it.

NG   Finally, you once described sociology as a parasitic subject that had no fundamental unity or essence of its own (Urry, 1995: 33). Perhaps surprisingly, you saw this as a positive trait, not least because it promoted a discipline marked by 'openness and a relative lack of authority and control' (Urry, 1995: 34). In *Sociology Beyond Societies* you come back to this point to say that this placed sociology in a strong position: because of its openness it could develop a new global agenda and with this overcome the loss of its key concept, 'society'.

Are you still so optimistic? And, given that complexity theory posits 'the connectedness of science with its system of investigation' (Urry, 2002: 37), how do you see your own work as changing the system it is analysing?

JU   Following on from what I have said above, I will answer this question in a roundabout way. Cosmopolitanism will, in part, reconfigure how the social sciences develop in a post-societal era of global complexity. It will lead to the spread of theories of global complexity as one of the means of capturing, representing and performing the new world ordering that remains balanced 'on the edge of chaos'. Complexity theories seem irreducibly part of the emergent systems *of* global complexity. Thus, one is going with the flow, so to speak, if one develops the implications of the complexity sciences for the multitude of global systems that are currently haunting the world's population.

Can sociology go with this flow? I am not sure but I do think this is the way to pose the issue of sociology's future. It also is not a question of what the interconnections are that I might have with the system, so much as the degree to which systems are emerging that may produce concepts, theories and methods that are constituents of one or more such systems, rather than being constituents of previous 'societal' systems. So, the question is not so much to be a parasite, although this is a necessary feature of a successful 'undisciplined discipline'; it is rather to be able to be part of the processes of self-making of one or more of these global fluids, and especially of what I have termed 'the cosmopolitan global fluid'. *Sociology Beyond Societies* and *Global Complexity* are tiny droplets placed in the rivers of debate that may help to shift sociology's system into a complex future.

REFERENCES

Barber, B. (1996) *Jihad vs McWorld: How Globalism and Tribalism Are Reshaping the World*. New York: Ballantine.

Lash, S. and Urry, J. (1994) *Economies of Signs and Space*. London: Sage.

Urry, J. (1995) *Consuming Places*. London: Routledge.

Urry, J. (2000) *Sociology Beyond Societies: Mobilities for the Twenty-First Century*. London: Routledge.

Urry, J. (2002) *Global Complexity*. Cambridge: Polity.

CHAPTER 7

Saskia Sassen: Space and Power

NG   Since the early 1990s you have approached the question of globalization from a number of different angles, and analysed, among other things, inequalities in the world economy (Sassen, 2000), the transnational mobility of people and money (Sassen, 1998), immigration trends and policies (Sassen, 1999) and global changes in state power and political sovereignty (Sassen, 1996). This body of work seems to be unified by a basic underlying position, namely that the study of globalization is to take urban geography seriously, and with this place the city (or city networks) at the centre of its analysis. But why approach the question of globalization in this way? What may be gained by focusing on the nature and geography of urban space, and what is sociological about such an approach?

SS   You are right in emphasizing the fact that I have tried to study globalization through various specific, often localized processes rather than through an encompassing overview of global processes. You are also right in seeing that the city is a key space where I keep returning in my research. But I would neither say that I put the city at the centre of globalization, nor that it should be at the centre of its study. Each historic phase brings with it strategic articulators of dynamics, processes, and institutional orders. The city is today one of these, along with others. The city was also a crucial articulator in earlier phases, notably the city-states of the Renaissance and the world cities studied by Braudel.

More generally, we know that there have long been cross-border economic processes – flows of capital, labour, goods, raw materials and travellers. And over the centuries there have been enormous fluctuations in the degree of openness or closure of the organizational forms within which these flows have taken place. In the last hundred years, the inter-state system came to provide the dominant organizational form for cross-border flows, with national states as its key actors. It is this condition that has changed dramatically since the early 1990s as a result of privatization, deregulation, the opening up of national economies to foreign firms, and the growing participation of national economic actors in global markets.

In this context we see a re-scaling of the strategic territories that articulate the new system. With the partial unbundling or at least weakening of the national as a spatial unit come conditions for the ascendance of other spatial units and scales. Among these are the sub-national, notably cities and regions; cross-border regions encompassing two or more sub-national entities; and supra-national entities, i.e. global digitized markets and free-trade blocs. The dynamics and processes that get territorialized or are sited at these diverse scales can in principle be regional, national and global. There is a proliferation of specialized global circuits for economic activities that both contribute to and constitute these new scales and are enhanced by their emergence.

The organizational architecture for cross-border flows that emerges from these re-scalings and articulations increasingly diverges from that of the inter-state system. The key articulators now include not only national states, but also firms and markets whose global operations are facilitated by new policies and cross-border standards produced by willing or not-so-willing states. Among the empirical referents for these non-state forms of articulation are the growing number of cross-border mergers and acquisitions, the expanding networks of foreign affiliates, and the growing numbers of financial centres that are becoming incorporated into global financial markets. As a result of these and other processes, a growing number of cities today play an increasingly important role in directly linking their national economies with global circuits. As cross-border transactions of all kinds grow, so do the networks binding particular configurations of cities. Today we have about 40 global cities, with five major ones at the top (New York, London, Tokyo, Paris and Frankfurt) and then several levels of such cities. This, in turn, contributes to the formation of new geographies of centrality that connect cities in a growing variety of cross-border networks. It is against this larger picture that I see cities as strategic sites today.

NG By focusing on city structures and networks it would seem that you bypass approaches that simply oppose 'the national' to 'the global'. For example, you talk of cities not only as spaces where the global and the local might meet, but also as places which, in certain circumstances, become disconnected from both regions and nation-states (Sassen, 1998: xxvi). You term such places 'global cities'. But what is meant by the term 'global' here? Is globalization to be seen as a movement towards the concentration of economic powers or services in key cities (e.g. London, New York, Tokyo) or as a process of spatial expansion of particular economic and political forms across the globe, or both? Put simply, does globalization involve processes of centralization *and* dispersal?

SS   Indeed, a focus on cities does force me to see that the global is not simply that which operates outside the national, and, in that sense, to see also that the national and the global are not mutually exclusive domains. The global city is a thick environment that endogenizes the global and filters it through 'national' institutional orders and imaginaries. It also helps render visible global internal (national) components of the economy and, especially, the imaginaries of various groups. Studying globalization in this manner means you can engage in thick descriptions and do empirical research in specific sites rather than having to position yourself as a global observer. Now that I have been at it for a while I can see that no matter what feature I am studying, over the last 15 years or more I have gravitated towards these thick environments. It feels like a hundred years of digging.

As for the second element in your question – what I mean by the global and by globalization in using this type of approach – it touches on a distinction that is dear to me and has gotten me into lots of trouble, especially when I started this work.

Let me start by asking the question: what is it we are trying to name with the term 'globalization'? In my reading of the evidence it is actually two distinct sets of dynamics. One of these involves the formation of explicitly global institutions and processes, such as the World Trade Organization, global financial markets, the new cosmopolitanism, the War Crimes Tribunals. The practices and organizational forms through which these dynamics operate are constitutive of what is typically thought of as global scales. They are formally global institutions, some more institutionalized (the WTO, the War Crimes Tribunals) than others (the new cosmopolitanism), but still recognized as global no matter how particular and national the focus of their work.

The second set of processes I think are part of globalization do not necessarily scale at the global level as such, yet, I argue, are part of globalization. These processes take place deep inside territories and institutional domains that have largely been constructed in national terms over the last several hundred years in much, though by no means all, of the world. What makes these processes part of globalization even though localized in national, indeed sub-national settings, is that they involve transboundary networks and formations connecting or articulating multiple local or 'national' processes and actors. Among these processes I include cross-border networks of activists engaged in specific localized struggles with an explicit or implicit global agenda, as is the case with many human rights and environmental organizations; particular aspects of the work of states, e.g. certain monetary and fiscal policies critical to the constitution of global markets that are hence being implemented in a growing number of countries; the use of international human rights instruments in *national* courts; non-cosmopolitan forms of global politics and imaginaries that remain deeply attached or focused on localized issues and struggles, yet are part of global lateral networks containing multiple other such localized efforts. A particular challenge in the work of identifying these types of processes and actors as part of globalization is the need to decode at least some of what continues to be experienced and represented as national.

In my work I have particularly wanted to focus on these types of practices and dynamics and have insisted in conceptualizing them as also constitutive of globalization even though we do not usually recognize them as such. When the social sciences focus on globalization – still rare enough deep in the academy – it is typically not on these types of practices and dynamics but rather on the self-evidently global scale. And although the social sciences have made important contributions to the study of this self-evident global scale by establishing the fact of multiple globalizations, only some of which correspond to neo-liberal corporate economic globalization, there is much work left to do. At least some of this work entails distinguishing (a) the various scales that global processes constitute, ranging from supra-national and global to sub-national, and (b) the specific contents and institutional locations of this multi-scalar globalization. Geography, more than any other of the social sciences today, has contributed to a critical stance towards scale, recognizing the historicity of scales and resisting the reification of the national scale so present in most of social science (see Sassen, 2003).

All of this indicates that what I mean by the global is not only an extension of certain forms to the globe, but also a repositioning of what we have historically constructed and experienced as the local and the national. Further, this repositioning happens in many different and specific ways and in a growing number of domains – economic, political, cultural and ideational.

And now to the final issue you raise in your question: the contradictory notion (very present in my work indeed) that globalization involves both centralization and dispersal. This dynamic gets at the heart of how I have conceptualized the rise of global cities. One of the key hypotheses in my global city model is that the more far-flung and dispersed the network of a firm's offices, factories and service outlets, the more central management functions become complex and weighty. When the sector is globalized and involved in uncertain and speculative markets, the pressures and complexity of these functions are such that firms need to buy some of these functions from specialized service firms. The latter need to operate in thick, varied environments that also are nodes where multiple global information loops intersect producing added value in the form of knowledge, better understanding and insights. Global cities are such environments. The key dynamic is that the more global a firm's operations, the more its central functions are subject to agglomeration economies. And the key condition is that the firm is an integrated corporation that seeks to maintain control and centralize profit appropriation – rather than distribute control and profits in parallel to its service and production functions.

NG   In the preface to the second edition of *The Global City* (Sassen, 2001) you talk of a new 'conceptual architecture' for the study of globalization. Does this mean that a new sociological methodology is needed for the study of global forms? If so, what might this look like?

SS   Yes, it does mean for me that we need new conceptual architectures. But it does not mean that we have to throw all existing research techniques and data sets out the window. I use this term 'conceptual architecture' with care: an organizing logic that can accommodate multiple diverse components operating at different scales (e.g. data about various localized dynamics and self-evidently global ones) without losing analytic closure (maintaining at least a modicum of such closure). Studying the global, then, entails not only a focus on that which is explicitly global in scale, but also a focus on locally scaled practices and conditions that are articulated with global dynamics, and a focus on the multiplication of cross-border connections among various localities. Further, it entails recognizing that many of the globally scaled dynamics, such as the global capital market, actually are partly embedded in sub-national sites and move between these differently scaled practices and organizational forms. For instance, the global capital market is constituted both through electronic markets with global span, and through locally embedded conditions, i.e. financial centres.

A focus on such sub-nationally based processes and dynamics of globalization requires methodologies and theorizations that engage not only global scalings but also sub-national scalings as components of *global* processes, thereby destabilizing older hierarchies of scale and conceptions of nested scalings. Studying global processes and conditions that get constituted subnationally has some advantages over studies of globally scaled dynamics; but it also poses specific challenges. It does make possible the use of long-standing research techniques, from quantitative to qualitative, in the study of globalization. It also gives us a bridge for using the wealth of national and sub-national data sets as well as specialized types of scholarship, such as area studies. Both types of studies, however, need to be situated in conceptual architectures that are not quite those held by the researchers who generated these research techniques and data sets, as their efforts mostly had little to do with globalization.

One central task we face is to decode particular aspects of what is still represented or experienced as 'national', which may in fact have shifted away from what had historically been considered or constituted as national. This is in many ways a research and theorization logic that is present in global city studies. But there is a difference: today we have come around to recognize and code a variety of components in global cities as part of the global. There is a broader range of conditions and dynamics that are still coded and represented as local and national. They are to be distinguished from those now recognized global city components. In my current research project, I focus on how this all works out in the realm of the political.

NG A large section of *The Global City* (Sassen, 2001: 197–325) addresses 'The Social Order of the Global City'. But what do you mean by the term 'social' here? Is there a connection between the social and society, or between societies and nation-states? Or does the emergence of global cities mark the birth of new transnational social forms?

SS Let me answer your question about the specific issue of social forms in combination with the question you ask about the social order of the global city. You ask if my work signals the need for a new sociological methodology for the analysis of social forms, and whether the global city marks the emergence of new, transnational social forms. My answer is yes and no.

First, on the methodology. Yes, in the sense in which I spoke earlier about the need for new conceptual architectures to study some of this, including social forms. No, in the sense that not everything – research techniques and data sets – is new. Rather, the design of these new conceptual framings allows us to use techniques and data sets produced with different questions in mind. And not just in sociology.

Secondly, on the emergence of new types of transnational social forms. Indeed, I think we are seeing this. The global city is a very specific type of site for these processes. It endogenizes global dynamics that transform existing social alignments. And it enables even the disadvantaged to develop transnational strategies and subjectivities. Often this enablement is at heart a *prise de conscience*. What I mean here is that it is not always a new social form as such but rather a subjective, self-reflexive repositioning of an old social practice or condition in a transnational framing. Transnational immigrant households, and even communities, are perhaps emblematic of this.

There are, however, also new social forms. The most familiar instance is the new transnational elites in various professions, from accountants to art curators – the accountants evidently being as creative as the curators. There are also new social forms that may look like they have nothing to do with globalization, but are in fact deeply articulated with it, even though intermediated through a variety of local dynamics, such as the housing market. These are not trans-national *per se*, but they are globalization-linked new social forms. For instance, I interpret the vast growth of homelessness and its transformed composition in global cities as representing a new social form. We have long had homelessness, but it can get constituted through different social forms. Today, in major global cities it is deeply linked with the need for global actors to develop urban space in ways and in quantities that have produced a vast displacement of low-income residents. Thus, in terms of the social composition of homelessness we see more families, more women and children. This is clearly so in London and New York. In Tokyo, the numbers are far smaller and it is largely elderly men and women. Here is where the global city is a powerful lens through which to examine globalization in its concrete, on-the-ground operation, deep inside what is still the national realm.

In my current research on political aspects, I am trying to get at these on-the-ground operations, still deeply coded in national terms, and in that sense hermetic to the standard approaches for the study of globalization. On a more theorized level, this work also includes a specification of the formation of new social forces that come together and get actualized in global cities. Thus, these cities are the spaces where global corporate capital hits the ground and becomes embedded in processes of social reproduction, including that of its managers and professionals. In this regard, the global city is the site where global capital begins to constitute itself as a social force, one in contest with the other emergent social forces in global cities – the new types of urban workforces constituted largely through minoritized workers – whether natives or immigrants.

NG   You also use the term 'social geography' (Sassen, 2001: 256–84). What is meant by this term?

SS   Yes, I somehow find concepts such as geography and architecture enor-mously useful. I think it has to do with the fact that a term such as 'social structure', which is the one I would be expected to use as a sociologist, has become a sort of designator rather than a heuristic tool. Perhaps I am trying to get at something akin to Beck's memorable *zombie categories*. Geography and architecture are working categories for me in my work of interpreting empirical details and patterns.

So when I use social geography in the case of an examination of global cities, I am getting at at least two matters. One is the notion that there are multiple and distinct socio-spatial formations present in a city. A given built environ-ment can be inhabited by more than one of these. For instance, Wall Street at night is the locus for a social geography that is partly constituted in the immigrant community of Northern Manhattan, and very different from that of the high-income areas of the city and the suburbs where most of Wall Street's top professionals live. The second is that I use the notion of social geography to deconstruct and then resynthesize assemblages of micropractices and their spatial patterning. In brief, both of these uses allow me to work with a dynamic, spatially sensitive analytic grid for examining, what can I say, social structurations.

NG   It seems that this social geography is closely tied to the study of economic globalization, and more specifically to the mapping of inequalities existing within *and* between cities. Does your definition of global social forms result from the mapping of such inequalities? For example, you use the term 'class' in your work. Is class synonymous with 'the social' (as it is for most Marxist social theorists), and is it an overridingly economic category resulting from 'income polarization'? Or is class something different when studied at the level of the city? Is it possible to argue, like Zygmunt Bauman, that we are witnessing the emergence of new global class formations?

SS   This is not an easy question for me. When I use class in *The Global City* I am capturing at least two features of class. One is related to class dynamics: its instantiation in concrete, thick environments. In other words, class becomes activated under particular conditions; it is not simply an attribute. Further, it has multiple locations in which it becomes activated. The city is one of them, the factory is another, and, we now know, the ethnic or immigrant community is another. The global city is a very acute location today for activating class dynamics. In this type of conceptualization or use of class, I leave somewhat unexamined the issue of the genesis, or nature, of class and hence the whole debate between Marxist formulations and the more nuts-and-bolts, often empiricist, interpretations/definitions of US sociology especially.

Class for me is not simply an economic category. I would say in much US sociology it is a bit that way and it works as an attribute. I resist that. Hence I focus on class dynamics and their activation. Once you introduce a specific concrete focus, class activation is the moment when class ceases to be a hermetic category, though there is a lot of interpreting that goes on before you get there. But once you are there, class is a complex, thick social condition and event that includes economic, spatial, subjective and ideational elements. I do not know exactly – you are making me think here – where I would go from here if I were a class theorist. Would I wind up in a different place because my starting point is a thick environment where some of the most powerful dynamics of today's world hit the ground and encounter some of the most disadvantaged people from all over the world constituted as 'workers'? Interesting. I think that the way I deal with class leads me to focus or capture the formation of social forces in global cities. I am not certain whether class as we have used it would best capture the nature of these social forces as I described them briefly above.

NG Further to this, you place great emphasis on global cities as sites of 'post-industrial production' with their 'own infrastructure of activities, firms and jobs' (Sassen, 1998: xxiii; 2000: 84–5). How are these sites and these forms of production connected to the emergence of 'new class alignments' and to what you call the 'practice of global control'?

SS Yes, I emphasize – over and over, one might say in the hope of melting down any opposition here – that global cities are production sites. What they are uniquely positioned to produce is a capability: the capability for global control of the operations of global markets and firms. This is, then, a very different type of production site from that we usually think of, and it has a different meaning to the common understanding of post-industrial production. Secondly, this is a different way of conceptualizing high-level professional work and their outputs. The usual one is to emphasize the high levels of human capital involved and to emphasize the output, a highly specialized service. I want to emphasize the multiple material practices and human resources that need to be brought together in order to produce global control capability. This includes the sphere of social reproduction for both the top-level professional workers and the low-wage service workers. By new class alignments I am signalling that production of this crucial input for economic globalization (global control capability) articulates workers, professionals, owners of capital, control practices, the components of social reproduction, and the political subjectivities that get mobilized under these new conditions, into specific socio-spatial and political formations. In this sense, also, the city represents the moment in the complex process that is global capitalism, when the latter can be actualized as a social force rather than being the abstraction of an electronic market.

NG Aside from class inequalities, you also point to 'enormous' economic inequalities between men and women in global cities such as New York, London and Tokyo (see Sassen, 2001: 250). In your book *Globalization and Its Discontents* you take up this issue by outlining a 'feminist analytics of the global economy' (Sassen, 1998: 81–109). Your argument here addresses, first, the 'incipient unbundling of the exclusive territoriality of the nation-state' and second, changes in political sovereignty that may come with the emergence of international law. But why did you select these two issues as a way of opening up 'an analytic terrain' for feminist enquiry into globalization? And why did you choose to avoid analysis of global forms of patriarchy?

SS The reason for starting the analysis with the broader issues of how legitimate power is reconstituted at a time of economic globalization is that I did not want to start with the empirical or analytic categories through which the specific condition of women is usually examined. The empirical recording of inequalities between men and women is part of the story, but I argue that these inequalities have been around under all kinds of highly diverse socio-political and economic systems. I am interested in understanding the specific con-ditionalities of gendering today, and, even more narrowly, the specific condi-tionalities of gendering underlying the new global economic system dominated by finance. Finance is as far removed as you can get from the analytic categories of feminist scholarship. It is not enough to measure ongoing inequalities and oppressions if the purpose is to understand how the current phase constructs these, or at least some of these outcomes. One question, then, might indeed be: how do the current transformations destabilize older forms of patriarchy and to what extent do they contribute to their reduction or their re-invention? I also emphasize how the particular production issue crucial to global cities – global control capability – positions women in very specific ways in these globalized sectors, both at the top and at the bottom of the system.

NG In taking this position in *Globalization and Its Discontents* you seem to place great faith in the democratizing forces of international law. You say, for example, that 'Once the sovereign state is no longer viewed as the exclusive representative of its population in the international arena, women and other nonstate actors can gain more representation in international law; contribute to the making of international law; and give new meaning to older forms of international participation, such as women's long-standing work in interna-tional peace efforts' (Sassen, 1998: 94). Is the nation-state, then, to be viewed as the main cause of the problem here? If so, why do there continue to be such 'enormous' inequalities between men and women even in global cities that have disconnected themselves from national-state boundaries? And what evidence is there that international law will work to counter *de facto* economic inequalities between men and women?

SS When I emphasize developments in international law or in the new constitutions that allow individuals of particular groups, such as indigenous peoples, to go directly to international forums for claim-making and bypass national states, I am not necessarily positing that this is the solution to inequality. Not at all. There are two matters I am trying to get at. The more general argument is that globalization destabilizes existing formalized hierarchies of power, of legitimacy and for claim-making. In so doing it produces openings, both rhetorical and practical, for new types of actors and claims. These include a variety of actors and claims: from multinationals and their enormous claims on national states and on global cities, to the new politics of claim-making by disadvantaged people especially in cities. Even at its best, e.g. the Keynesian state, by formalizing inclusions/entitlements formalizes exclusions. When national states privatize and deregulate they not only reduce entitlements for the included, they also create possibilities for the excluded to emerge as political actors in their own right.

The second matter is what instruments can serve struggles for equality (this holds for all kinds of groups, notably indigenous peoples who are using international forums for claim-making). Law by itself is not enough, but it is one of the instrumentalities. Past experience suggests that it will take struggle and mobilization to make law work for the pursuit of equality and enablement.

As for the question about global cities then having to reflect this effect and being places of lessened inequality ... it does not quite work that way. The logic is a different one; it points to political possibilities rather than reduced inequality. Global cities are sites where the new trends towards inequality materialize in highly concentrated doses, and in that sense these cities are almost a natural experiment situation. One component of these trends towards inequality is the large low-wage workforce, which has had few if any entitlements in the past, and is highly internationalized and feminized. Today it has acquired a new type of visibility and what I call 'presence' – presence to power and to itself. I interpret this as the beginning of a micropolitics, of new types of political subjectivities, and as the beginning of the formation of a social force that finds itself in contestation with global capital as it hits the ground in these cities.

NG   You also say that with the emergence of global cities comes the possibility of transnational politics (Sassen, 1998: xx). What might this politics look like? You talk of a politics 'going beyond the politics of culture though at least partly likely to be embedded in it'. What do you mean by this?

SS   Continuing with the preceding answer, these new types of micropolitics and subjectivities can be transnational. The large numbers of people from all over the world who often encounter each other for the first time in the streets, workplaces and neighbourhoods of today's global cities, including encounters with co-ethnics who are in highly professional jobs (i.e. a class encounter) produce a kind of transnationalism right there in situ, in one city. The city endogenizes the transnational in the microstructures of daily life. We see an emergent recognition of globality, often in the form of recognizing the recurrent struggles and inequities in city after city, a recognition enabled by global media and by the visibility of the global in these cities.

Some of this goes beyond the politics of culture we have seen since the early 1980s which has been much less embedded in these questions of globalization and globality. Some of it takes the politics of culture to the global scale. The latter case is illustrated by some of the issues concerning gay, lesbian and queer struggles and claim-making. As someone concerned with how actual practices can shape and reshape, destabilize and strengthen formal institutions, I find that the city, especially today's large cities, are strategic spaces where some of these dynamics are made legible, and perhaps also produced. In this regard, urban space becomes productive of these forms of subjectivity among the disadvantaged and enables them to emerge as a social force. Global cities around the world are the terrain where a multiplicity of globalization processes assume concrete, localized forms. These localized forms are, in good part, what globalization is about. Thus, they are also sites where some of the new forms of power can be engaged.

What is being engendered today in terms of political practices and political subjectivity in the global city is quite different from what it might have been in the medieval city of Weber. In the medieval city we see a set of practices that allowed the burghers to set up systems for owning and protecting property and to implement various immunities against despots of all sorts. Today's citizenship practices have to do with the production of 'presence' by those without power, and a politics that claims rights to the city. What the two situations share is the notion that through these practices new forms of citizenship are being constituted and that the city is a key site for this type of political work, and is, indeed, partly constituted through these dynamics (see Sassen, 2002). After the long historical phase that saw the ascendance of the national state and the scaling of key economic dynamics at the national level, the city is once again today a scale for strategic economic and political dynamics.

NG   A further proposition outlined in *Globalization and Its Discontents* is that global cities might become 'strategic sites for disempowered actors' (Sassen, 1998: xxi). How might this be the case?

SS   It is precisely the coexistence of the sharp concentrations of the powerful and the powerless that gives the global city also a strategic political character. If we consider that large cities concentrate both the leading sectors of global capital and a growing share of disadvantaged populations – immigrants, many of the disadvantaged women, people of colour generally, and, in the megacities of developing countries, masses of shanty-dwellers – then we can see that cities have become a strategic terrain for a whole series of conflicts and contradictions. We can then think of cities also as one of the sites for the contradictions of the globalization of capital. This brings us back to some of the earlier historical formations around questions of citizenship and struggles for entitlements, and the prominent roles played by cities and civil society. The large city of today emerges as a strategic site for these new types of operations. It is one of the nexuses where the formation of new claims materializes and assumes concrete forms. The loss of power at the national level produces the possibility for new forms of power and politics at the sub-national level. The national as container of social processes and power is cracked. This cracked casing opens up possibilities for a geography of politics that links sub-national spaces. Cities are foremost in this new geography. One question this engenders is how and whether we are seeing the formation of new types of politics that localize in these cities.

NG   How does this vision of politics connect to your work on migration and immigration? In *Guests and Aliens* you discuss the '*de facto* transnationalization of immigration policy making' (1999: 156). The purpose *de jure* of such policy, however, is surely to reinforce the borders of particular nation-states. Indeed, it is interesting that all the data cited in the appendix to your book details the flow of people between different nations. Given this, how does your work on immigration connect to your writings on global cities? For surely global cities are still in some way located within the legal jurisdiction of a nation or a region?

SS   We might start by noting that immigration is one of the localizations of the global. It is a major process through which a new transnational political economy and translocal household strategies are being constituted. It is one largely embedded in major cities insofar as most immigrants, certainly in the developed world, whether in the US, Japan or Western Europe, are concentrated in major cities. It is, in my reading, one of the constitutive processes of globalization today, even though not recognized or represented as such in mainstream accounts of the global economy.

As for the last question you ask here, the relation between my work on global cities and my work on immigration, there are at least two connections. Global cities tend to be crucial destinations for immigrants, even though not always the final destination. Second, global cities are very special types of politico-cultural environments. What we might bring in here, to frame the question of immigrants in the global city, is the significance of the city today as a setting for engendering new types of often informal political practices, and new types of incompletely formalized political subjects. Immigrants, including unauthorized ones, can participate and often are involved in these practices and emerge as such informal subjects. The global city is a partly denationalized space both for global capital and for a broad mix of groups that are either immigrants or minoritized citizens.

NG   Perhaps what is at stake here is the question of state sovereignty. In your book *Losing Control?* (Sassen, 1996) you talk of the emergence of a 'new geography of power'. What exactly is this 'new geography'? And how does 'power' itself change in nature with the emergence of new forms of global politics?

SS   We are seeing a repositioning of the state in a broader field of power and a reconfiguring of the work of states. This broader field of power is partly constituted through the formation of a new private institutional order linked to the global economy, but also through the growing importance of a variety of other institutional orders, from the new roles of the international network of NGOs to the international human rights regime.

I have been working on these issues for the last few years, and it is my new project since the global city work. My argument is not that we are seeing the end of states but, rather, that states are not the only or the most important strategic agents in the new emergent global institutional order. Secondly, states, including dominant states, have undergone profound transformations in the sense that they have begun to function as the institutional home for the operation of powerful dynamics of denationalization of what were once national agendas. This raises a question about what is national in several of the key institutional components of states (central banks, ministries of finance, specialized regulatory agencies) linked to the implementation and regulation of economic globalization. We can also raise this question in regard to the growing introduction of international human rights instruments in national legal and judiciary work.

The changed condition of the state is often explained in terms of a decrease in regulatory capacities resulting from some of the basic policies associated with economic globalization: deregulation of a broad range of markets, economic sectors and national borders, and privatization of public sector firms. But in my reading of the evidence, this new geography of power confronting states entails a far more differentiated process than notions of an overall decline in the significance of the state suggest. And it entails a more transformative process of the state than the notion of a simple loss of power suggests.

Let me elaborate on this by focusing on economic globalization. One of the marking features of this new (mostly but not exclusively) private institutional order in formation is its capacity to privatize what was heretofore public, and to denationalize what were once national authorities and policy agendas. This capacity to privatize and denationalize entails specific transformations of the national state, more precisely of some of its components. Of particular concern in this regard is that this new institutional order also has normative authority – a new normativity that is not embedded in what has been and to some extent remains the master normativity of modern times, *raison d'état*. Rather, this new normativity comes from the world of private power yet installs itself in the public realm, and in so doing contributes to denationalize what had historically been constructed as national-state agendas.

The structural foundations for my argument lie in the current forms of economic globalization. Economic globalization, in my conception, does not only have to do with the crossing of geographical borders captured in measures of international investment and trade. It also has to do with the relocation of national public governance functions to transnational private arenas and with the development inside national states – through legislative acts, court rulings, executive orders – of the mechanisms necessary to accommodate new types of rights/entitlements for global capital in what are still national territories in principle under the exclusive authority of their states. The accommodation of the interests of foreign firms and investors under these conditions entails a negotiation. The mode of this negotiation in the current phase has tended in a direction that I describe as a denationalizing of several highly specialized national institutional orders. Geared towards governing key aspects of the global economy, both the particular transformations inside the state and the new emergent privatized institutional order are partial and incipient but strategic. Both have the capacity to alter crucial conditions for liberal democracy and for the organizational architecture for international law, its scope and its exclusivity. In this sense, both have the capacity to alter the scope of state authority and the inter-state system, the crucial institutional domains through which the 'rule of law' is implemented.

NG   You have also written about 'electronic space and power' (Sassen, 1998: 177–94). You say that we are witnessing the 'spatialization of inequality' in both the 'geography of the communications infrastructure' and in 'the emergent geographies in electronic space itself' (1998: 182). Does this mean that electronic space to some extent mirrors the political terrain of physical space? And is digital power simply a mirror image of other non-digital forms?

SS   Yes, digital space is partly inscribed by the larger power dynamics and cultural forms of the institutional orders or larger societies within which it is embedded. But digital power is not simply a mirror image of that world.

Let me elaborate on this. These new types of networks and technologies are deeply imbricated with other dynamics; in some cases the new ITs are merely derivative – a mere instrumentality of these dynamics – and in other cases they are constitutive. Yet, even when partial, digitization is contributing to the re-scaling of a variety of processes with resulting implications for, among others, territorial boundaries, national regulatory frames and, more generally, the place of inter-state relations in the expanding world of cross-border relations.

The widespread practice of confining interpretation to a technological reading of the technical capabilities of the new technologies is very problematic. Such an interpretation neutralizes or renders invisible the material conditions and practices, place-boundedness, and thick social environments within and through which these technologies operate. Another consequence of this type of reading is to assume that a new technology will *ipso facto* replace all older technologies that are less efficient, or slower, at executing the tasks the new technology is best at. We know that historically this is not the case. Such readings also lead, ironically, to a continuing reliance on analytic categoriza-tions that were developed under other spatial and historical conditions, that is, conditions preceding the current digital era. Thus, the tendency is to conceive of the digital as simply and exclusively digital and the non-digital (whether represented in terms of the physical/material or the actual, which are all problematic though common conceptions) as simply and exclusively that, non-digital. These either/or categorizations filter out alternative conceptualizations, thereby precluding a more complex reading of the intersection and/or inter-action of digitization with social, material and place-bound conditions.

We can illustrate this using one of the key effects of these technologies: the enhanced mobility of capital and the growing dematerialization of economic activities. Both mobility and dematerialization are usually seen as mere func-tions of the new technologies. This understanding erases the fact that it takes multiple material conditions, including infrastructural and legal, to achieve this outcome. Once we recognize that the hypermobility of the instrument, or the dematerialization of the actual piece of real estate, had to be *produced*, we introduce non-digital variables into our analysis of the digital. One of the implications for resource-poor states or organizations in an international sys-tem with enormous diversity in resources is that simply having access to these technologies does not necessarily alter their position in that system because it takes a wide array of other resources to maximize the economic benefits of these technologies.

Obversely, much of what happens in electronic space is deeply inflected by the cultures, the material practices, the legal systems and the imaginaries that take place outside electronic space. Much of what we think of when it comes to cyberspace would lack any meaning or referent if we were to exclude the world outside cyberspace. Thus, much of the digital composition of financial markets is inflected by the agendas that drive global finance which are not technological *per se.* Digital space and digitization are not exclusive conditions that stand outside the non-digital. Digital space is embedded in the larger societal, cultural, subjective, economic, imaginary structurations of lived experience and the systems within which we exist and operate.

NG   Finally, are new social forms emerging as life itself becomes increasingly digitalized, or does digitalization spell not only the end to all distinctions between public and private space, but to the very idea of 'the social'?

SS   For this type of analysis we need to go beyond the impacts of these technologies on society. Impacts are only one of several forms of intersection. In the social sciences most of the focus has been on impacts, with the new technologies functioning as the independent variable that variously alters the dependent variable (organization of work, social practices, whatever the social condition under study). But there are other forms of intersection, including the constitution of new domains (for instance, electronic financial markets, large-scale Internet-based conversations) and major transformations in old domains (e.g. computer-aided design or surgery).

Understanding the place of these new computer-centred network technologies and their capabilities from a social science perspective requires avoiding a purely technological interpretation, and recognizing (a) the embeddedness and (b) the variable outcomes of these technologies for different economic, political, and social orders. They can indeed be constitutive of new social dynamics, but they can also be derivative or merely reproduce older conditions. Further, some of their capabilities are distinct and exclusive to these technologies, and others simply amplify the effects of older technologies.

The issue is not to deny the weight of technology, but rather to develop analytic categories that allow us to examine the complex imbrications of technology and society. We want to go beyond the very common notion that understanding this interaction can be reduced to the question of impacts – more precisely, the impacts of these technologies on the specific domains constructed as objects of study in the various social sciences. These technologies have also shaped whole new socio-technical systems and practices. It also means examining the specific ways in which these technologies are embedded in often very specialized and distinct contexts. And it requires examining the mediating cultures that organize the relation between these technologies and the users or the objectives of their use. These mediating cultures can be highly diverse and specific; for example, when the objective is control and surveillance the practices and dispositions involved are likely to be different from those involved in using electronic markets or engaging in large-scale computer-based conversations.

We can start with the recognition that these new technologies and their associated information and communication dynamics are characterized by variability and specificity. That is, they are likely to be present in ways that are uneven and contradictory across sectors, unfolding in particular contexts, and hence difficult to generalize. The uneven and often contradictory character of these technologies and their associated information and communication structures also signal that these technologies should not be viewed simply as factor endowments. This type of view is present in much of the literature, often implicitly, and presents these technologies as a function of the specifics of a region or an actor – ranging from regions and actors fully endowed or with full access, to those without access. Rather, we can view these technologies also as a function of the operational logics of social forms such as networks and markets. Technologies relating, for instance, to the Internet, satellite surveillance, and data banks can be strongly associated with co-operative policies and practices (e.g. transborder access to IT infrastructures, data, and human capital or greater transparency), or they can be linked to conflict, such as applications of IT in the military, the identity politics of ethnic groups involved in violent conflicts, the contentious politics of activists, and the competition for economic supremacy among states.

REFERENCES

Sassen, S. (1996) *Losing Control? Sovereignty in an Age of Globalization*. New York: Columbia University Press.

Sassen, S. (1998) *Globalization and Its Discontents: Essays on the New Mobility of People and Money*. New York: New Press.

Sassen, S. (1999) *Guests and Aliens*. New York: New Press.

Sassen, S. (2000) *Cities in a World Economy* (2nd ed) (1st ed, 1994). Thousand Oaks, CA: Pine Forge.

Sassen, S. (2001) *The Global City: New York, London, Tokyo* (2nd ed) (1st ed, 1991). Princeton, NJ: Princeton University Press.

Sassen, S. (2002) 'The Repositioning of Citizenship', *Berkeley Journal of Sociology*, Vol. 46, pp. 4–25.

Sassen, S. (2003) 'Globalization or Denationalization?', *Review of International Political Economy*, Vol. 10, No. 1, pp. 1–22.

CHAPTER 8

Ulrich Beck: The Cosmopolitan Turn

NG   In your work *What is Globalization?* you say that globalization calls into question the 'methodological nationalism' of modern sociology, namely the presupposition that 'we live and act in the self-enclosed spaces of national states and their respective national societies' (Beck, 2000a: 20). How do you suggest we should proceed in the face of this challenge? How, for example, might we conceive of society or *the social* beyond the territorial limits of nation-states? Or, more simply, how do you suggest we break from what you call the 'territorial orthodoxy' of social theory?

UB   First, let us redefine the main argument. Methodological nationalism is about a situation where the social sciences – not only sociology but also political science, law, history, economics and so on – are to some extent still prisoners of the nation-state. It is about a situation where we do not talk about *the* society but about societies in the plural. In other words, there is a seemingly self-evident association of society with the nation-state, to the extent that society is defined by the nation-state. And this is not just a belief like racism or sexism, but a way in which social science is conducted, organizes itself and produces data. We cannot just get away from it by taking an Enlightenment approach to this nation-based position, because as sociologists we have got methodological nationalism in our flesh and bones. All our basic concepts are related to it. If you think about power, state, identities, politics, class, family and neighbourhood not only in theoretical terms but also in terms of empirical research, the focus is always the structures or dynamics of Britain, Germany, France, and so on. Nowadays there are about 198 or so nation-states, 198 societies and so 198 sociologies concentrating on national territories as defined units of society! Even comparative research still presupposes these national units. And this ontology of society and politics is produced in a frame of reference that also presupposes the distinction or opposition between the national and the international. Society is not only national society, for at the same time it is produced internationally, and a clear distinction is made between what is inside and what is outside, what is domestic politics and what is foreign politics, what is our society, our identity and then the identity of others. There is a strong relationship between this national-international opposition and universalism as well. For if you concentrate on a particular society and from this make an argument about society in general, you end up taking a particular space of experience and then universalizing it into the basic logic of society itself. Most of the classics do this, as does most sociological theory that universalizes: it picks up a historical experience, first of all a European experience or an experience of being at the centre of the world, and from this produces universal concepts about society in general.

This approach can and must be criticized. In the beginning it was very productive, as this was the way classical sociological theory worked, but now, how should we proceed? There are two directions you have to take. The first one is to find out that the spaces of experience are no longer exclusive. We are living in an age of flows – flows of capital, cultural flows, flows of information and risks, of which the terrorist risk is only the latest so far in the evolution of global risk society. In everyday life it is the same: more and more people are living in two or more national spaces. And this is the crucial point: for them there is more, not less – more and new spaces of experience, more languages, more traditions, uncertainties and clashes of culture in one's biography, leading, in turn, to the reworking, retelling and revision of identity and vision, both of the past and the future. There is a continuous negotiation between ascribed realities – roles, traditional backgrounds and their expectations – and now cognitive and imaginative possibilities. In order to understand these more fluid life-forms, these *transnational realities*, we have to overcome methodological nationalism. And to do this we have to start from below. We have to be specific, follow the transnationally networked actors and at the same time redefine the basic sociological categories in a cosmopolitan horizon – what Weber calls *Wertbeziehung* [value-relevance].

Weber was thinking in the national-universal 'value horizon' (the 'light', which gives meaning to an epoch). But at the beginning of the twenty-first century a 'cosmopolitan turn' comparable to the 'linguistic turn' in the 1970s is necessary. We have to change from a national to a cosmopolitan 'horizon', 'light', 'perspective', and have to realize that the European experience is twinned with, or underpinned by, lots of other experiences, as we have learned through postcolonial theory. There is not only the Atlantic or Western perspective but also many other perspectives that we must take into account. So, I would make a distinction between universalism and cosmopolitanism. Universalism, as I said before, takes an implication from a particular society or historical experience and extends it to a theory of *the* society. This is especially true for American sociology, which presupposes that the world outside is like the US – but poorer, less modern. But cosmopolitanism or globality is when this universal framework is criticized from different historical backgrounds and experiences. There are not only different paths to modernity – revolution, colonialism and imperialism – but also different modernities, both inside the Western world (for example, the Scandinavian model) and externally as well.

There is no longer a privileged position from which to conceptualize the field of society, and there is no longer a privileged Western position or even a privileged postcolonial perspective, but many different perspectives on modernity. We live in an age of *entangled modernities* that have different views of the history and the future of modernity at the same time. If you wanted a metaphor or parallel development to this, it would be something like the movement from a Newtonian point of view to an Einsteinian point of view. Methodological nationalism is to some extent a Newtonian point of view in the social sciences, while the perspective I am looking for is something more like Einstein's theory of the social and the political, which realizes that modernization disenchants and dissolves its own taken-for-granted foundations. The notion in, for example, Talcott Parsons' writings that each society is a closed and self-equilibrating system, dissolves. Einsteinian sociology is about a 'meta-change' – a change of the co-ordinates of change to exist at different speeds and to have different impacts. Thus – as far as I can see – there is never going to be one mathematical theory of post-national development, as many aspects of different perspectives have to be taken into account. This means that we have to redefine the basic concepts of the social sciences, and this is one direction in which we have to go.

The other direction is empirical research. When I talk about reflexive modernization, this term is used to signify a new empirical curiosity. Most of our concepts are misleading to some extent. Let me take 'household' as an example. Household, like class, family, consumption and so on, is one of those basic units that we need to produce data on. But what is a household in an age of flows and networks? This is a very simple question but one that is very difficult to answer. You find forms of living apart, living together, living apart together, my children, your children, our children, divorce and remarriage. The situation is very complicated, especially if you take transnational 'family networks' into account as well. There are even different definitions of who belongs to the family and who doesn't from different members of family networks. And to speak in a more systematic way, households are differentiated in geographical, social and economic terms and it is hard to bind all these dimensions together. One of the projects we are running in the Research Centre for Reflexive Modernization in Munich addresses this question of how to redefine households today. The French sociologist Kaufman (1999) gives us quite a nice idea of how to redefine households by looking at what a couple is. This redefinition cannot be done by looking at sexual relationships or by looking at marriage. His idea instead is that a couple can be defined by two people buying a single washing machine, because then everyday involvement gets started and something like a social definition of the situation in terms of identity begins, and so on. This is only one example. But in answer to your question I would say this: we have not only to, first of all, criticize methodological nationalism and its impact upon the social sciences in theory and research, but secondly to build a new frame of reference which redefines the basic concepts of the social sciences from transnational and cosmopolitan perspectives. This is to be done by empirical research in different areas in order to find out how reality beyond sociological categories is transforming itself. My idea is for real or concrete science, or what Weber called *Wirklichkeitswissenschaft*, to redefine mainstream sociology, which today is methodologically sophisticated but which nevertheless continues to work with zombie categories.

NG Part of your argument is that sociology should shift its focus to the analysis of new 'transnational social spaces'. But what are such spaces, and how do transnational social forms differ from those we have seen before?

UB Take, for example, the domain of media. Of course, here the national frame continues to prevail. But, at the same time, media industries and cultures have been changing dramatically by producing and reproducing all kinds of transnational connections, transformations and confrontations. The consequence is that cultural bonds and loyalties begin to transcend national boundaries and nation-state control: people using transnational channels live here as well as there. But how can we conceptualize Turkish- and German-speaking transmigrants living in Berlin while taking into account their transnational contexts and aspirations? The tendency is to put German Turks or Turkish Germans in one or the other national frame, rather than address specifically their 'as-well-as-ness' forms of life, consciousness, networks and aspirations, and the difference, challenges and richness of being positioned transnationally. Here, again, is the main point: even when we talk about 'diasporic cultures' we still argue and still are trapped in the national horizon or gaze, and presuppose the national imaginary or norm of given territorial and national either-or identities. This is why sociology is blind for the coming into being of a new reality in which everyday practices like cooking, eating, talking and even making love or watching TV involve exceptional levels of cosmopolitan interdependence.

Globalization happens not out there but *in here*. It transforms people and places from within. Thus, talking of a cosmopolitan sociology does not mean, for example, Wallerstein's world system theory or a global sociology that tries to picture the totality of the globe at once. It does not mean giving an enlarged vision of the national point of view. It does not mean either the John Meyer position, which similarly puts global cultural norms at the beginning of the argument and then tries to find out how they are distributed all over the world. This is a sophisticated research programme, but it takes a kind of unification as a main idea of development, and this is an approach to which I am opposed. Instead, a cosmopolitan perspective is needed. A cosmopolitan perspective is related to places as well. Just take a look at your own urban neighbourhood. Are there not more and more culturally mixed people living their lives locally and at the same time in, let's say, India, Russia, Turkey, etc.? This is what I mean: the macro-cosmos of cultural diversity – and conflict! – in the global society is existing in the micro-cosmos and in the countryside as well. A 'banal cosmopolitanism' is emerging that is comparable with the 'banal nationalism' characteristic of the first modernity (most evident in the waving of national flags). The metaphor for this banal cosmopolitanism is the supermarket. Here you have a global array of foodstuffs and cuisines routinely available in almost every town across the world. To be more systematic: the point of the cosmopolitan perspective is *not* to construct a false opposition between the national and the transnational. We need to reconceptualize the transnational as integral to the very redefinition of the national. It is changing the national or the local from within.

The cosmopolitan is a difficult concept, and it is symptomatic that we have to use old concepts and traditions that produce many misunderstandings in order to define the new situation. What makes cosmopolitanism so interesting from a social science perspective is that it is a pre-national and a post-national concept at the same time. This is because there are at least two traditions of cosmopolitanism in the European context. The first 'cosmopolitan moment' was in the ancient world, in Greek philosophy that redefined the relation between 'us' and 'them' in 'as well as' categories and not 'either-or' categories. Every human being is located by birth in two worlds, two communities: the 'cosmos' (that is world) and the 'polis' (i.e. the city-state). To be more precise, individuals are rooted in one cosmos but in different cities, territories, ethnicities, hierarchies – nations – religions at the same time. The second cosmopolitan moment is in the Enlightenment tradition of the eighteenth and nineteenth centuries, and emerged in the debate over how to relate, combine, synthesize or integrate national and cosmopolitan perspectives by giving priority to the latter. But, to cut a long story short, I will define the cosmopolitan through a simple metaphor: it means having roots and wings at the same time. It means not being a global player; it is not the perspective for those privileged to inhabit frequent traveller lounges. It is rooted, rather, in the sensitivities and solidarities that organize most people's sense of identity and location in the world; it is redefining the local in a translocal perspective. This means combining local, national and global perspectives in special conceptual frames of references. How can this work? 'Rooted cosmopolitanism' – having roots and wings – comes into being where universal ideas, philosophies and ethics spread among people at all levels of society. Universalistic values and obligations and particularistic local cultures mix to produce new forms of both. They produce new forms of localism that are open to the world.

This happens through the 'globalization of emotions'. Its political implications are huge. Let us take, for example, the demonstrations against the Iraq war that took place in February 2003. There are, of course, many explanations for these demonstrations, but one crucial element is that scores of war films and thousands of TV images of the suffering of the war's victims have formed this sensibility to the fate of others. Hollywood or newsmen may have manipulated the tears that have embarrassed us in our cinema seats and in our armchairs, but they have enlarged our emotional imagination and have cosmopolitanized it, and us, from within. We now have a cosmopolitan imagination, including the otherness of the other in our self-definition, in a way no previous generation has done. We imagine the families – just like our own ones – in a Baghdad suburb, whose lives are hanging in the balance. It is this imagination that includes the consequences of one's own national decision to others. This is the background for the outburst of democratic culture around the globe, and it has implications for what I call 'methodological cosmopolitanism'. One of its laws is that global phenomena can and must be studied locally. Globalization not only de-places but also re-places, and by superimposing place on place it creates a new kind of place.

The result is – or should be – a new sociology of place. Locality must be rediscovered, but not – and this is the next common misunderstanding – in its old form. The old structure of locality was to be encapsulated; its new form is to exist as a set of superimposed nodes of multiple global networks. In this way, you can organize cosmopolitan sociology on a local level, for example by comparing localities. To do this you would have to find out about what I call the 'inner cosmopolitanization' of places, cities and nations, or 'cosmopolitanization from within'. This means not just treating globalization as an additional point of view, i.e. that you have the national space and then an additional global relation to this. For even if you talk about 'interconnectedness', as David Held does so nicely, you still presuppose national units that are getting more and more interconnected. I think we have to go at least one step further and talk about how these national spaces are being cosmopolitanized from within. We have quite a few indicators that enable us to study this process. To take some of these: dual citizenship (the legal basis and practice in dealing with migrants etc.), development in the export and import of cultural commodities, who speaks how many languages, media research covering symbols of banal cosmopolitanism, and educational issues (representation of minorities in professional fields, public services, political parties). Also, how many bi-national couples are there in specific countries? How many bi-national children are growing up? And what about transmigrants? There has been an interesting shift of perspective in the migration literature. Migration has long been studied as a process of leaving one place and going to another. These places were seen to be related to some extent, but still the migrant was seen to disappear from one space and then arrive in a new country in order to be part of that country. But nowadays we find that these two spaces are combined not only in personal ways, but also in all kinds of social relationships. One example of this kind of international setting is the military. In terms of personnel, NATO's upper echelon has already completely succumbed to the attack of the cosmopolitan virus. Most missions are now miniature cosmopolitan societies, in which officers and troops from all member countries mix and co-operate even more so than in multinational corporations. Large-scale military exercises have not only become transnational in their means but also in their ends. The main objective of most such exercises is to improve international military co-ordination and integration, in other words, to foster military transnationalization.

One thing I find interesting about the military sphere, when placed in historical perspective, is how it highlights just how short the national phase of social organization really has been. The idea that armies should be national, in the sense of being ethnically homogeneous, is something that could never even have been considered by the empire builders of the past. All the great world conquests of Western history, from Caesar to Napoleon, were only possible on the basis of multiethnic armies. Empires could only be erected and secured by employing states from beyond one's original borders. In fact, the willingness of Rome to open up its citizenship to an ever-increasing circle of military recruits was a major factor in making its victories possible. When you take this long view of military history, multicultural armies have been history's rule. So how did we get to the modern exception, where ideas of an ethnically homogeneous nation, state and national army not only dominate our military thinking, but also seem like unchangeable facts of nature? Against this historical background, the question we really have to ask is: what made homogeneous national armies possible? What conditions were necessary for this transition to occur? And if these conditions no longer hold, perhaps we should not be surprised if our armies start to revert to the historical rule.

We should also keep this historical background in mind when we hear about the army's new 'cosmopolitan mission' in a post-national, multiethnic world, or its conversion into the knighthood of a new crusade. Multiethnicity was never incompatible with empire, and the original crusades were not models of tolerance. So there are good reasons why the transition we are facing in Germany today, from a national duty to a professional army oriented towards international 'peacekeeping missions' – a phrase that would have made Orwell smile – is regarded with ambivalence. This critical attitude is good, and it should be the attitude we take in general towards cosmopolitanization. But cosmopolitanization is not a scenario where everything becomes good. Rather, it throws up entirely new kinds of risks. And one of these is the risk that the very concept of 'cosmopolitan society' might offer an effective ideological legitimation for the imperial powers of capital and the military.

NG   How can we examine this idea of 'cosmopolitanization from within' at an empirical level?

UB   The most sophisticated studies of this form of cosmopolitanism have come through the analysis of global cities. Saskia Sassen, Manuel Castells, Kevin Robins, John Eade, Martin Albrow and many others argue that cities cannot be studied in a national map. Rather, they are places where interconnections between a global space or transnational space and local space can really be studied. And from this model we can go on to find out how many of these spaces are being cosmopolitanized from within. But let me first clarify an issue that is very important here: there has to be a clear distinction between the perspective of the actor and the perspective of the observer in both the national and cosmopolitan perspectives. Let me explain this. There is a body of beliefs that equalizes society with the national imagination; if it is held by social actors, I call it a 'national perspective', if it is held by scientific observers, I call it 'methodological nationalism'. A parallel distinction has to be made between a 'cosmopolitan perspective' (actor) and 'methodological cosmopolitanism' (social scientist). At any rate, the decisive point is that the 'national perspective', which structures social and political action, can no longer serve as a premise for the perspective of the social science observer. In order to understand even processes of renationalization throughout the globe, we need a methodological cosmopolitanism, because such processes have to be understood as a reaction to cosmopolitanization from within.

However, an important line of enquiry concerns whether there are limits to the cosmopolitanization of national societies. On the one hand, the national space of experience has been denationalized; it has been overlaid by cosmopolitan experiences. On the other hand, social life is still bound into the same national institutions as before (as concerns education, money, political rights, language and most institutions of the public sphere). In these crucial ways, what might be at bottom a cosmopolitan microcosm is still filtered in along national and state lines. The relation between national structures and transnational realities is thus full of contradiction and contingency. And it is easy to go wrong here in two different directions: in one direction looms the cosmopolitan error, and in the other the national one. The *cosmopolitan error* is to act as though everything I have described as 'cosmopolitanization' can be directly extrapolated into consciousness and action, or, in other words, to start from the assumption that this *globalization from within* of nations automatically leads to cosmopolitan sensibilities in people. Looked at realistically, the opposite, namely the resurgence of national reflexes, is a more probable first reaction. But despite this, everything we have said still remains true. Many crucial things that occur in national space cannot be explained in national terms or even really properly located there. There is a split between reality and perception. But because of these appearances and because of nationalist counter-reactions, breaking out of this *national error* is not only difficult, it may even be becoming harder.

The key point is that cosmopolitanization might only partly be happening. Cosmopolitanization is not a linear process as there is a lot of resistance to it, and forms of renationalization are appearing as a reaction to globalization. But even if this is true, we need a cosmopolitan perspective to analyse this situation. In the first modernity there was a combination of the national perspective and methodological nationalism. In the second modernity this breaks up, and we can no longer be sure how much of social reality is structured by national dynamics and actors. A cosmopolitan perspective is needed to analyse this, meaning that we have to build a frame of reference that is directed by methodological cosmopolitanism. We cannot simply think about the rise of new nationalisms in, say, British terms or in the German context, but we have to see them as a reaction to the ongoing processes of globalization and ongoing cosmopolitanization from within.

NG Do you see the need for a new methodology here? How, for example, might sociologists work beyond the confines of 'methodological nationalism' to look at transnational spaces of 'action, living and perception'? And what methods might be used to analyse new dependencies between national states and what you call 'world society'?

UB There are quite a few different aspects of such a methodology. I am talking of methodological cosmopolitanism, and this implies, as I have said already, redefinition of concepts from a cosmopolitan perspective. I try to do this in my latest book *Macht und Gegenmacht im globalen Zeitalter* (2002) (to be published in English as *Power in the Global Age* by Polity in 2004), in which I try to redefine the concept of power or *Herrschaft*, which so far has been pretty much related to the nation-state (the work of Weber is an example). First of all, we have to open this concept up, and see that the global economy is a very important power player on the global scale, as are transnational institutions like the World Bank, the International Monetary Fund, and so on. But global civil movements are important too, as are global uncivil movements, such as transnational forms of terrorism. In my new work, I try to redefine spaces and strategies of power in relation not only to national and international relationships, but also to all these different actors who possess different ways of redefining the basic norms of global power today. I think we have to go on to do this in relation to class, to politics, and to households. So there is a lot of work to be done. And secondly, we need to organize empirical research in these kinds of fields. This research cannot be done by one person or in a national setting only, and so we have to organize transnational research units. Different perspectives from different points of view must be included in order for us to find out how powers inside of Western nation-states are to be reconceptualized. You can do this in different fields, and it not only applies to the concept of power but also to that of risk as well. It is very important to look at the subject of global risk in different dimensions, such as environmental, financial or terrorist risks on a global scale. Today (in 2003) the Americans fight Iraq in the first war against risk – the risk of transnational terrorism. To me, this is a rather strange mix up of centuries – trying to get back into control by military means in an age of manufactured uncertainties. In terms of my theory, it must end up being counterproductive: the militarization of international relations is a reaction to the increasing terrorist threat. But the logic and implications of these risks have to be studied in different national contexts because they are related to national and international contexts at the same time, and they mix the 'inner' and the 'outer' in new forms. This research has to be done in case studies and through special organizational forms. We try to do this work in the Research Centre for Reflexive Modernization in Munich.

NG In your *British Journal of Sociology Millennium Lecture* (published as 'The Cosmopolitan Perspective' (Beck, 2000b: 79–105)) you claimed that the basic concepts of social analysis – family, class and nation-state – are now outdated, and exist today only as 'zombie concepts' (concepts that live on after their death). But if this is the case, what do you think the key concepts of sociology actually are, or should be?

UB In order to understand the ongoing 'meta-change' we might need some new concepts, but we should start by recoding or redefining existing concepts. For even in a transnational world we have to study politics and the state and power, and we have to study social inequalities – and indeed across the globe inequalities seem to have increased – but it is less clear that social class is a useful idea to serve as the principal unit of analysis. Provocatively, I developed the argument that individualization is the 'social structure' of the second modernity and that it produces non-linear, open-ended and ambivalent consequences. One consequence is that poverty is no longer a characteristic of those within the working class, for middle-class youngsters, elderly people, widows and individuals with high educational certificates may experience poverty as well. The cosmopolitan world is a world of high contrasts living side by side, which is something the category of class doesn't grasp. There are 'citadels' next to scenes from *Apocalypse Now*. And if you look at poverty in transnational terms you find that actors living in transnational spaces define themselves in different national hierarchies and class structures. They might live, for example, in Britain as a taxi driver while at the same time working in New Delhi or relating to their family there. To do this they have to relate exclusive frames of positioning in their own lives, and also balance these lives to some extent. It is very interesting to see how this is being done. But you cannot understand how a British Indian taxi driver is living a transnational life-form if you only look at this life from a national, British point of view. Instead, you have to relate this world of experience and acting to a place and position in the Indian class system as well. You have to make these interconnections, and you might find that there are different value-judgements too, and they might be quite astonishing. This is because people who look very underprivileged in a national perspective can look quite different in a transnational perspective, and from the perspective of their family in India might be perceived as being middle-class. This is not true for everyone, but it is very interesting to find out about these different positions. A transnational or cosmopolitan perspective does this by taking into account different national perspectives and relating them to special positions inside and outside specific national contexts. This can be done, for example, for global players, and for the relationship between capital and labour as well, for labour cannot locate itself across the globe to the same extent that the actors of capital can.

One point of class struggle in a post-national perspective, then, is about how different actors relate themselves to different national frames of reference. The problem, then, is this: what kinds of spaces of reference have to be taken into account? This research has to be done in all kinds of fields. And it might be done on a very local level. If you look, for example, at London, it is a network of transnational networks. But if you use terms such as 'identity' or 'diaspora' or 'hybrid' you would miss this as you already presuppose the dominance of a national perspective. For example, as Asu Aksoy and Kevin Robins show so nicely in their research, Turkish-speaking migrants want to get away both from Turkishness and Britishness, or in other words they want to get away from the national cultural 'logic' or 'identity' that positions them uncomfortably 'between cultures', and which means them being 'rootedless', 'homeless',

'. . . less'. They neither want to copy a given (national) identity nor do they feel incomplete or 'less' than 'mononationals'. Their inbetweenness is more than this – maybe more of a burden or maybe richer than just having one identity. But basically and most importantly, this existence is different because it is not fixed, not homogeneous, not exclusive, not only related to one traditional context, but experimental, controversial and reflexive: to reflect upon the inconsistencies of one's own life is a matter of survival. The transnational perspective is the ironic perspective to cultures, an outside-inside stance. If 'irony' is capable of questioning the 'natural' categories of the national belief system, then living transnationally contains irony as the *conditio humana*. And, indeed, transnationalism makes fun of itself just as it does of dominant cultures, as you can find in the postcolonial literature: *the Empire writes back*.

The same holds with other concepts. If you talk about diaspora in a classical sense it means you want to be integrated into a foreign country that is an integrated national space, and so you are already using national categories. You have to be very careful in opening up spaces of self-definition. You have to be careful in positioning transnational players and actors, in seeing how they relate to national contexts, and in looking at what kinds of reflection or non-reflection are going on. Maybe we need some new categories rather than using identity, integration, assimilation, hybrid and diaspora, which are all preoccupied by a national perspective. But we would have to make this shift in a very sophisticated way, with maybe some new concepts that are close to the specific people, networks and experiences we are working with.

NG   One concept you seem keen to hold on to or perhaps reformulate is that of society. You have spoken of risk society, world society and even 'world risk society' (Beck, 1999). Others, meanwhile, have suggested that we are currently witnessing the end of society or the death of the social. How would you respond to such arguments? Would you ever be tempted to treat society and the social as zombie concepts?

UB   This is a very interesting and challenging question. I am a sociologist who wants to defend sociology against the ongoing offensive against social science. I don't think we can substitute for society a concept of culture or of civilization, or that we can substitute for society a concept of network. Classical sociology conceptualized society in a very sophisticated way. It used all kinds of different ideas to define society and to give it an important perspective in relation to the economy and politics. So, I would turn the question around and say that economics, political science and cultural studies all fail to grasp what is new about the processes of globalization and cosmopolitanization. For what is new about these processes is the redefinition of society: *thinking society anew is the* *issue.* All the other concepts we have talked of only have a very specialized or single point of view, but society can and should be a concept which integrates many different elements: culture, politics, values, religion, technological developments, global risk dynamics, and so on. The main issue is how cosmopolitanism is being institutionalized, how institutions themselves are changing in the face of this, and what kinds of unseen, unwanted consequences and dynamics they induce. Questions of redefinition and renegotiation, then, should concentrate on the concept of society. This is one of the reasons why I am opposed to postmodern theory. Postmodern theories give up on the analysis of institutions, and don't acknowledge the construction of new institutions in complex relationships that are to some extent post-national and post-Enlightenment.

One of the main examples of this, for me, is Europe. Europe is to some extent a post-national construction and cannot be understood in national categories at all, but it is not postmodern. To cut a long story short, the new Europe tries to answer the modernization of barbarism by redefining modernity. Let me go into a bit more detail to explain this. Social scientific reflection on the Holocaust has brought forth a discourse of despair, and with good reason. According to Horkheimer and Adorno it is the dialectic of the Enlightenment itself that generates perversion. This supposition of causality between modernity and barbarism continues to be felt in Zygmunt Bauman's (1989) book *Modernity and the Holocaust*. But this despairing farewell to modernity doesn't have to be the last word on the matter. Indeed, one could even say that it is blind to the ways in which the creation of the European Union has initiated a struggle over institutions with the aim of countering European horror with European values and methods: the Old World invents itself anew. In this sense, the memory of the Holocaust becomes a beacon that warns of the ever-present modernization of barbarism. The mass graves of the twentieth century – of the World Wars, the Holocaust, the atomic bombs of Hiroshima and Nagasaki, of Stalinist death camps and genocides – bear testimony to this. Yet an unreflected and unbroken link also exists between European pessimism, the critique of modernity and postmodernity which makes this despair a permanent feature – Jürgen Habermas is right on this point. To put it a little differently, there is a paradoxical coalition between the Europe of nations and the Europe of postmodernity, because the theoreticians of postmodernity deny the possibility and reality of combating the horror of European history with more Europe, or a radicalized, cosmopolitan Europe. National modernity and postmodernity both cause Europe-blindness.

'Europeanization' means struggling to find institutional responses to the barbarism of European modernity, and, by the same token, taking leave of postmodernity, which fails to recognize this very issue. In this sense, cosmopolitan Europe constitutes an institutionalized critique of itself: cosmopolitan Europe generates a *genuinely European internal contradiction* – morally, legally and politically. If the traditions from which colonialistic, nationalistic and genocidal horror originates are European, then so are the values and legal categories against which these acts are measured (for example, in the Nürnberg Trial) as crimes against humanity under the spotlight of world publicity. The new Europe tries to overcome a military history through post-national institutions. And to understand this we need a cosmopolitan frame of reference that is at the same time post- to both the national and the postmodern perspective. It is only through such an approach that we can find out what type of power relations and regional frameworks European institutions are trying to establish.

NG   Part of your approach to this question of the social is to look at new processes of individualization. In *Risk Society* you define individualization as 'the beginning of a *new mode of societalization*' (Beck 1992: 127; original emphasis). What does this mean?

UB   Individualization doesn't start with the individual – this would be a complete misunderstanding. Individualization, in the second half of the twentieth century, is a product of the state, mainly the welfare state, which addresses its rights and services to the individual – not to the family, class or ethnicities. In this way, the social state enforces individualization and empowers it. The result is that individuals no longer need to participate in the functioning of society. So again, the same theoretical motif: individualization undercuts the foundations of the social state that produces it. Thus, what I mean by individualization is *institutionalized individualism*. Individualization is not just chosen by people: it is not the ideal perspective of the actor by himself. It is an institutionalized process, and if you look at it through empirical research you can see it in two dimensions. First of all, you can study how legal and educational institutions are producing individualized life-forms through basic political, civil and social rights, most of which are centred on the individual. You can see this in the development of family law and the law of divorce: all the risks and implications are being transferred to the individual as an actor who defines his/her own situation. The second dimension is empirical research that looks at how people redefine relationships in their personal lives: how they react to their own self-definition and to the definition of others. Reaction to this individualized situation can be very ambivalent. There is not a one-way picture of individualization in self-perception, for it can be that in relation to highly individualized life-forms people pick up conventional life-forms as a new utopia. You have to distinguish these fields of empirical research.

But individualization itself goes back to the nineteenth century, and you can find roots of it even earlier in the Renaissance and the Middle Ages. It is a process that goes further back than the first, industrial modernity. But what happens in the second modernity, in the second part of the twentieth century, is that there is a qualitative change. Individualization in the Western context becomes generalized so there is no longer a given playscript of how everyday relationships, the family, sexual relations, careers and so on are to be handled. Traditions are being dissolved, or at least are no longer able to resolve the conflicts and dilemmas that arise in our personal lives. So, for the first time, people have to define their own lives in a radical, post-traditional way. And this is what is new: we have a discrepancy between, on the one hand, highly individualized life-forms, and on the other, institutions which still conceptualize these life-forms in given collective categories (like class and family). This collapse of perspective is new and has to be studied.

NG   Your work on individualization and globalization calls, to some extent, for the re-invention of sociological practice and theory. But instead of writing a book called the 're-invention of sociology' you wrote *The Reinvention of Politics* (1997) (which also happens to be the title of your first contribution to the *Reflexive Modernization* debate (Beck, Giddens and Lash, 1994: 1–55)). Is there a connection between these projects? Or should politics and sociology be kept firmly apart?

UB   We have to be careful not to mix up sociology with politics, but at the same time be sensitive to the political redefinition of the social. The opposition between society and politics, the social and the political, is breaking down – at the local as well as the global level. Your question contains a very interesting point because society is no longer given. Society can no longer be defined in pre-given terms, and so has to be negotiated and redefined. Against structuralism and system theory, *the actor is back*, and so society and sociology can no longer be separated from politics. We need a political theory of the social theory of the political. Therefore, I am strongly opposed to structuralism (which believes in the reproduction of structures) or system theory *à la* Luhmann. Such approaches tend to become metaphysical in a world that depends on actors, decisions and unseen consequences. That is why, even in *Risk Society*, I speak of subpolitics. Subpoliticization is not only occurring in national space but also transnationally as well. National and transnational institution building is taking place that is related to the actors of mobile capital on one hand, and to civil society actors on the other. This is a transnational subpoliticization of the interconnectedness of societies, but this process is political as well as social because it redefines institutions. And when institutions are redefined they to some extent become given institutions once again. So, we are in an open situation that involves a politicization of all kinds of institutions against the background of fixed façades. This is a political process; one which is not simply related to the political system but which opens up the restructuring and redefinition of political institutions to all kinds of subpolitical actors, including terrorist networks.

NG Your argument for the re-invention of politics emerges through your analysis of reflexive modernity and risk society. In the course of this analysis you make an argument for 'the fragility of social life' (Beck, 1997: 51–7). But why is it that, in your account, modernity has become politicized at the same time as social life has become increasingly fragile? What is the connection between these two processes? And why exactly is *social* life so fragile today?

UB This again is a very important and sophisticated question. But there is always a misunderstanding about risk and risk society. Risk normally means calculable uncertainty or insecurity, so we have the means to redefine uncertainty in a way that can produce some kind of certainty and security again. But risk society means that we don't have these means. It is about an age where in all fields new manufactured uncertainties and insecurities evolve; manufactured because they are products of the processes of civilizing and modernization, and uncertain because our means to calculate and make these uncertainties certain again don't work any more. This situation is, of course, related to the development of new technologies in risk society, in the fields of atomic energy, genetics, biotechnology and nowadays nanotechnology as well. In each of these fields, processes of redefining technology to solve the problem of uncertainty produce, in turn, new kinds of uncertainties that cannot be solved by this technology. The latest example of this is nanotechnology, which tries to solve problems by producing systems that at the same time enforce the unknown consequences of what is being produced. In this way, the distinction between knowledge and unawareness is breaking down: what we know nowadays is that we neither know nor control the consequences of the decisions we take today. This is not only true for technological developments, but also, say, of calculating your own biography under the conditions of a flexible labour market, and with divorce and remarriage becoming normal, and so on. We have a democratization of insecurities and risk to the extent that in all fields the expectations and norms of the institutionalized calculability of the first modernity are breaking down, or at least not really producing social securities. But society has so far been thought of through principles of calculation. If you look, for example, at Parsons, society is an answer to uncertainty, and institutions are seen to produce certainties in response to uncertainties produced by all kinds of modern processes. But today we are in a situation where this assumption no longer really works. Individualized actors now have to negotiate their life conditions for themselves, for institutions are no longer capable of producing the securities previously promised by the nation-state, welfare state societies of the first modernity.

NG   These ideas about the risk and the politicization of modernity seem closely tied to your pursuit of new democratic forms. You frequently refer to 'reflexive democracy' and to 'cosmopolitan democracy'. Are these two different things?

UB   No, not really, they are related to each other. Democracy is, of course, one of those concepts that has to be redefined at a transnational and cosmo-politan level. But so far we have not been very good at it. David Held has made a start, but I am not completely convinced that we have found the answers yet. Democracy does not have the same power in a cosmopolitan constellation as it had in the national context. This is because transnationalization means infor-malization, that is, an informal power relationship with an informal network and informal memberships. So, one of the basic questions is: how are we to formalize the informal in order to democratize it?

New forms of reflexive and cosmopolitan forms of democracy are related, even if I did not realize this straight away. This is because you can think about subpoliticization in democratic terms. This, however, does not have to mean that you are building new forms and frames for negotiation that include democratic procedures at all levels. For example, how are the weak states represented in the WTO and IMF? Why is there no participation of NGOs as actors of the global civil society in international organizations, as well as in national and local organizations? Of course, the main issue is: does the rule of law apply to *all* states, including the most powerful states? All that makes up democracy on the national level has to be redefined on the global level. Another example might be the planning of a highway: the connection of such a plan with local and metropolitan groups to negotiate this idea can be done not only in national but also transnational terms.

But there is a pessimistic view on transnationalization as well as an opti-mistic one. We have to think about the rise of a reflexive fundamentalism and a reflexive authoritarianism, as to some extent we are experiencing this now in response to the terrorist threat. One way to look at these terrorist networks is as 'NGOs of violence'. Like NGOs – non-governmental organizations – they are deterritorialized and decentralized. They are local on the one hand and transnational on the other. And they connect via the Internet. The way they organize their campaigns is, of course, different from the way Greenpeace or Amnesty International organize theirs. But just as the NGO scheme has been yoked to a wide variety of causes, so too with their transnational terrorist cousins. There is no reason why it must be fixed to Islamic terrorism. Theoretically it could be associated with all possible goals, ideologies and fundamentalist philosophies. But the most horrifying connection is that all the risk conflicts that are stored as potential could now be unleashed intentionally. The possibility of a genetically engineered plague has to be taken much, much more seriously now that we realize it could be released on purpose rather than only by mistake. The same is true for the risks of a nuclear accident. The effect of terrorist risk is to intensify all other risks. And many reactions to this summary of threats are not enforcing civil rights but really dissolving these rights at national and transnational levels. These levels have to be distinguished, kept in mind and conceptualized at the same time.

NG   Your attempt at 're-inventing the political' is based upon a call for social democracy to be more inclusive. But to what extent is this possible? Does not democracy necessarily work by an act of exclusion at some level, by, for example, granting legitimacy, representation and perhaps ascendancy to particular political values and not others? Is there any way around this? And what do you see to be the core political or cultural values around which an inclusive democracy might operate?

UB   Well, again here the cosmopolitan perspective helps. It contains a specific modus of inclusion as well as a value perspective. What makes cosmopolitanism so interesting for a social theory of modern societies is its thinking and living in terms of inclusive oppositions: nature is associated with society, the object is part of subjectivity, otherness of the other is included in one's own self-identity and self-definition, and the logic of exclusive oppositions is rejected. Nature is no longer separated from national or international society, either as a subject or object (this is what global risk society is about). 'We' are not opposed to the 'Them' etc. The world is generating a growing number of such mixed cases, which make less sense according to the 'either-or' logic of nationality than to the 'this-as-well-as-that' logic of transnationality. A cosmopolitan sociology is an antidote to ethnocentrism and nationalism. But it should not be mistaken for multicultural euphoria. There is a big difference between multiculturalism and cosmopolitanism in the social sciences. Multiculturalists tend to develop essentialist arguments in their zeal to defend the rights and cultures of migrants and aboriginal minorities within a given political context. And they tend to be biased optimistically. On the contrary, cosmopolitanism starts from a strict anti-essentialism and from the hard-won insight that there is an invariable connection between ethnocentrism, the hatred of foreigners and violence. With this in mind, it tries to advance over the concept of 'hybridization' because it avoids the dangers inherent in using biological metaphors for human difference.

Let me come back to your question. You seem to presuppose that systems of inclusion and exclusion are constitutive to all forms of life and politics. Some argue – as does Michael Walzer – that human beings cannot be loyal to universalistic institutions but identify closely to national or local ones. This might have been true for an either-or world but no longer holds for the as-well-as world we are living in. Here, the opposition between universalistic and particularistic institutions, cultures, and spaces of experience collapses. Systems of exclusion are often grounded in nationalist or statist ideology. They relate to what Weber has analysed as the closure and monopolization of opportunities. But in a cosmopolitan perspective the main question is: are there different *modes* of inclusion and exclusion that relate to the world of overlapping loyalties and dialogical imaginations of the second modernity? Take, for example, Kant's attempt. He envisioned the *ius cosmopoliticum*, which is an exercise in moral exhortation; it is an appeal to co-nationals to transcend the parochial world of sovereign states by respecting the rights of all humanity. Thinking about cosmopolitan democracy – who is to be included, excluded and how – presupposes to find out about the nature of post-national communities or national communities cosmopoliticized from within. What does this mean in terms of political participation? There is a long way to go. Some are proposing dual citizenship in the EU: a European citizenship including two national citizenships. This would change quite a lot. Maybe this is one of a number of ways to construct overlapping democracies for overlapping life-forms.

NG In your writings on democracy you speak often of the rise of 'transnational civil society' and new 'subpolitical' forms, but rarely use terms such as 'power' or 'domination'. How do you think the nature of power has changed with the onset of reflexive modernization?

UB This is the topic of my new book *Power in the Global Age*. To some extent I changed my mind in this book because now I think that power is one of the most important issues of the global game. This game involves the redefinition of the rules of power that play out not quite on a national but on a transnational level. Of course, many different actors mix with many different perspectives and instruments of power. But the main argument of the book is that we have to redefine the state. This is because civil movements by themselves are not able to enact political laws and institutions but depend on states. In this context, a central new distinction has to be made between sovereignty and autonomy. The nation-state is built on equating the two. From the nation-state perspective, economic interdependence, cultural diversification and military, juridical and technological co-operation all lead to a loss of autonomy and thus sovereignty. But if sovereignty is measured in terms of political success, it is then possible to conceive the same situation very differently: a decrease of autonomy can lead to an increase in sovereignty.

Nation-states that barricade their borders will be ultimately ill equipped to cope with problems that have their origins in a transnational world. Cosmopolitan states, by contrast, address the same problem by emphasizing the necessity of solidarity with foreigners both inside and outside of national borders. They do this by connecting self-determination with responsibility for others. It is not a matter of limiting or negating self-determination; on the contrary, it is a matter of freeing self-determination from its national Cyclopean vision and connecting it to the world's concerns. Cosmopolitan states do not make war against terror; they struggle against the *causes* of terror. They seek to restore the regenerative power of politics to shape and persuade. And they do this by searching for global solutions to burning problems that can't be solved by individual nations on their own.

The cosmopolitan state is not a global state, it is not US or UN institutions as a world government, but a national state that is bound into co-operative networks and which combines different national perspectives in building a nation that acknowledges the difference of others. Cosmopolitan states are founded upon the principle of national indifference, that is to say, of the national indifference of the state. In the sixteenth century, the Peace of Westphalia ended the religious civil war we call the Thirty Years War through the separation of church and state. In a similar manner, the separation of state and nation can be the solution to the world and civil wars of the twentieth and twenty-first centuries, in the same way that an a-religious state finally made possible the peaceful coexistence of multiple national and religious identities to exist side by side through the principle of constitutional tolerance. The main example of such a historical experiment is the EU. So, I think it is quite important to develop a perspective of the political evolution of the state and state concepts. We are not witnessing the end of the state, but rather the changing of the content of the nation-state in many directions. One direction is the transnational or cosmopolitan state, which relates politics and state power in new interesting ways to both the economy and power of transnational movements.

NG   In your work on globalization and political reflexivity you also talk of the possibility of forging a new (global) social contract (see Beck, 2000a: 14). What might such a contract look like? And can such a contract be truly universal, or is it destined to be exclusive in some way?

UB This contract needs to be specified in some kind of institutional design. Part of the contract could attempt to solve the dilemmas that come up between national sovereignty on one side, and human rights issues on the other. Humanitarian intervention means that national sovereignty and law have been undermined by the enforcement of global norms, possibly against the interests of national states and national politics. A global contract would, in part, be designed to handle this new situation.

Let me give you a different interpretation of the same issue. In talking about the possibility of an Iraq war you find an opposition which is pretty much arguing in the national perspective, saying it is about oil against blood or about a geo-strategic intervention of the US military and political forces in this area, and so on. This may be true to some extent, but does not really get the point because it still presupposes the national-international distinction, and pre-supposes international law as a given system to judge all kinds of acting. But if it is true that we are beyond the distinction between the national and inter-national, we have to redefine or reform international law. All the global chal-lenges like climate change, global food risks, environmental risks, terrorist threats and so on are beyond the nation-state and even beyond the distinction between the national and the international. So, to some extent we have to open up the system of international law to these new challenges. There has to be a reformist perspective through which we can find norms that enable us to cri-ticize the enforcement of power and norms at a transnational level. This would be part of the new social contract. And this means that we need some new institutional architecture for relating different spaces of power – the European, American, Asian spaces – into a system of balanced powers following some kinds of rules that have yet to be developed.

NG What role do you think sociologists should have in drawing up a new social contract? Should sociologists themselves be legislators (in Bauman's sense) rather than interpreters, and should sociology itself have a normative function?

UB This is a very difficult question. First of all I would say that sociologists should start doing their jobs in the right way: they should start redefining society beyond their zombie categories. There is a lot of work to be done. But this work would make sociology interesting for a broad public again, for there would be a clash of perspectives between a sociology that redefines the situation in transnational or non-national terms and the national-bound actors and institutions. A cosmopolitan sociology throws light onto the coming into being of transnational spaces of experience, and identifies institutions not only out-side but also inside the national container. Such a sociology takes a critical

stance to society and its self-understandings. It emancipates itself from methodological nationalism and holds a mirror to the national perspective of actors,
showing what is wrong with it and why. This is the conflict that sociologists
really have to pick up on and be able to research. And this research could be
done, for example, in relation to the question of Europe. There is no sociology
of Europe so far; only a nation-based sociology that summarizes national
perspectives by themselves or by making, at most, comparative analyses
between nation-states. But even the question of whether there is a European
society has yet to have been addressed systematically. There is still no political
theory that allows us to understand European politics as, to some extent,
beyond the nation-state.

But, first of all, sociologists should redefine themselves, and this would be a
very important contribution. I started with my Ph.D. on the conflict over value-
judgements in the social sciences. I compared all kinds of perspectives and got
very confused! In the end, I said that the most important contribution of
sociologists to the public and to politics is not their value-judgements, for
society can produce its own value-judgements. The most important contribution of sociology lies in defining reality in terms of what Weber called
Wertbeziehungen (value-relevancies or value-relationships). The cosmopolitan
perspective on social reality is one of these new value-relationships. It produces
a new kind of definition of these social and political opportunities for action
and their dark sides. This could be a very challenging and important contribution for the value development and political development of society itself.
It is not a positive outlook. It is about 'The Cosmopolitan Society and its
Enemies' (Beck, 2002b). For in a sense, the enemies of the emerging cosmopolitan society struck back on 11 September 2001.

NG Finally, in *The Reinvention of Politics* you stress the importance of
sociological (self-)criticism. You draw the conclusion that 'if society is self-
critical, an uncritical society will become false and a critical one conformist',
but add that 'a criticism of criticism, however, is yet to be invented' (1997:
177). What do you mean by this? Are you making a case for the development of
new forms of critical theory?

UB Yes, from the beginning the toolbox of my theory and its elements – risk
society, reflexive modernization, radical individualization and now the 'cosmopolitan turn' – are designed to combine into a new critical theory. My
description of modern society – as one that is a threat to itself by its very
existence – opposes the concepts of classical sociological theory. I am neither
talking of more or less functioning systems (as Parsons and Luhmann do), nor
of crisis (as Marx did). To me the functioning causes the complications. The

victory of modernity dissolves or defeats modernity, or, to be more precise, induces its meta-change. The crisis is what is systematic, what is the norm, and so it is not 'crisis' anymore but a meta-change. In all my theoretical work I try to capture these basic ambivalences of a world that is threatening, transforming and redefining itself in one and the same movement. The 'either-or' is succeeded by the 'as-well-as'. But we have to be specific about this as-well-as *conditio humana*. It is much easier to say what the as-well-as world is *not* about than to say what it is about. In order to do this, I try to re-invent cosmopolitanism as an intellectual tradition preceding and succeeding the national perspective and its built-in either-or logic. The zeal is to overcome 'national sociology' with its false universalistic understandings of the social world and open up nation-state centred society and politics – sociology, political science and history. This needs a new critical theory with cosmopolitan intent. A paradigmatic change is necessary: a shift from methodological nationalism to methodological cosmopolitanism, *a cosmopolitan turn*. We need to construct a conceptual horizon that highlights a new configuration of the world. Previously, the national cosmos could be decomposed into a clear distinction between the inside and outside. Between the two, the nation-state governed and order was established. In the inner space of experience, the central themes of work, politics, law, social inequality, justice and cultural identity were negotiated against the background of the nation, which was the guarantor of a collective unity of action. In the international realm, the corresponding concept of 'multiculturalism' was developed. Multiculturalism, by means of delimitation from and exclusion of the foreign, mirrored and crystallized the national self-image. Thus, the national/international distinction always represented more than a distinction, it actually functioned as a permanent self-affirming prophecy.

In the cosmopolitan turn, it becomes suddenly obvious that it is neither possible to clearly distinguish between the national and the international, nor, in a similar way, to convincingly contrast homogeneous units. National spaces have become denationalized, so that the national is no longer national, just as the international is no longer international. The state is not collapsing but changing, and new actors, a new global power game and new realities are arising, as are new mappings of space and time and new co-ordinates for the social and the political, co-ordinates which have to be theoretically and empirically researched and elaborated. This means that the fundamental concepts of 'modern society' and their relationships must be re-examined and re-invented. Household, family, class, social inequality, democracy, power, state, commerce, public, community, justice, law, history and politics all must be released from the fetters of methodological nationalism and must be reconceptualized and empirically established within the framework of a cosmopolitan social and political science, which remains to be developed. So the cosmopolitan turn sums up to quite a list of understatements: only these tiny challenges?! But otherwise sociology is turning into a museum of antiquated ideas.

REFERENCES

Bauman, Z. (1989) *Modernity and the Holocaust*. Cambridge: Polity.

Beck, U. (1992) *Risk Society*. London: Sage.

Beck, U. (1997) *The Reinvention of Politics*. Cambridge: Polity.

Beck, U. (1999) *World Risk Society*. Cambridge: Polity.

Beck, U. (2000a) *What is Globalization?* Cambridge: Polity.

Beck, U. (2000b) 'The Cosmopolitan Perspective', *British Journal of Sociology*, Vol. 51, No. 1, pp. 79–105.

Beck, U. (2002a) *Macht und Gegenmacht im globalen Zeitalter*. Frankfurt: Suhrkamp.

Beck, U. (2002b) 'The Cosmopolitan Society and Its Enemies', *Theory, Culture & Society*, Vol. 19, Nos 1–2, pp. 17–44.

Beck, U., Giddens, A. and Lash, S. (1994) *Reflexive Modernization*. Cambridge: Polity.

Kaufman, J.-C. (1999) *Sociologie du couple*. Paris: PUF.

CHAPTER 9

Nikolas Rose: Governing the Social

NG   What initially attracted you to the discipline of sociology?

NR   In fact, I was originally trained as a biologist. I went to Sussex University in 1965 to read biology, partly inspired by my brother who was a biologist, but also because I had been fascinated by biology since I was young, and developments in molecular biology and genetics seemed very interesting and important. But 1965–7 were very dramatic political years, especially for people at university, and gradually I found my interests moving from small creatures like fruit flies to larger animals, and from larger animals to human beings. At that point I shifted from reading for a degree in biology to reading for one in biology and psychology. But soon after I left university, although I kept up my interest in psychology, it became clear to me that the kinds of social, political and ethical questions I was interested in didn't really admit of psychological answers. I came to think that psychology, at least in the form it then existed, was something that had to be explained, rather than something that could itself explain much about human beings and their social interactions. And that coincided with me becoming much more explicitly politically engaged. I was reading a lot of Marx, and in fact I became a Marxist long before I became a sociologist.

NG   You recently described yourself as an ex-Marxist. In what ways did the work of Marx inform your early position. And at what point did you break from Marx, and why?

NR   Marx was important to me for two reasons. First, because at that point I felt Marx's writings, and the kinds of work they had given rise to, gave the best possible grasp of the forms of inequality and injustice which were disturbing and troubling – not just for me but for a whole generation of radicals in that period in the late 1960s and early 1970s. So, to that extent, it was a substantive interest. But secondly, Marx attracted me because it was a highly developed theoretical attempt to grasp the nature of our social world. It seemed to be much more successful in doing that than the kinds of social science that I had a glancing acquaintance with. All those things that have now become rather unfashionable about Marxist theory – the fact that it was a totalizing explanation, the fact that it could link developments in economic life with developments in cultural life and developments in political life, the fact that it had a global grasp, the fact that critique was not just something external to the theory but was something built into the very fabric of the theory – all these things seemed very powerful. As I read Marx and Marxism, I become increasingly influenced by a particular interpretation of Marx: the Althusserian interpretation. Again, at that point it seemed to me to be the most rigorous attempt to develop a coherent theoretical approach to these kinds of questions. It was an approach, and this was very important to me at the time, that worked with Marxist concepts but which was not an economically determinist Marxism. This was important because the kinds of politics I was involved with were the politics of education, of culture, of cultural and subjective transformation. Economistic Marxism, which relegated these things to superstructure, didn't seem to me to have any grasp whatsoever of these issues, namely issues of advertising and mass media, issues of the role of psychology as a discipline, issues to do with psychiatry or education, and so on. Althusser's famous concept of the relative autonomy of the ideological at that point gave me an intellectual and a conceptual grasp of how one might go about analysing these things. This concept seemed to me to be tremendously difficult in those days. That classic paper 'Ideology and Ideological State Apparatuses' (see Althusser, 1977) was the most difficult paper that I had ever read, despite the fact that reading it now it looks like good old-fashioned functionalism. But, nonetheless, it gave a clear role and significance to educational institutions, psychological apparatuses and so on, and seemed to give some clues as to how one could analyse them. But quite soon, the Althusserian problematic was shown to be liable to many of the criticisms which it had developed of Marxism, in particular the criticisms of essentialism, of totalization and of teleology. And, perhaps more important, the concepts were not very helpful in analysing the details of specific practices and how they worked. Like a whole generation of British Althusserians, I became increasingly dissatisfied with what the Althusserian theoretical apparatus could provide, and increasingly aware that it had very similar problems to the theories it was criticizing. Althusser's work certainly helped me to think theoretically and conceptually, but the actual concepts that he himself produced were not able to do the kinds of work that I was interested in. And at that point I encountered the work of Michel Foucault.

NG   What was it that specifically attracted you to the work of Foucault?

NR Well, if we are talking historically and biographically, I had started working with a group of people around a journal which I helped set up called *Ideology and Consciousness* (*I&C*), which was initially conceived as a Marxist journal addressing questions of ideology and subjectivity, both terms which I would now be reluctant to use in any technical sense. But at the time, the prospect of developing a kind of Althusserian psychoanalytic theory of the constitution of the subject seemed an attractive one, a politically significant one, and a conceptually possible one. Foucault's books, starting with *The Order of Things* (1970), helped me break from thinking about subjectivity in terms of the constitution of particular types of human psychology. They helped me find a different way of thinking about subjectivity, and helped me break from the idea of ideology as something that in some way or other disguises, dissimulates and reproduces certain relations of production. Foucault's books weren't just critical, rather they seemed to make possible a more positive analysis of the organization of discourse, and of the kinds of objects and possibilities that discourses help produce and regulate. *I&C* was translating some of Foucault's work into English and publishing long accounts of the work of his collaborators, like Jacques Donzelot's (1980) book *The Policing of Families* – which we reviewed before it was translated into English. At the same time, in my own work and for my Ph.D. thesis, I was trying to wrestle with the question of the nature and history of psychology as a discipline (the discipline I had come out of). I tried to do this first of all in a kind of Althusserian way that didn't work, and then by using the work of Foucault, which did! This approach seemed to me to be tremendously powerful at making sense of the emergence of these forms of knowledge of human beings, their correlated institutional and technical forms, and the forms of subjectivity that were being brought into existence. Reading Foucault's work and using his concepts seemed to make a whole dimension of reality visible which to some extent had been a bit obscured before, as you couldn't get conceptual grips upon it when you either had to relate it to an economic base or to a particular subject, or to see it as performing an ideological function for the reproduction of the relations of production. And that is what I tried to do – to develop this approach to the development of psychology as a kind of *savoir*, as a kind of know-how, as a form of expertise that had played a key role not just in dealing with the problems of human beings in an advanced industrial world, but also in actually creating the kinds of human beings we take ourselves to be and are taken to be by others. That was what my doctoral thesis ended up as – after ten years – which was then published as *The Psychological Complex* (Rose, 1985) and which I still think is a very good book, despite the fact that it more or less sank without trace at the time.

NG How does the theme of governmentality play out in this approach to sociology and psychology?

NR I wouldn't have put my work under the sign of governmentality at that time. But, looking at it now, it seems to me that the kinds of insights that were offered by Foucault's concepts, even in the stage before the whole language of governmentality became so popular, operated in something like the same terms. The idea of governmentality points one to explore the different mentalities of government (and government here covers all those attempts to manage the conduct of human individuals) to shape conduct, or attempt to shape conduct through specific means to particular ends. And this, in turn, involves various ways of understanding who human beings are and what determines their conduct. The psychological is the form of knowledge and the type of expertise, and the mode of practice *par excellence*, of the conduct of conduct – the conduct of conduct at the micro-level, whether it be the schoolchild in the classroom, the mother and her maternal behaviour in the home, or the prisoner. The advantage of this way of thinking, for me, was that it didn't just enable you to redescribe conceptually something that you could describe in other terms, which is what a lot of sociological concepts seem to do. Rather, it actually provided a way of bringing new relations and aspects of practice into focus, and of unpacking the ways they operated in a great deal of detail.

At the same time, I also became involved in another self-produced journal, a journal about contemporary politics called *Politics and Power*. I was working on this with a group of people who were largely from the same intellectual and political background as me. Many of them were ex-Althusserian Marxists who had become disillusioned with the capacities of Marxism to provide the analytical tools for looking at what was going on in democratic societies, and who were interested in the kinds of developments that were going on politically in Europe under the sign then of Euro-communism. Many of them were involved in feminist and socialist-feminist theory and politics. This kind of feminism seemed to me to exemplify a new way of thinking about the power relations that were intrinsic in certain practices, and of strategies to transform them in the here and now, whether they be in the bedroom, the kitchen, or in the workplace. In the post-Marxist period – this is how it felt for many of us then – the question was: how could one analyse these kinds of practices and bring them into some kind of connection with more general issues which had more conventionally formed the focus of politics – issues of the state, government, large-scale apparatuses of social policy, and so on? Before I really understood the concept, it seemed to me that the idea of governmentality, or *the conduct of conduct*, provided a way in. When it came to linking up more general rationales for governing a whole political space with the micropractices of what went on in hospitals, in social work departments, in the regulation of different sorts of aspects of social and economic life, governmentality seemed to provide a way of doing the kind of work which the Althusserian concepts like 'the relative autonomy of the state' couldn't do. One could side-step some issues that had hung up radical political theory – like the question of the state – and just ask some other questions. For example: according to what rationales are we governed? In relation to what ends are we governed? How – by what techniques – are we governed? What is the scope of government? What are the limits of government? Who are the agents of government – that is to say, what entities do the governing, because they are clearly not just the politicians in parliament nor the civil service? And what is the relationship between the political and the non-political – as both are involved to some extent in the government of conduct? These were the kinds of questions that came into view, and that was when my own work moved away (for about ten years, although never entirely away) from the analysis of the psychiatric, psychological, psy-domain towards more general questions of governmentality.

NG You use the terms 'conduct of conduct' (Rose, 1999a: 3) and also sometimes the 'will to govern' (Rose, 1999a: 5). These terms appear to have a Nietzschean ring to them. In using the work of Foucault have you at the same time developed a position in relation to Nietzsche?

NR The simple answer to that is 'no'! I haven't developed a position in relation to Nietzsche. I am not a philosopher. I read Nietzsche, I learn from Nietzsche, I try and guard myself against the temptation of taking this or that aphorism and using it as if it demonstrates something – since whatever Nietzsche's aphorisms are, they are not demonstrations. So, I haven't developed a position in relation to Nietzsche. But I read Nietzsche to set my thought into motion. Nietzsche's writings kick you in a certain direction and make you think about familiar things in new ways. And then the task is to think. I'll leave it to the philosophers to have positions about Nietzsche.

NG You counter-pose domination, or what you call 'the crushing of the capacity for action' (Rose, 1999a: 4), to governmentality, which presupposes the freedom of the governed. What is the connection between these practices? Are we shifting from one to the other?

NR If one looks at the way in which Western societies have governed themselves for about the last 200 or 300 years, it is clear that the governmental rationalities that we could term 'liberal' have legitimated themselves, justified themselves, and sought to govern in the name of some idea of freedom. But that idea of freedom has always been limited. There have always been certain subjects who have not been considered capable of bearing the weight of freedom. Conventionally, children, slaves, women in certain respects, and some subjects of the colonies were excluded from the capacities of freedom and they had to be governed in other ways. And, along another dimension, there were those who had forfeited their rights to bear the weight of freedom: lawbreakers, the mad, and an array of other figures varying across time and place. But even if one thinks of the government, or the conduct of the conduct of children, the mad, prisoners and so forth, I don't think it is very helpful to counter-pose rationalities that claim to work through freedom to those that think that they must eliminate the capacity to act in their subjects. Even in reformatory institutions such as the prison, psychiatric hospitals and the old asylums of the nineteenth century, the rationale was to shape conduct in certain ways – to recreate the capacity to act according to the disciplines that freedom requires. Of course, the reality was that the techniques used in those institutions often did not live up to those grand justifications, and systematically degraded and dominated those within them, usually for reasons of institutional order and control. No one who visited an old asylum or prison in the 1950s or 1960s would say that they were technologies to create the possibility of freedom in their inmates. Discipline and the maintenance of order depended often on very brutal ways of crushing the capacities to act of those who were within those institutions – often extending to those who worked there. But I think that the rationale for these kinds of institution has always been predicated upon the idea that they are essential to freedom, or perhaps that the constraint of some is necessary for the freedom of the majority, or that such constraint will restore the constrained to the status of free subjects. However, the reality of most of these institutions has been to work in very different ways. Hence, the critique of these institutions, which goes along their whole history, has very often operated by saying: 'Look, you are claiming to be able to reform the prisoner, but how can you reform the prisoner when you are actually brutalizing people within the prison?' Or: 'You are claiming to be able to cure or at least to reform the person in the psychiatric hospital, but how can you do that when you are brutally suppressing them with chains or with drugs?'

As far as the colonies are concerned, we would need to make some further distinctions. Colonial governmentalities exemplify a variety of relations between government, freedom and domination. And metropolitan states often worked out techniques of government in the colonies. The colonies were experiments in government, and where the colonizing powers were themselves liberal they were not exempt from criticisms in the name of freedom. Once more, the argument was made: 'Look, you are claiming to govern in line with the values of liberty and autonomy of freedom, but how can you rationalize this example of colonial brutality against that standard?' And then, of course, there were many conventional rejoinders. For one group, it would be: 'These people, this race of people, do not have the capacity to bear the burdens of freedom – they are too child-like, they do not have the intellectual capacity, they are too close to the savages.' For others, it would run along the lines that you have got to be cruel to be kind, you have to use harsh and coercive measures because only in that way can you bring people into the ambit of civility where they can exercise the disciplines of freedom.

So, I am certainly not saying that we have reached the sunny uplands of freedom. What I am saying is that a certain ideal about freedom – a certain ideal that one should govern in the name of freedom and that, with exceptions that must be justified, the subjects one governs are subjects who have some kind of natural right to be free – has become central both to the justification of the attempt to shape the conduct of others, and to their critique. This is not to say that they represent the reality of what is going on, but that they are the terms in which those who govern have to be able to justify themselves if they are to claim to govern legitimately.

NG You say in your book *Powers of Freedom* that governmentality doesn't simply involve practices of rationalization but also reflexivity (see Rose, 1999a: 7). What type of political reason underpins or results from these two different types of practice?

NR By reflexivity I mean something very specific. I am not talking about reflexivity in the sense that it is used in accounts, say, of 'reflexive moder-nization', although there is certainly a connection between the two uses. I am arguing that reflexivity is a characteristic of certain mentalities of government – perhaps of all 'liberal' mentalities of government. This reflexivity involves a constant reflection by those who govern and their critics about whether we are governing too much, or governing in the right kind of way, or achieving our objectives, or having perverse effects. Reflexivity is this kind of constant reflection on how one governs. This happens at the macropolitical level through the constant subjecting of those who exercise power to a certain kind of critique, and to a critique they exercise on themselves. It also happens at the micro-level as doctors and social workers, and all those others involved in the conduct of conduct, are constantly being questioned by others and questioning themselves about whether they are doing their jobs the right way, whether they are being effective, about what right they have to intervene (for example, whether social workers have the right to intervene into a family to remove a child they think is being abused), or whether the family has the right to its privacy, and so forth. This constant questioning characterizes the forms of liberal political rationality that have developed in the West.

But this questioning does not infuse every political rationality. State socialism was a political rationality – one that has been insufficiently investigated in these kinds of terms – but one that doesn't involve this kind of reflexivity. This kind of questioning of the limit was not intrinsic to such a rationality – nor, for example, to theological political rationalities such as that of the Taliban in Afghanistan. Others may pose such questions to these mentalities of government, but such questions are often unintelligible to those who govern, and they are certainly not questions that such rationalities pose to themselves. For Foucault, as he argues in his essays on Enlightenment, this kind of questioning is characteristic of an attitude to ourselves in the present that comes into being around the time of the Enlightenment. The questioning – of who we are, of what we are doing, of what we can hope for, of whether it is justified for us to be doing what we are doing, or of whether we are doing too much or too little – is the attitude he calls, after Kant, the attitude of Enlightenment. But as I have said, this is not a chronological claim, i.e. a claim that all rationalities of government since Kant are enlightened. For even from the limited examples we have just discussed, it is clear one could not claim that.

NG   On the other side of things you say that governmentality presupposes the freedom of the governed. What might such a limited form of freedom look like?

NR   I think there are two types of questions here. The first is a general conceptual question. The way in which the concept of government is set up implies action upon action, that is to say that it implies ends are achieved by acting on entities – human beings in this case – that have the capacities to act. And if one takes the capacity to act to be a form of freedom, albeit a rather 'thin' sense of freedom, then the idea of the capacity to act in the things that are acted upon is built into the very idea of what it is to govern. That is one way in which government is predicated upon the idea that you are governing entities that can act. But it is a different kind of question to ask if this freedom is the same if you are governing your flock as it is if you are governing a group of schoolchildren, or as it is if you are governing your family, or governing citizens in a society. In relation to this kind of question, one would need to ask: 'what exactly is the capacity to act that is presupposed in the schoolchild, in the political subject, in the family member, and so on?' In this sense, the presuppositions about the capacity to act have a very definite history. What we have come to call freedom today involves one particular sense of the capacity to act. We have come to understand freedom in ways that are culturally and historically specific, but nonetheless they form the horizon of our thought around freedom. Autonomy, self-fulfilment, lack of constraint – all those terms that became so familiar to us in the political rhetorics of the 1980s – seem to define the limits and the substance of what we call freedom today. And I want just to make two kinds of remarks about this. First, I started doing my work on freedom precisely because freedom at that historical moment had become such a powerful and salient political concept. I thought one needed to work on this concept, not through a project of deconstruction (to bring out what was hidden or repressed, or the unspoken or unspeakable) but through historical work to see the way in which this specific sense of freedom had been carved out. Second, although it is hard, I think that it is entirely possible to recover other forms of freedom that don't take the form of self-fulfilment, autonomy, choice, or self-direction – forms which don't place the self and its capacities at the centre of an ethic of freedom. To take a simplistic example, perhaps the monastic life, which is a life lived in the maximum of constraints about time and space and conduct and so on, is nonetheless a life of enormous freedom, a freedom that provides us with a different set of possibilities than the kinds of freedom which we think we have today.

NG You present your book *Powers of Freedom* as a genealogy of freedom. Is there an underlying political objective to this work?

NR As I have already hinted, the political objective had to do with the salience of the language and the ethics of a certain kind of freedom in the politics of the late twentieth century. To that extent, the studies I did at that time were a genealogy, at least in the way that I understand the term. That is to say, they start from a problem in the present and trace back the contingent historical circumstances that have given that problem its possibility and salience. Genealogy forges certain conceptual tools that enable one to understand the coming into existence of that problem in the present. That problem for me was the problem of freedom. But this certainly doesn't mean that if I were starting this work today I would start with the question of freedom. I would probably start with the question of ethics, or the question of community, and from that starting point, the lines one would trace back would be different. So, in answer to your question, an underlying political objective did shape my concerns in this work. It wasn't so much a political objective as a political problem, a question of how you could make the question of freedom amenable to analysis, especially as it seemed to me that this question of freedom, and a certain way of posing this question of freedom, had become the common ground not just of the politics of the Right but also of the politics of the Left. It seemed impossible to move politically beyond demands for the maximization of autonomy, of choice, of individual rights, and so forth. I wanted to try to make it possible for myself to think politically outside that space.

NG   Following up on this question of method, your idea of genealogy clearly comes from the work of Foucault, but you also claim to follow Deleuze's idea of an empirical methodology (Rose, 1999a: 11–12). What does such a methodology look like? Is it similar in form and intent to a genealogy?

NR   I wouldn't claim to be a Deleuzian. I think my relationship to Deleuze is a bit like my relationship to Nietzsche. I wouldn't even claim to understand Deleuze, and I am not sure such a relationship of understanding is possible! Probably my relationship to Deleuze is of the worst possible kind in that I creep up on his work and steal a few concepts and then run off and use them in whatever way seems most productive for me. No doubt this is a very bad practice.

But you asked me about empiricism. We are all familiar with the ways in which empiricism as a philosophical doctrine has been criticized, especially criticisms of the claim that all knowledge is derived from sensations or experience, or that statements only have meaning when they can be related to the experience of the senses. But when I talk about empiricism *à la* Deleuze, this is not at all what I mean. I mean instead an attempt to set up a constant dynamic engagement between thought and its object, and thus a concern with engaging with the specificities of situations, cases and elements. I take from Deleuze this way of thinking about the relation of thought to the empirical, in which there is a kind of resonance that occurs between thought and its object. The object is neither simply summoned up by thought (as implied in certain versions of constructionism), nor is it simply given, external to thought, or waiting to be discovered. In any event, it is not the case of a grand and universal epistemological position here, but of finding ways of thinking about specific events and the particularities of practices. As thought engages with these small actualities they are transformed, and new kinds of connections become possible. I am by no means a philosopher, but in my own rather clumsy and *ad hoc* way I have tried to develop a way of thinking in which concepts are most powerful when they are engaged in some way in an empirical field, and where concepts, as they engage with that field, transform it in certain ways and make it amenable to further changes. I'm afraid at present I don't really have an elaborate or sophisticated methodological language to characterize this position that I try to hold to in my own research. But that is what I was gesturing to with the idea of an empirical methodology. As for its links with genealogy, I think it is an ethos of enquiry quite close to that discussed by Foucault (1977) in his essay 'Nietzsche, Genealogy, History': a concern with the singularity of occurrences (without craving some general truth that lies behind them), and with the patience to accumulate little details and attend to small differences rather than discovering sameness, so that attention is shifted to the profusion and diversity of entangled events.

NG How does this empiricism connect to your idea of governmentality. You say they are close in spirit or ethos. How is this so?

NR For me, the most productive forms of analysis undertaken under the sign of governmentality do partake of this kind of spirit, ethos or attitude of empiricism. This is because what they seek to do is to show how, in very specific locales and fields, certain kinds of relations of thinking and doing are brought into existence, and how certain practices are constructed and certain technologies are assembled together. This demands a meticulous attention to the details of apparently small things, like the invention of a statistical index such as the gross national product, a device like an IQ test, or the development of a technique for gathering numbers and accumulating them in the form of a census (and then putting them into tables and using those tables as the basis of calculation or prediction). These studies require an attention to the details of the ways in which these fields are brought into existence and put together. All these little techniques have to be invented, or rather *assembled*, because many of them are not invented *ab initio* but are put together using bits and pieces that already exist in the field. This means that government is kind of an art of bricolage. And to work under the sign of empiricism is to accept that one needs to study these things at this kind of level.

NG You also talk, again in the spirit of Deleuze, of charting 'lines of force' (Rose, 1999a: 11). What do you mean by this? And do you think that accompanying 'lines of flight' might be developed from your writings?

NR The idea of lines of force seems to me to be a way of avoiding the rather tainted and problematic vocabulary of power, which always brings a whole host of static associations along in its wake – such as the idea that power is a quantifiable thing that can be possessed – however much one might try to avoid them. Deleuze's idea of lines of force seems to provide a means for thinking about relations of 'power' in a much more mobile and dynamic kind of way – in terms of relations, speeds, durations, flows and vectors. It is not easy to think in this way, but Deleuzian thought is incredibly mobile, and that is why it is something I continue to learn from.

   As far as lines of flight, well, I would not want to prescribe the lines of flight that my work might make possible. I think the maximum that I would hope for

– and I know these phrases have now become banal – is that this work tries to illuminate the contingent historical conditions and processes by which we have come to accept certain things as true. I try to do this in ways that make sense, for instance, to the social worker dealing with a family, or to the psychiatrist dealing with the question of whether or not a person ought to be constrained or given drugs, or to the economist asked to make predictions about 'the rate of growth' of 'the economy'. I don't see my work as trying to tell any of those people what to do, nor even as trying to unsettle them, as my sense is that many of them are already pretty unsettled as it is. But I hope to give them some concepts that might help them think their way out of their situation. *They* would have to develop the lines of flight though!

NG Another concept you discuss in some detail in your book *Powers of Freedom* is 'the social'. How do your writings on governmentality inform a theory of the social? Can we talk, as Baudrillard (1983) does, of the death of the social?

NR   I think we need to pose this as a question, or rather, today, we are posed this as a question: are we seeing 'the death of the social?' To address this question, we have to be quite precise about what we mean by 'the social'. The social is not the same as 'society', it is not the same as 'social life', and it is not the same as 'social relations'. I use the term 'social' in the same way as Jacques Donzelot used the term in his terrific book *The Policing of Families* (1980) written over twenty years ago. 'The social' names a certain sector of reality which begins to be brought into existence in the nineteenth century, and continues to exist in a relatively unquestioned way up into the second half of the twentieth century. At one level, the territory is indicated by the emergence – in English, French, German and many other languages – of the little word 'social'. This term starts to be used as the qualifier for all sorts of things, including social insurance, social rights, social workers and indeed of a whole discipline of the social that is sociology. The work that others and I have done on governmentality has tried to identify the conditions under which this 'social' – that formed the horizon of much ameliorist and radical thought – gets brought into existence.

At the risk of being boring, I would stress that some rather mundane and low-level processes bring this 'social' dimension of experience into existence before it gets theorized by the great theorists of the social like Durkheim. This was the work of the doctors and sanitary engineers in mapping out the spaces of disease and trying to sanitize them, the work of the police forces charting out criminal space, and the work of urban reformers mapping the conditions of the labouring classes in the great cities, and so forth. The documents, figures, maps and charts that they produced all gave a certain solidity to a set of phenomena that seemed not to be simply matters of individual activity, but which shaped the character and conditions of individual lives, fortunes and fates. It seemed that there were larger forces at work that went beyond just themselves and their individual families and localities, and which bound them together. Pretty soon, this idea of the social being not only formed the basis of a whole way of conceptualizing human existence, but also enabled ways of intervening in it in order to try and mitigate the worst and increase the best: social insurance or the politics of social right in France, and so on. So, we can see here the emergence of this 'social' that became the horizon of our thought at least up until the last decades of the twentieth century. On the one hand this gave rise to a political imperative: if government is to be legitimate or effective, it must be social. On the other hand, and related of course, it gave rise to an intellectual imperative: if this or that feature of human life is to be understood, we must pay attention to its social aspects. My research tries to understand how all these crucial implications of this little word 'social' came into existence. And perhaps the old cliché is relevant: Minerva's owl flies only at dusk. That is to say, it has only been possible to recognize the historicity of this 'social' horizon at a time when its hold over us has begun to fade. Donzelot, for instance, wrote his book at a time when many intellectuals and politicians were already beginning to question the inevitability of the belief that individuals were shaped and determined by society, that individual rights had to be subordinated to social obligations, and that insurance against risk was best secured by schemes of social provision, and so forth. These shifts were, and are, highly contested. That is what I mean by putting the question mark after the phrase 'the death of the social'. People still refer to society, of course; they have not simply erased that reference to all the forces and processes that bind human beings together beyond their individuality and their family relations. But the social vocabulary for accounting for these does not have a monopoly any more, with terms like 'community', for example, being the most common substitute these days for the idea of the social.

NG In line with this, you say that the social is not an inevitable horizon for our thought or political judgement (Rose, 1999a: 101). What do you mean by this?

NR I was formulating this argument at a certain historical moment, when many 'progressive' intellectuals and activists thought that the only riposte to the rise of post-social, individualized, community-based ways of thinking – the kinds of thinking most associated with Margaret Thatcher, Ronald Reagan and the neo-Liberals – was to try to re-invent the social. I felt that in doing so they often forgot that this social was a relatively recent historical phenomenon. More importantly, they forgot that in the 1960s and 1970s many radical critics of the Left thought that the role of critique was to draw attention to the downsides of this social, and argued, for example, that social policies by and large hadn't produced much in the way of redistribution of wealth, that the patronizing bureaucracy of the welfare state created dependency in its clients, and that the apparatus of welfare had created a bloated group of functionaries who made their careers and their salaries out of administering it, and so on. I was among those who were suggesting that one should not be nostalgic for the welfare state that was passing away. I was also suggesting that – given that the social is itself a historical phenomenon – there might be ways of inventing a radical post-social politics which would eliminate some of the downsides of that social, and which might at the same time maximize some of the upsides of practices premised on autonomy and choice.

NG   In the light of this, what do you think the connection is between society and community? Do you think that society is giving way to community?

NR   Well, I do think that in some ways, and in some respects, the social is giving way to community. Of course, I am trying to avoid the temptation you are offering me of providing a total theory of society and a diagnosis of social change – that is not the kind of thesis that attracts me. I am not saying society is giving way to community in the sense that we are at the end of one epoch, and at the beginning of another. I am proposing something a little more limited in these ways of thinking about who we are and about how we should govern, be governed and govern ourselves. And this is that in our ways of posing problems and in trying to resolve them, in our ways of naming techniques, technologies and personnel who operate in order to shape and govern conduct, the term and territory 'social' is giving way to the term 'community' and the territory 'community'. In the early twentieth century, at the time of the politics of social rights and social insurance, it seemed that freedom would have to be social or it would never exist. But now it seems, for many at least, that the social is a site of constraint. For many it seems that we must find our freedom in community, and that only in community can we find the combination of powers and relationships that can constitute what we think of as freedom. And while we have not spoken about citizenship, I think that citizenship is also mutating. The link between citizenship and the social, which was central to the welfare regimes of the twentieth century, is being replaced by a new link between the autonomous citizen and his or her community, which in turn gives a whole new ethical form to citizenship.

NG   You also say that society still exists but not in a social form. Might this mean that the social is giving way to the political?

NR   By using this formulation – 'society still exists but not in a social form' – I am trying to avoid that apocalyptic language that proclaims 'there is no such thing as society'. Clearly, from the point of view of sociologists who want to explore the networks of relations that exist between human beings in certain times and spaces, 'societies' still exist as loose frameworks for defining the object of study, although, perhaps, even here the concept imposes rather too much unity upon these networks. But 'society' in the way that sociologists such as Durkheim thought about it doesn't exist any more. For a hundred years, sociologists and others thought of societies as almost natural in kind – discrete, bounded and territorialized (usually by the nation-state) – with their own kind of relatively uniform culture, mores, family forms, patterns of socialization, and so forth. This idea of society is hardly sustainable today, conceptually or empirically. But that is not your question. You ask: 'has the social given way to the political?' If pressed to frame it in this kind of language, I would say that the social has given way to the ethical. That is to say, questions that were previously posed as social problems – Is it acceptable to take drugs? How should we deal with the problems of our young people? How can we understand the decline of the inner cities? How are we going to regenerate the American spirit (to use the language of the American communitarians)? – are now being thought of as ethical questions. For example: how can we re-establish the ethical basis of our way of life? How can we frame a new set of ethical relations that people will become attached to and which will guide their conduct, and so on?

NG   In spite of this, it seems to me that in contemporary social theory there has been a widespread attempt to regenerate or reinvigorate ideas of the social through the political. For example, Ulrich Beck (1997) talks of 're-inventing the political', Zygmunt Bauman (1999) is 'in search of politics', while Anthony Giddens (1998) lays down the basis of a Third Way. You yourself talk of 'reframing the political'. Does this mean that you take the position that there is no way beyond politics? And, if this is the case, would you follow Beck, Bauman and Giddens in attempting to rejuvenate the social through politics, or even through ethics?

NR   That is a massive question. I am not sure that I would want to rejuvenate the social. At least I would have to ask myself why I would want to do so. But nor do I think that there is any outside to politics. The difficulty is that all these words – the social, the political – are, to some extent, rhetorical terms. They don't have a fixed reference. For example, by designating something 'political' you are seeking to designate that aspect of existence as something that is amenable to struggle and transformation. When feminists say that the personal is political they are saying that we must think of issues – such as who does what to whom in the bedroom, who buys the toilet paper, who cleans the bath? – as related to the distribution of power, and as having important kinds of consequences that should be the subject of contestation. To that extent, I think it is always going to be possible to designate any aspect of experience as political if one wants to make it subject to legitimate contestation. And that is why I am wary about using the term 'the political'. To call something political, it seems to me, is a perfomative act: it is trying to pull something into the field of contestation, just as to call some question 'technical' is to try to remove it from the field of contestation.

My way of addressing this vast question that you pose is to say, then, that there is never going to be an end to politics. It is not a question of using politics to rejuvenate the social but a question of asking ourselves what new kinds of issues and problems we want to make subject to contestation. Maybe we want to take some that are no longer subject to contestation and make them subject to contestation, and in order to do that we would designate them political. But then who is the 'we', who is doing this designating? I no longer think it is the role of the intellectual to designate something political. The old model where it is the intellectual who reveals the hidden fractures, the suppressed power relations seems to me to have only a limited purchase. I think we need to start from the evident fact that people themselves in all sorts of circumstances, whether they are psychiatric patients or women in Islam, are making things subject to contestation. To some extent I think that the intellectual goes to where those questions are and sees of what service he or she can be.

NG Following up on this, would you say that it is a mistake to attempt to regenerate the social through community? In the concluding section to your paper 'Inventiveness in Politics' (Rose, 1999b) you seem to reject the 'ethopolitics' of the Third Way in favour of an alternative moralism that reasserts the 'systematic and structural nature of poverty, exploitation, degradation and powerlessness, both nationally and internationally'.

NR Yes, I would see it as a mistake to try to regenerate the social through community because both the term 'community' and the politics of community seem to me to be, in exactly the way you say, hyper-moralized. It is not just that communities don't exist but that the kind of ethics embodied in the contemporary language of community, which often seems to be a kind of civic Christianity, a civic religion, is not something that attracts me ethically. But the fact that I don't feel attracted to them is unimportant. Important political disputes are happening around the idea of community, and, of course, the idea of community can be turned on itself, transformed and used in all kinds of radical ways. It is not univocal. In fact, the point I was trying to make in *Powers of Freedom* was actually a rather specific one. It was to say that some of the problems that are being addressed and understood in terms of community in Third Way social democracy and American democratic and republican politics really need to be thought of differently. For instance, the idea that one can address poverty and inequalities of income through encouraging people to become jobseekers, and through the mechanisms of the market and the employment contract, seems to me to be astoundingly naïve in the light of everything one knows about the ways in which markets, market relations and contractual relations work. And the idea that these sorts of strategies should be used in certain limited sectors of the West, and that we should seek to revitalize our markets in these sectors, seems to me to betray an almost deliberate blindness to the kinds of super-exploitation of workers of other countries and of other regimes, who do not have access to those kinds of conditions – the exploitation of those on which the markets of the West fundamentally depend. Of course, these are issues that have been very much brought into the political field by anti-globalization movements. I may not agree with all the analyses that are used in the service of anti-globalization, but these movements have succeeded in confronting the political imagination of the West with that which it wishes to turn its back on, to exclude or ignore, and this is without doubt an incredibly valuable political act.

NG In the introduction to your *Powers of Freedom* book you suggest that conventional ways of analysing politics and power are now becoming obsolescent. This, in particular, is because such approaches have tended to analyse power relations at the level of the nation-state. This said, however, 'globalization' is not a term you use too often as a sociological concept. Why is this?

NR It is true that I don't use the term 'globalization'. This is because it seems to be a term worth analysing rather than using. What work is this term doing? Many analysts who I respect have pointed to the limits of the strong claims about globalization: the persistence of local and national economies, the fact that in many ways trade was more internationalized at the beginning of the twentieth century than it is now, and the fact that there are still very powerful national boundaries, national linguistic boundaries and boundaries on the mobility of individuals and labour as opposed to capital. So, the term has acquired a truth status that is rather problematic. But there is a second reason to be wary about the term 'globalization'. This is because it has become an operative term in some political and economic discourses. The fact that 'we live in the era of globalization' is used to argue through, to justify, to rationalize, and to strategize everything from the marketing of Coca-Cola to what we should do about the Internet. And that is why I don't use the term 'globalization'. But I do think it is crucial for the sorts of questions we have been talking about today to be explored in a transnational context. I am well aware that a common critique of some of the works of Foucault and his followers is that they have made large generalizations from studies of a small sector of North Western Europe in a limited historical period. Actually, I think critics have overestimated this tendency to generalize from the West, at least as far as analyses of governmentality are concerned. Recently, I have been reading research that has used concepts of governmentality to examine phenomena as diverse as the 'modernization' of Japanese subjectivity in the Meiji period, Chinese 'one child' policies, the Japanese colonization of Taiwan in the early part of the twentieth century, and the role of military force in the colonial government of India. These studies have brought the genealogies of these phenomena into detailed historical connections with the knowledges, rationalities and technologies deployed to govern populations in Europe and North America. These are the kinds of detailed, grey, meticulous studies that interest me. They don't make claims about global social processes but instead look at the movement and mobility of ideas from place to place, at the mobility of capital, at the mobility of people and at the mobility of strategies and politics, and in each case they do so by tracing out specific networks. That is what interests me rather than trying to pose these things initially from the point of view of globality and globalization, although perhaps it doesn't need to be an either/or.

NG   I will finish by going back to my last question. At the outset of *Powers of Freedom* (Rose, 1999a: 1) you say that many conventional ways of analysing politics and power are now obsolescent, not least because as we have entered the twenty-first century fundamental aspects of 'the political' have changed. In view of this, and speaking as a sociologist, do you think that not just political thought but also social thought needs to be 'reframed' (in line with the subtitle of *Powers of Freedom*)?

NR   The short answer is 'yes'. But, of course, it would be arrogant to say that social thought 'needs to' be reframed as social thought is already reframing itself. The kinds of work we just talked about under the sign of globalization (and which I would certainly have specific criticisms of) is, at another level, trying to reframe itself in just this kind of way. It is trying to move away from the central organizing concepts of nineteenth-century social theory, including the ideas of state, of society, of a unitary sphere of culture, of a national population and of institutions that were in some way nationally bounded. And it is trying to move away from the kind of analysis whose concession to 'else-where' was to place these discrete and bounded states in a 'comparative' framework. The kind of thought you have been talking about – whether it is thought about 'the end of society', 'sociology beyond society', 'globalization', or 'risk society' – is trying to find a way of reframing that thought that used to be called 'social'. Whether we should call this thought social any more I don't know. But I still quite like the term 'sociology', if one can keep 'the social' in brackets, because sociology, at its best, seems to have always indicated a space for inventiveness in thinking about these kinds of things. Unfortunately this inventiveness was disciplined and therefore subordinated and tamed across the middle decades of the twentieth century, but perhaps it is now becoming increasingly wild, unruly and inventive. At least, we can hope.

REFERENCES

Althusser, L. (1977) *Lenin and Philosophy*. London: New Left Books.

Baudrillard, J. (1983) *In the Shadow of the Silent Majorities*. New York: Semi-otext(e).

Bauman, Z. (1999) *In Search of Politics*. Cambridge: Polity.

Beck, U. (1997) *The Reinvention of Politics*. Cambridge: Polity.

Donzelot, J. (1980) *The Policing of Families*. London: Hutchinson.

Foucault, M. (1970) *The Order of Things*. London: Routledge.

Foucault, M. (1977) 'Nietzsche, Genealogy, History', in D. F. Bouchard (ed.) *Language, Counter-Memory, Practice*. Ithaca, NY: Cornell University Press.

Giddens, A. (1998) *The Third Way: The Renewal of Social Democracy*. Cambridge: Polity.

Rose, N. (1985) *The Psychological Complex: Psychology, Politics and Society in England, 1869–1939*. London: Routledge.

Rose, N. (1999a) *Powers of Freedom: Reframing Political Thought*. Cambridge: Cambridge University Press.

Rose, N. (1999b) 'Inventiveness in Politics', *Economy and Society*, Vol. 28, No. 3, pp. 467–93.

CHAPTER 10

Françoise Vergès: Postcolonial Challenges

NG You have spoken of the intimate historical relation that has existed, or perhaps still even exists, in France, between republicanism and colonization (Vergès, 1998: 90). A key part of your argument is that following France's formal abolition of slavery in 1848 'slaves became citizens *but* remained colonized' (Vergès, 2002a: 355; original emphasis). This idea of 'colonized citizenship' (see also Vergès, 1999a; 2002b) is particularly interesting when thought of in connection to the question of the social. First, it shows that the political rights on which the social (or what Rousseau called a 'social contract') was founded were particular rather than universal (and exclusive rather inclusive): the colonized subject was 'never quite a citizen, not quite French' (2002a: 355). Second, it suggests, more generally, that European modernity cannot be understood outside of the quest for empire, and that the social, as both a discourse and a mode of political organization, was shaped from its outset by a relation between colonizer and colonized. Would you agree with this? And if so, to what extent do you think it is necessary to rethink classical ideas of the social, or social theory more generally, in terms of the challenges presented by different (post)colonial histories?

FV I have indeed insisted on the intimate relation between French republicanism and colonialism. We certainly have historical research on this link but political philosophers have, for the most part, remained indifferent to it. Why is this so? I think because colonialism is not yet fully considered a 'political' question, certainly not a 'philosophical' one. The racism and Eurocentrism of Enlightenment philosophers has been discussed, their defence or attack on slavery assessed, their support of colonization questioned, but there is a tendency to dismiss these events as occurring 'before our time', thus deserving a chapter but certainly not becoming a central question. There is, of course, the work of postcolonial thinkers, and the names of Achille Mbembe, Dipesh Chakravorty, Gayatri Spivak, Arjun Appadurai, Anthony Appiah, Edward Said, and Kuan-Hsing Chen come to mind. Their writings have changed the ways in which life, death, desire, happiness and identity are discussed. However, the link between French republicanism and colonialism as a political and not simply a historical link remains to be fully explored, particularly now that republicanism is again a central question of the political debate (the Republic is summoned when racism, citizenship, integration of migrants, borders, multiculturalism, values are discussed), and also because aspects of French colonial republicanism, such as the 'civilizing mission' and justified interference in sovereign countries, have returned to haunt us.

The colonial – chattel slavery, politics of force, state of exception – is quite often played down when rights, citizenship, emancipation and freedom (central questions for the West) are discussed. The colonial is considered an episode in history that should not be allowed to undermine the European sense of its own superiority. Europe should make amends, some excuses are in order, but we should restrain from questioning the entire canon. Europe's colonial domination has been the subject of a profound forgetting. This forgetting should be seen as a symptom: it is vital, for instance, to place the history of slavery outside of the official story of modernity. Slavery *must* belong to a premodern era, before the Enlightenment. I think though that we have far from exhausted the debate about colonial domination and modernity, terror and European colonial domination, and the racialization of labour and European colonial domination. We need to continue the work inaugurated by Frantz Fanon, Aimé Césaire, C. L. R. James and others who aspired to reconceptualize European history by bringing back from margins European raciology and recognizing its intrinsic role in the modern government and power. As Paul Gilroy has written: 'we should strive ... to keep the wound open a bit longer' (Gilroy, 2003: 57).

Apologies for Enlightenment philosophers' mistakes remain of the 'child-of-the-time' school: knowledge was sparse, everyone was racist and pro-slavery, it is easy to judge in retrospect. Another argument usually centres on a threat: if we ask Western philosophers to pass the test set up by postcolonial thinkers, none would emerge unscathed and the entire body of philosophy would be dismissed, thereby comforting those who reject all of its claims, and crushing under the weight of history those who are victims because they would no longer be able to find in Western philosophy the counter-tradition of emancipation, freedom and equality. Is this what we want? Scholarship is certainly not about distributing good and bad marks but about reminding contemporary thinkers of the blind spots of Western history so as to open up the debate on a legacy: to receive, to reject part of the legacy, to interpret it, to transmit it. I am thinking here of Derrida's remarks on legacy, on heritage: it implies a gesture of choosing, of reinterpretation so that new things or histories may appear. In terms of the colonial: how are we to judge the crimes (who will judge, and with what laws?)? And how is it possible to avoid the pitfalls of revisionism?

In France, the colonial remains a minor concern for historians and philosophers. Two discourses dominate the approach on colonialism: the discourse of indignation, denunciation and remorse on the one hand, and revisionist discourse on the other. Indignation, denunciation and remorse – discovering the crimes of colonization, being indignant about them, denouncing them and asking the State to express remorse – constitute a necessary gesture. Indignation is a respectable sentiment. It is that sentiment of anger provoked by an act that insults my idea of justice and my ethics: 'I cannot remain passive. I must intervene! I must do something.' It often leads to curiosity: 'How and why could this happen?' The impulse to act following a movement of indignation is a political sentiment. But when indignation becomes a 'profession', when it secures my conviction of being 'right', it leads to righteousness, to a position without risk: 'I am always on the right side, I do not need to look further at the complexity of situations'. Literature on colonialism has often adopted the style, tone and vocabulary of denunciation, maintaining the confusion between denunciation and analysis. The history of colonial crimes needs to be continued but what do we really learn from it? That colonizers were brutal, that they violated the principles that Europe claimed as defining its identity? This represents a first step, the end of an illusion, but tends to keep the debate within the frame of the tribunal: victims and torturers, judges and lawyers, witnesses and prosecutors. The tribunal may represent one space to deconstruct the past, to reappropriate a history, to listen to the voices of the victims and punish the guilty, but it cannot constitute the entire space where political conflicts are played out. The demand for remorse, for repentance by the State and its institutions (army, police, administration), belongs to the politics of reparation and pardon which constitutes a new field of politics and law. The democratic State must speak *and* act against the crimes committed in its name to reaffirm its will to protect and respect the fundamental rights of the human subject. The public expression of remorse seeks to answer to a demand for justice, punishing violent, murderous acts which were not 'crimes' when they occurred, or were accomplished by governments seen as illegitimate (dictatorships, totalitarian governments). It is about asking that a place be made in collective memory for the nameless victims, for the disappeared, for the dead without graves. Again, this has been an important development in the democratization of public space. However, it is also interesting to observe upon which 'crimes' (where the colonial is concerned) the discourse about remorse is organized. In France, it has been torture in Algeria. The denunciation of torture during the Algerian war certainly constitutes a necessary moment but it also masks the fact that torture was the founding act of colonization in Algeria. Torture during the Algerian war of independence is the visible tip of a complex and long history of spoliation, violence and brutality. Focusing on that moment exonerates the French Republic from its responsibility in the colonization of Algeria and its complicity in denying rights to millions of Algerians, shifting the responsibility of violence upon a small group of armed renegades. Colonization was always a state of exception. But denunciation and remorse cannot focus on *exceptional* moments. It must ask why the state of exception was a norm of French republicanism.

The second dominant discourse in France is a revisionist discourse. The debate is presented under two headings: first, how many bridges, hospitals, schools were built during colonialism and how many since? (the accountant's sheet heavily tilted towards the colonial era), or second, what system can be said to violate human rights more openly? (the righteous missionary's sheet heavily tilted towards the colonial era). Influential intellectuals of the '1968 generation' (as they call themselves) have been very active in revising the colonial. Constituted of former *gauchistes* or former *nouveaux philosophes*, the revisionists have decided that their defence of the colonized was a symptom of their own infantilism, which they need now to denounce and renounce, warning younger generations against a similar disease. When they discovered the Gulag and the crimes of totalitarian communism, the revisionists replaced the opposition between imperialism and anti-imperialism with the opposition between totalitarianism and democracy. This later became the defining terrain upon which a democratic ideal would be invented. The colonized had proven their incapacity to espouse democratic ideals, and Europe needed to be protected against their resentment, envy and destructive impulse. Pascal Bruckner recommended that Europe dismiss the white man's sob and get rid of the burden of colonial guilt. Alexandre Adler claimed that we must do justice to colonization and recognize its 'grandeur' (24 April 1997). Jean-Pierre Le Dantec (former director of *La Cause du Peuple*) declared: 'We invented the Third World'. Socialist leaders followed with an appeal: 'Let's stop being ashamed!', insisting on the fact that 'without the Republic' the colonized would not have acquired the tools of their liberation. It has been an exercise in depoliticization and dehistoricization, a reconfiguration of the political terrain, a shift from power to morals as the central notion of politics. It sets up the Gulag versus the plantation, a worthless and stupid opposition. It sets up a temporal rupture between the evils of a premodern era (slavery, colonization) and the evils of modernity (totalitarianism, genocide). This division between 'premodern' slavery and 'modern' forms of violence obscures the analysis of predatory politics and restores the superiority of Europe. The analysis of the colonial deserves better than that. It is not that the colonial is the key to reading current forms of inequality, racism, discrimination and predatory economy, but it participated in the European imagination, and informed its notion of the sovereign, the citizen, the Nation.

In France, it would be stupid to contend that Republican colonialism disappeared one day in 1962 with the end of the war in Algeria. The hybrid figure of Republican colonialism is difficult to define and delimit because it refers to two apparently opposed visions and practices. The French Republic is the territory of the sovereign people. Its inhabitants are *citizens*. The colony is the territory of the state of exception and of the politics of force, its inhabitants are *subjects*. Logically, the existence of the republic excludes the existence of the colony. Yet, in France, the Republic was the condition of the colony. There cannot be an analysis of the Republic, of citizenship, of the territory of the national which does not include the colonial moment. Étienne Balibar in *L'Europe, l'Amérique, la guerre* (Balibar, 2003) argues that the analysis of barbarism and violence must be done with the analysis of its circulation between the colonized territories and their metropole. He reminds us that the analysis remains unfinished. Europe must revise the narrative of violence (the illusory division between North and South, the fantasy that violence in the colony did not affect the North) and learn a *leçon d'altérité* [lesson of alterity]. This is what I have tried to do. In a recent book, with Pascal Blanchard and Nicolas Bancel (Vergès, Blanchard and Bancel, 2003), I return to the figure of the Colonial Republic, and look at the ways in which it organized French political thought. Why were the colonized excluded from the social contract? From freedom? Why were natural rights not 'natural' in the colony? Why, as Hannah Arendt (1973: 185) has pondered, did race become a 'principle of the body politic'? Arendt is among the few philosophers to take the question of the relation between Europe (as the cradle of 'democracy and civilization') and imperialism seriously. She remarked that natives were 'natural' human beings who lacked the specifically human character, the specifically human reality, so that when Europeans massacred them they somehow were not aware they had committed murder (Arendt, 1973: 192). In the colony, Europeans refined their use of racism and bureaucracy, the destructive violence of which they would later witness in Europe.

NG In your book *Monsters and Revolutionaries* you read the history of (French) colonialism according to the logic of (Marcel Mauss') gift-exchange. In this reading, the gift from colonizer to colonized (and vice versa) can never be returned: 'the colonized, constructed as "receivers", were not recognized as equals, and thus their reciprocal *don* [gift] could never satisfy the metropole' (1999b: 7). According to Mauss' argument, a complex web of *social* relations emerges through gift giving. But in the context of colonialization what does this mean? Does a specific and quite different set of social relations emerge in cases where one or both groups are always in (symbolic or real) debt to the other?

FV I did not read the problematic of the colonial debt in economic terms. I was, of course, looking at slavery and its abolition and at colonization in the French empire. Colonization, as a system of debts, built a specific set of social relations. It is interesting to observe to what extent the notion of 'generosity' was used in French colonial discourse. Colonization was an expression of France's generosity: France had a duty, a mission, a 'civilizing mission'. It would conquer the hearts of the colonized, and bring light into a world of darkness. The empire was an expression of the universal, which, from the French Revolution, became associated with the principles and goals of the Republic. The colonized were indebted to France, which never hesitated to bring its science, technology and pedagogy to the backward territories.

Europe had received from Rome the mission to bring Christianity to the world. It would *save* the world from evil, bringing the populations enslaved by godless spirits and deities the light of God, its generous love. The secularization of the Christian mission through French republicanism imposed a similar doctrine of salvation. France would not convert colonized peoples to God but to the ideals of the Enlightenment, to the republican ideal that brings salvation to the world. Peoples would be saved from tyrants, and they would discover liberty and equality. Saint-Just declared that the 'French people vote for the freedom of the world' [*le peuple français vote la liberté du monde*]. The French Republic was the true inheritor of Rome: barbarians were colonized for their own good. And that they do not know that they need to be colonized is further proof that they need to be colonized. They do not know it yet, but once they discover the truth, they will be thankful and our armies will be covered with flowers. It was a story of *revelation and redemption*, a story of a generous power bringing liberty throughout the world out of its good heart, and which expected to be *loved* in return. Athens and Rome were destroyed because their colonial practices nurtured resentment and hatred. Slavery and its corruption had eaten the *Ancien Régime*. French colonialism would avoid these pitfalls because it would export fraternity and equality. The French Republic[1] would be the mother of colonized peoples and later their children. The *Ancien Régime* was patriarchal and indifferent to the feelings of the colonized – the Republic would be maternal and generous. Love would be the foundation of the relation between the republic and the colony, and hence love rather than hatred would return to France. The rhetoric of love is as important as the rhetoric of generosity. Colonizers would often be shocked to discover that they were not loved. Narratives abound about the feelings of 'betrayal' and 'deceitfulness' of natives.

The rhetoric of generosity and of love in politics frames social relations within the economy and symbolism of the debt: 'What you owe us' and 'what is owed to us'. Generosity and love masked the violence of colonial relations and justified colonial 'humanitarian' intervention. This was particularly true of the French abolitionist doctrine. Indeed, after the abolition of slavery in the French colonies in 1848, the French Republicans launched a series of colonial attacks which they justified on the grounds of abolitionism. They were saving Algerians, Malagasy from the slave traders (usually 'Muslim') and with this bringing modernity. Their love of freedom and their disinterested desire to free peoples around the world legitimated their intervention on sovereign soil and the newly freed could not but be indebted to them.

The discourse on debt in politics introduces the debate thus: what is owed to me rather than what action should I take now in the present, what future can I imagine? I am always caught within the temporality of a past action: this was done to me, therefore I am indebted. French colonial discourse on the debt foreclosed any discussion of the present and the future. As an aside, it is interesting to note that the politics of decolonization sought to look towards the future (with all the limits of its vision of the future), whereas postcolonial politics has insisted on the recovery of the past: the past defines the present and the future. Decolonization thinkers rejected the determinism of the past ('I am not the slave of slavery', Fanon famously wrote) whereas an important current of postcolonial thought has argued that recovery of the past, that reparation of the wound is the horizon of politics. I am not arguing that we should return to decolonization but I think it is interesting to ponder the different postures and the importance that memory has taken.

NG In a recent article, you have argued that the 'colonial impulse' or the 'model of colonialization' is still with us today (2002a: 351). You also talk of the emergence of the 'postcolonial colony' (2002a: 352) as a new form of social organization. What is the 'postcolonial colony', and how does it differ, at the level of social organization, from the types of colonialism we have seen before?

FV The notion of the postcolonial colony must be refined because I have used it to refer to two different situations (even if the observation of one informs the other). The first use designates a territory freed of the colonial status which has not entirely lost its colonial structure. Its inhabitants are now citizens, and it may be under democratic rule. I was speaking of the French overseas territories still under French rule (New Caledonia, Antilles, Guyana, Tahiti and other Pacific dependencies, Réunion) that are now also considered European regions (called regions of the 'ultra-periphery'). The colonial still structures the relation between France and these local societies. Since they chose to remain 'French', they must find a way of existing within the rigid framework of the 'one and indivisible' republic. The political debate about what kind of link must exist is thus entirely framed within the question of 'status'. What status can be imagined which would acknowledge the specificity of the postcolonial territory (geographical distance, post-slavery society, society of colonized natives and settlers, connection with geographical region, local economy) and the iron principle of French republicanism? It is important to define these links in juridical terms, but I think that the importance given to the juridical aspect has obscured the political debate on both sides. The question of national independence, except in New Caledonia, has never mobilized an important part of the population. Yet the rhetoric of independence, of the politics of identity has framed the discourse of most intellectuals of the French postcolony. This has led to a confusion. In France, there is support for the politics of identity. The French still favour the romantic ideal of the Nation: it is as if freedom cannot be thought of outside of the idea of nation. In the overseas departments (Antilles, Réunion), there is a fixation on 'what France has done to us', 'what France owes us'. This leads us to ignore the political debate about Europe and France as multicultural, multireligious, multiethnic spaces with their pockets of dire poverty and exclusion. Postcolonial French overseas territories do not participate in this debate though they could constitute a base for discussing relations between Europe and 'its others' as they, because of history and culture, are hybrid societies. Colonies are 'postcolonial colonies' because the debate is still framed within the colonial political: the construction of the freed nation is the only condition of existence. This was true of Algeria, Indochina and African colonies and could have been true of the territories I am speaking about. But we (postcolonial of French overseas territories) 'chose' to remain within the French Republic. I would argue that we *must* take part in the debate about Europe, about globalization, about Europe and the United States. That contribution is part of our emancipation from the colonial. Creole societies were multicultural, multireligious and multiethnic from the beginning. What Europe is discovering, we experienced through loss, forced relocation, forced immigration, violence and resistance. Other colonies (New Caledonia for instance) know what it is to live on a territory divided between camps (Kanaks forced to abandon their villages and to regroup into camps; Whites into segregated towns). We know about being silenced, about genocide, about death organizing the social (slavery), and also about living together on a territory and inventing new ways of coexisting, new cultural and social practices.

I was also speaking of another space: the grey zones of current globalization. This space accompanies new forms of colonization connected with globalization, which is not similar in pattern to the colonization of the nineteenth century. Let me give some examples very quickly: the transportation of plundered resources no longer requires in all cases the building of roads, rails and military compounds to protect them. Oil can be exploited without such things.

Helicopters can go and pick up gold and diamonds on secured areas, leaving the surroundings to warlords, famine, whatever. The workforce no longer needs to be local, and there is no need for the problems of forced labour (an army to force it, a police to control it, revolts). Labour can be transported from elsewhere, and for a temporary period. It can be made more docile. For instance, more than 10,000 Chinese women work in the free-trade zones of Mauritius. The agreement between both governments is worked out concretely by agencies that recruit women in rural areas. The women come for two years and must go back after this time. They are forbidden to organize – Mauritian unions cannot talk to them – and they are warned that they must not 'lose the face of the Chinese State' with rebellious actions. The costs of organizing the movement of these women across distances are minor compared with the advantages. Meanwhile, in Spain, farmers have recently chosen to recruit thousands of women from Eastern Europe to pick fruit and vegetables. They are seen as more docile than North African men, who until now constituted the migrant seasonal workforce. They are chosen married and with children as a further guarantee they will go back to their country. Racism against North African men, rejection by Europe of its south, and the desire of the Eastern Europeans to earn euros and be considered 'good Europeans' (compared with 'Muslim' men) all play a part in this new organization of migrancy. And with the new scramble for African oil, we can foresee the drawing of new borders, new territories of colonization and of those spaces which seem to 'fall' from the surface of the earth, away from our consciousness, even in our visual world: the *grey zones*. We can expect further poverty, corruption and violence. Since the late 1970s, Nigeria has received over £300 billion in oil revenues, but per capita income is less than $1 a day. In Angola, $1 billion vanished in 2002 between the Angolan presidency, the central bank and the state oil company (see *Guardian*, 17 June 2003, p. 2), yet its population lives in limbo, in a grey zone. They do not even 'count' as bodies, for they are no longer needed to produce wealth. They can live or die, it does not matter much to the State. The State can import the workforce; can lease private armies, so why would it need these bodies? Grey zones are thus the territories on which people who do *not* count live (the State no longer needs to collect taxes, to raise armies among them, does not need their children for its future or their existence to construct its legitimacy), and where new routes of trafficking in human beings emerge.

NG You have said that 'we need to examine new forms of colonization and their order of knowledge' (Vergès, 2002a: 352). What methodological procedures or tools might be used in order to do this? Your study of the political history of Réunion is framed in the terms of a genealogy (Vergès, 1999b: 12–13). You have also recently spoken of the possibility of pursuing a genealogy of different modes of 'writing "Africa"' (Vergès, 2002c: 607). Does this mean that you think genealogy, in Foucault's sense, to be useful in the unmasking and exploration of new colonial powers? If so, how?

FV Genealogy in Foucault's sense can be one tool, but the study of current forms of colonization requires other methodological procedures. My own writing is closely connected with reading the present, using literature, philosophy and psychoanalysis along with social sciences. The fragmented reality of the postcolony – its heterogeneity along with continuous aspects of some elements of the colonial – demands a multidisciplinary approach. It looks like an old recipe, and 'what's new?' you could say, but I do think this is the way to approach the multilayered complexity of new forms of colonization. I am thinking of the work done by WISER, a centre of research based at the Wits University, Johannesburg with Achille Mbembe as Senior Researcher, or of the project I am helping to set up right now, the *Maison des civilizations et de l'unité réunionnaise*, which will seek to study the diasporic linkages and formations, and processes of creolization, in the Indian Ocean world today.

NG In your postscript to a recent collection on postcolonialism you cite Edouard Glissant's claim that 'the entire world is experiencing the process of creolization' (Vergès, 2002a: 350). Is this a claim with which you would agree?

FV When Edouard Glissant claims that the 'entire world is experiencing the process of creolization', I am sceptical of the optimism of the claim and wary of its totalizing aspect. I think it is too soon to support such a claim. We need more studies on sites where processes of creolization might emerge (global cities, regions). My hypothesis is that processes of creolization will exist alongside other processes produced by contact and conflict, such as indifferent multiculturalism, apartheid, segregation and the creation of ethnic enclaves. Will creolization appear as the only alternative process to hegemonic strategies of identification? I am not sure. In the current process of globalization, new forms of identification can be observed whose layers of complexity cannot be exhausted with the notion of creolization. I also think that it is impossible, really impossible, to claim that the 'entire world' is experiencing creolization. The 'entire world' is too complex, too diverse to experience one single process. Glissant's argument is extremely attractive, astute and attuned to the postmodern and postcolonial condition, but it simply cannot be applied to the 'entire world'. The upheavals and transformations produced by current globalization – increased migrations, new routes of migration, new global cities, regionalization, the speed of information, financial exchanges – lay the grounds for new processes of mixing whose contours we do not yet know.

Historically, creolization emerged in slave society, in the first globalization processes produced by the slave trade and European colonization. It describes a process constantly at work whereby new slaves are integrated and creolized by slaves who arrived earlier. We know that masters were careful about diversifying their community of slaves to foreclose and weaken loyalty and solidarity. They later learned to live and work side by side, to understand each other by creating and adopting the Creole language, and to adopt and adapt each other's beliefs, rituals and practices. Newcomers could not survive if they sought to protect the 'authenticity' of their beliefs, rituals and practices. The system of the plantation required slaves to forget the past, their roots and their culture, while providing the grounds for preserving bits and pieces of their culture which were mixed with creolized practices. It was a requirement that went against the masters' policy of dividing but which they could not control. The plantation was the matrix of creolization, the machine through which slaves and masters went. People were thrown on the island by the yoke of history. On Réunion, even the whites coming to the island were not wealthy Europeans or young aristocrats seeking fortune, but poor peasants from the poorer regions of France and Europe forced to emigrate by the State. They had no choice. The process of creolization was fragile as it was regularly threatened by new arrivals and weakened by the masters' regulations. It was nonetheless this very fragility that was the condition of creolization. Creolization was a dialectical movement of forgetting, adopting, transforming what was adopted, and creating rituals and practices that could be shared by diverse groups, who, however, always brought their own singular approach to them. For instance, death was framed within a mix of Afro-Malagasy and Hindu understandings of filiation, genealogy and time, to which each group added its own contributions.

There is *no creolization without conflict* between affirmed contrasts and the movement towards unity. When Indian indentured workers arrived on Réunion, they clashed with the emancipated slaves and sought to distinguish themselves from bonded workers: they were free, they claimed, and not Blacks. And yet they adopted Creole ways of being and living while bringing their own rituals, practices and beliefs which the population creolized before adopting them. The coexistence of conflict, tension and cohabitation produced a unity, the Creole world, which was, in turn, questioned by new contrasts. Both contrasts and unity were produced by the same structures: slavery and colonialism. The process of creolization as a process creating structures of identification, cultural practices, ways of being and understanding time, space, and the world, was not forged in relation to a sovereign territory. Creolization began with displacement (which we should not romanticize) creating other forms of inhabiting the territory. It was the experience of *being a foreigner*. The new country was the territory of enslavement, deportation and exile, but also of a new world and culture. Cultures arrived in bits and pieces. The alienation of slavery, the 'social death' of slavery, the forced relocation, the fact of having no choice, produced a radically different relation to the territory.

Creolization must be a process constantly at work in which 'diffusion' and 'spread' of elements go along with appropriation and adoption, which implies the agency of the recipient. Many of those interactions do not take place between equals. Creolization is not a harmonious process: there are practices of exclusion and discrimination. It is, as Aimé Césaire proposed in his 1956 letter to Maurice Thorez, about finding a viable way of avoiding 'two paths to doom: by segregation, by walling yourself in the particular; or by dilution, by thinning off into the emptiness of the "universal"' (Césaire, 1957). It is about *not* having the choice to share a territory with others, whom we have chosen and whose ways of being and living are not 'ours'. Creolization challenges the 'truth' of identity. It suggests that loss is not necessarily a lack. It is not a series of homogeneous parts that can be subtracted or added at will; it is a dynamic process, a movement. Not from A to B, or A plus B, but bits of A plus altered A plus bits of B ... There is an African proverb, which I like a lot and which expresses what I am trying to say: *Qui que tu sois devenu, tu ne sais pas ce que tu es* [Whomever you have become, you do not know who you are]. It is about something in progress, not about a fixed thing. All this may look abstract, but to me it was brought out by the experience of living on a land without a pre-colonial past, a land of estrangement for each inhabitant, with no roots, no origins but the act of colonization.

Is my understanding of creolization that different from Glissant's? Not that much, it seems. To Glissant, the *relation* is central and he takes the notion of creolization to a new global level. Widespread cultural encounters, fragmentation of cultures, and 'extreme multilingualism is the inevitable destiny of all countries. Modern communications further exacerbate contact and diversity' (Dash, 1995: 179). Glissant argues that it is inevitable that increasing 'chaos' (the increasing encounters of cultures when none of them can claim to represent a totality) will lead to creolization, which he prefers to the concept of *métissage* because with creolization there is always a part of the unexpected (whereas the outcome of *métissage* can be calculated) (see Glissant, 1996: 19). Creolization 'demands that the heterogeneous elements in relation valorize each other, in other words that there is no degradation or diminution of the subject [*de l'être*] through this contact, this mixing' (Glissant, 1996: 18). I differ from Glissant's generalization of the process of creolization and from his tendency to claim creolization as the best thing under the sun. To me, there is no 'best thing', there are conflicts, arrangements, negotiations, limits to arrangements, desires to master, control and oppress. The process of creolization is not the rule in situations of contacts between cultures (historically, it was rather the exception). Contacts between cultures do not necessarily produce creolization; they can produce apartheid, separatism, multiculturalism and indifferent cohabitation. Creolization, as I said, requires the forgetting of origins, which survive only as reconstructed and transformed. In the current era of globalization, the politics and economy of predation, trafficking in human beings, brutality and force are organizing new territories of power and resistance. There are new global cities. Are we witnessing processes of creolization in these territories? They are not exactly reproducing the conditions of the plantation upon which the process of creolization emerged. If creolization is understood as a process of mixing, we can certainly argue that we are witnessing them. They might produce a unity as well (creolization = diversity *and* unity challenged by diversity, which in turn experiences a process of unification, etc.). However, it is not a *global* process and 'the entire world' is not experiencing the process of creolization. Rather, I think that we are witnessing processes of creolization along with processes of contact, apartheid, indifferent multiculturalism and new forms of contact and conflict. On the same territory – a city, a region – these different processes may coexist, overlap, or be in conflict. Further, it remains to be seen to what extent processes of creolization can resist the pressure of the politics of identity. Are these processes still at work in the current era of liberal globalization? Can they be extended to current situations of contact? Is current globalization producing similar situations as the globalization of the era of slave trade, characterized by trafficking in human beings, predation, brutality and force?

NG   You have described 'Creole cultures' as being (at least at their point of emergence) 'profoundly diverse and mobile' (2001: 170). But what might this mean for an understanding of the social? In such cultures, do social relations develop that are also diverse and mobile? Or are all social relations today increasingly diverse, fluid and mobile regardless of processes of creolization?

FV   I will not argue that social relations are diverse and mobile like Creole cultures. Postcolonial theory has sought to distinguish the social and the cultural, working out their interconnections but also their points of separation. Creole cultures are diverse and mobile because diversity and mobility are the conditions of their creation and survival. Once they become fixed and territorialized, they are no longer Creole but national, though Creole culture can exist alongside national culture (in Mauritius, there is a national culture and discourse around the 'rainbow nation' and Creole culture refers to the culture of the descendants of slaves usually ignored by the national discourse).

Social relations in Creole cultures of post-slavery societies were shaped by the economic and symbolic system of slavery and colonialism, then by postcolonial economic dependency. They were not fluid and flexible but rather organized by a system of death, of *bio-power*. Social relations today are certainly increasingly diverse, fluid and mobile in form. This has been observed and analysed. However, I am more interested in the new forms of trafficking in human beings, the new predatory economy with its grey zones, its spaces regulated by death. The sources of predation are more diverse: the African continent is no longer the source of human beings as things, women have joined in great numbers the flows of forced migration (in modern slavery, it was mainly men who were trafficked), the territories on which that kind of labour is used are no longer the plantation with its rigid organization, they are mobile, diverse. What kind of social relations will these new forms produce? I am following the debates around these issues. We lack a vocabulary to speak of the politics of brutality and force and the economy of plunder that have emerged in recent times. We describe them, but we are not sure about the *theory* that will help us to understand how they work. On a global level, we witness an increasing number of 'useless' individuals excluded from social citizenship, along with a privatization of the attributes of sovereignty when they are not 'captured' by warlords, terrorists and gangs. This new development has made obsolete the rivalry between powers for the conquest of territories. What capital needs now is a 'securization' of transnational zones of productivity, of the sites of extraction of wealth, and to keep the useless out of these sites.

NG How might the idea of creolization be thought alongside what you call the process of *métissage* or miscegenation? Why does this latter concept occupy such a pivotal position in your work, and why is it of importance today?

FV The concept of *métissage* or miscegenation no longer occupies the pivotal position it used to in my work. I became interested in the concept because I wanted to understand why European colonialism had been haunted by the figure of the *métis*, a monster, a hybrid, a potential criminal and revolutionary. Then the concept was forgotten. Decolonization was certainly not interested in *métissage* (too much of a third space) but in national identity and national culture. In the late 1980s, early 1990s, the concept became fashionable again. It was criticized for its relation with biology and for having a binary structure, but it has remained very much in use, notably in the world of arts, fashion, and music. I wanted to challenge the romanticization, the idealization of *métissage* and resituate its emergence in its historical and political moment. I showed how important it has been for colonial power, but also for the movements of decolonization, to control and discipline the *métis*. It did not mean that the *métis* was the next redemptive figure but that its forceful rejection was a symptom worthy of enquiry. My work challenged the discourse of purity and the politics of identity as truth, and suggested that the site of identification is always a site of anxiety.

The work I did was extremely useful because I had to de-idealize a number of figures. I am sorry to be biographical here, but it helps to explain. I grew up in a family of activists, communists engaged in the anti-colonialist movement on Réunion Island. My grandfather had denounced French colonialism in Indochina, my father was a founder of the communist party in Réunion, my mother was a feminist, my uncle a lawyer defending Algerian nationalists, and my aunt a heroine of the Algerian war. During my teens, I witnessed a lot of violence, political repression, a stifled public debate, and controlled media. You could not play the *maloya*, the music slaves had created, in public. School was about France, France, France. I idealized *le peuple*, rejected French culture, and blamed France for everything. Working around the figure of the *métis* was a work of de-idealization, of reinterpreting the legacy, of going beyond the division between victims and torturers.

The figure of the *métis* is still important in my work but more as a reminder of the temptation of purity, of the desire to deny uncertainty. It is also a reminder that one can live without a fixed genealogy, with a broken filiation but without experiencing lack. It is about living with loss. One may not need roots to be grounded. The market has loved the *métis*, the hybrid for a series of reasons. One is the market's capacity to absorb new images, to be attentive to new markets. In the world of advertising and arts, young creators are aware of the ideas and texts of cultural studies. They aspire to a world in which ideologies do not dominate. They tend to reject strongly the idea of purity and are attracted to the world of the in-between and transversality. Power, however, is not central to their vision of the world. The subversive power of hybridity and *métissage* was contained in their capacity to challenge the notions of purity and authenticity upon which the ideas of national territory and culture, the ideas of who belongs and who does not, were built. As such, they are still subversive in the West as well as in the postcolonial world against groups trying to reconfigure notions of purity and authenticity. Further, we cannot abstract social relations and the new forms of exploitation which are producing new figures of the monstrous.

NG   How might your position on creolization and *métissage* be situated in connection to recent debates around hybridity, multiculturalism and 'cultural globalization'? You have expressed your reluctance to make generalizations about transformations that are occurring in 'the current context of globalization' (Vergès, 2001: 180). Does this mean that you reject the concept of globalization itself, or simply certain understandings of this concept?

FV   I do not reject the concept of globalization itself but also I do not think I can make generalizations about transformations occurring in the current context. It is a little too soon to make generalizations. The late Barbara Christian (1994) spoke of 'The Race for Theory' when race became a pivotal concept in the understanding of culture, history and politics in the US. She meant that people were racing to find a theory, that the competition was fierce and bloody, but also that race had become theory, and consequently that politics, power, economy were forgotten or marginalized in the process. I am often reminded of her essay in our current times when there is a race to find the theory of globalization without trying first to understand what is happening.

Creolization, *métissage*, hybridity, multiculturalism, cultural globalization are tools to interpret the emerging situations. For instance, if we look at the global-city of Dubai, which concept will better describe the multilayered structures of cultural, financial and sexual exchanges that are at work? Traders from east and west Africa, from Russia, Iran, India, the Gulf Emirates, Madagascar, China come to the city; women from the Philippines are maids, Europeans are engineers, bankers and technicians, and Palestinians work in the administration.

NG   Recently, you have also introduced the term 'cosmopolitanism' into your writings (Vergès, 2001). More precisely, you have drawn a distinction between what you call 'creole universalist cosmopolitanism' and 'creole cosmopolitanism as revolutionary internationalism'. What exactly are these different forms of cosmopolitanism? And what might this focus on cosmopolitanism bring to our understanding of (post)colonial subjectivities and societies?

FV   In trying to see how notions elaborated in the West are worked out in the non-European world, I noticed that there existed a notion of cosmopolitanism in the non-European world. It emerged from the conceptualization of a common condition and the refusal to be excluded from humanity. Being colonized was the common condition, yet the world was not divided between masters and slaves but between oppressors and oppressed, and connections could be made with peoples everywhere. This cosmopolitanism is a kind of 'citizenship of the world' but based on an understanding of inequality and exploitation. 'Creole universalist cosmopolitanism' was more humanist than 'creole cosmopolitanism as revolutionary internationalism': it sought to embrace the ideals of the Enlightenment which, once adopted throughout the world, would bring peace and progress, but, again, with a strong attack against European imperialism. Because of their non-relation with a sovereign territory, Creoles saw themselves as 'inhabiting' the world, as lacking a strong sense of 'nationality', and they identified themselves with other peoples rejecting racialism and nationalism. By contrast, 'Creole cosmopolitanism as revolutionary internationalism' was indebted to the practices and discourses of decolonization, to 'the colonized of the world unite' kind of thing. It was a revolutionary understanding of cosmopolitanism, a 'cosmopolitics' if you wish.

NG   You also draw on Fanon's use of the term *vertigo*. You say that vertigo is 'provoked by the gap between group identification and identification with a shared humanity' (2001: 177). Underlying this statement seems to be a distinction between political struggle demanding loyalty to a group and struggle for identification within 'the community of human beings'. Marx saw this as the difference between struggle for political emancipation and human emancipation. But where do you locate yourself within this political arena? You talk of a 'politics of emancipation'. What are the aims of such a politics, and what practices might it involve?

FV   You are right, my distinction between political struggle demanding loyalty to a group and struggle for identification within 'the community of human beings' echoes Marx's difference between struggle for political emancipation and human emancipation. However, I do not separate the two as Marx does. I do think that political emancipation raises the question of what kind of community of human beings we wish to invent. I refute Marx's belief in inevitable progress. I see political struggle as a series of conflicts and negotiations that do not find an 'end'. I imagine incremental changes, resistance against politics of predation and plunder, and for that, the need to rethink the community of human beings. I do not believe that one class, one group, or even the *multitudes* will bring emancipation. It is an uneven process. For instance, if we look at the situation of women, we can see a lot of regression. This situation is no longer at the forefront of the agenda, whether in health, education, or political rights, even though women now constitute the target of trafficking (a lot of new jobs no longer demand physical force). But if we look at resistance against monumental projects such as dams, we witness new forms of resistance. In summary, a new definition of the human free of the Enlightenment's ideals is needed: reason, progress, integrating psychoanalytical notions (desire to expand, to dominate), anthropological approaches and geopolitical analysis. The politics of emancipation would seek to integrate these approaches and does not promise 'freedom' and 'peace', but recognizes the need to control and curb the cruelty and brutality of the economy of plunder. Its practices: on the legal front – seeking to indict plunderers, to expand the laws protecting the weak, etc. – knowing that this is just one aspect of the struggle but understanding that to 'dismantle the master's house, we can use the master's tools'; and on the political front, to organize transnational movements, or a 'cosmopolitanism from below' (see, for instance, Arjun Appadurai's (2000) study of homeless networks between Bombay and Johannesburg).

NG   Finally, to return to my opening question, you declared the following: 'the legacy of slavery contaminated republican democracy; it instituted a culture of demonization and violence with which we still live today. Its predatory character has not disappeared from human relations and we must confront that reality' (1999a: 7). In response, what role would you assign social theory in the attempt to confront this situation?

FV   I think we can no longer oppose to capital its alternative pole, its 'progressive' aspect – abolitionism to slavery, nationalism to colonialism, socialism to liberalism. There was a form of 'binarism' to this – hegemony and its alternative. Today, it looks like the choice between two forms of barbarism, soft and hard. We are still extremely protected in Western Europe. We cannot escape noticing it when we travel to Africa, Asia, Latin America and Eastern Europe (and to some places of Western Europe, but even there it does not compare). Will we be able to build a theory that matches the transnationalism of capital? (I do not consider that *Empire* by Michael Hardt and Toni Negri (2001) constitutes an answer, but I do not even wish to explain why. It is for me such a Eurocentric manifesto.) But do we even wish to build *a* theory? I am not sure. We do need concepts, and as we noticed with colonialism we need to make them adaptable to different situations (i.e. nothing like the notion of 'the' working class which hindered for so long the understanding of colonial situations), but *a* theory? However, social theory must perform critical analysis of notions such as the nation, immaterial work, transnational capital and resistance. Revising the analysis of slavery as an economy of plunder and a politics of force and brutality might contribute to this endeavour.

NOTES

1. I understand that my indifferent use of French colonialism, the French Republic and France might confuse the reader. I cannot go into any detail here about what I think the three figures share. Their territories overlap quite often.

REFERENCES

Appadurai, A. (2000) 'Spectral Housing and Urban Cleansing: Notes on Millennial Mumbai', *Public Culture*, Vol. 12, No. 3, pp. 627–51.

Arendt, H. (1973) *The Origins of Totalitarianism*. New York: Harcourt Brace.

Balibar, E. (2003) *L'Europe, l'Amérique, la guerre: Réflexions sur la médiation européenne*. Paris: La Découverte.

Césaire, A. (1957) *Letter to Maurice Thorez*. Paris: Présence Africaine.

Christian, B. (1994) 'The Race for Theory', in R. C. Davis and R. Schleifer (eds) *Contemporary Literary Criticism: Literary and Cultural Studies*. New York: Longman.

Dash, J. M. (1995) *Edouard Glissant*. Cambridge: Cambridge University Press.

Gilroy, P. (2003) 'Mapping the Black Diaspora', *Art Press*, June, pp. 57–9.

Glissant, E. (1996) *Introduction à une poétique du divers*. Paris: Gallimard.

Hardt, M. and Negri, A. (2001) *Empire*. Cambridge, MA: Harvard University Press.

Vergès, F. (1998) 'Memories and Names of Algeria', *Parallax*, Vol. 4, No. 2, pp. 88–91.

Vergès, F. (1999a) 'Colonizing Citizenship', *Radical Philosophy*, No. 95, pp. 3–7.

Vergès, F. (1999b) *Monsters and Revolutionaries: Colonial Family Romances and Métissage*. Durham, NC: Duke University Press.

Vergès, F. (2001) 'Vertigo and Emancipation, Creole Cosmopolitanism and Cultural Politics', *Theory, Culture & Society*, Vol. 18, No. 2, pp. 169–83.

Vergès, F. (2002a) 'Post-Scriptum', in D. T. Goldberg and A. Quayson (eds) *Relocating Postcolonialism*. Oxford: Blackwell.

Vergès, F. (2002b) 'Race and Slavery: The Politics of Recovery and Reparation', in P. Osbourne and S. Sandford (eds) *Philosophies of Race and Ethnicity*. London: Continuum.

Vergès, F. (2002c) 'The Power of Words', *Public Culture*, Vol. 14, No. 3, pp. 607–10.

Vergès, F., Blanchard, P. and Bancel, N. (2003) *La République coloniale. Essai sur une utopie*. Paris: Albin Michel.

Index